THE BEAUTY INDUSTRY SURVIVAL GUIDE
A Salon Professional's Handbook

by Tina Alberino

Copyright

The Beauty Industry Survival Guide
© 2015 by Dread Machine Publications

Printed in the United States of America.

First Edition: January 2015
10 9 8 7 6 5 4 3 2 1

Alberino, Tina.
 The Beauty Industry Survival Guide: A Salon Professional's Handbook—1st ed.
 ISBN- NUMBER 978-0-9909100-0-8

All rights reserved. No part of this book may be used or reproduced in any manner whatsoever without written permission.
 Super cool author portrait designed by Windmyll at www.Artcorgi.com.

Contents

Foreword 1
Fresh Meat 3
   The Real Pros & Cons 3
      Pros 4
      Cons 6
   Your Projections Are Worthless 8
   Seek Knowledge 11
   Mentors: Beauty Industry Demigods 16
   End Your Other Life 18
Salon Survival 21
   Mind Your Manners 21
      Professional Etiquette 21
      Nothing is Sacred 28
   Coworkers: Funky Martians, Delightful Whackadoodles, and Crazypants Predators 30
      Common Beauty Industry Personalities 31
   Clients: The Difficult, Toxic, and Soul-Sucking Varieties 40
      Difficult Client Subtypes & Strategies 41
      Das Boot: Toxic Client Dismissal Procedure 47
   Salon Emergencies: "Danger, Will Robinson!" 50
Staff Classification 57
   Booth/Studio Renters 57
   (Microsalon Owners) 57
   Employees 58
   Independent Contractors 59
      The IRS 20 Factor Test, Clarified for the Beauty Industry 60
      Proper Uses of the IC Classification 68
      Vocab Lesson: Lions, Tigers, and "Subcontractors" 71
Freelancers: Beauty Industry Gypsies 75

Employment: Working for The Man 83
Your Numerous Opportunities 83
Employee Rights 89
Compensation, Overtime, and Benefits 91
The FLSA, Free Services, and Being "Engaged To Wait" 97
Wage Theft 100
Diplomatic Dispute Resolution 110
Not-So-Diplomatic Dispute Resolution 112
Punish the Wicked 114
Finding a Job 117
Step 1: Your Professional Packet 119
Step 2: Prep 127
Step 3: Research 129
Step 4: Recon 134
Step 5: Making Contact 137
Step 6: The Interview 138
Interview Questions From the Desk of Satan 139
Step 7: Turn the Tables 149
Employment Contracts 101 156
Non-Solicitation & Non-Disclosure Agreements 158
Non-Compete Agreements 161
Binding Arbitration 163
"Training" Agreements 165
"Take This Job and Shove It" 168
Resign Without Burning Bridges 170

Microsalon Ownership 101 173
Booth/Studio Salons 173
On-Location/On-Site 173
Mobile Salons 174
Home Salons 174
Recommendations for Microsalon Owners 175
Booth/Studio Rental 176
Renters: Know Your Role 178
Commercial Leases 101 182

Mobile Salons 191
    Pros 191
    Cons 192
    Tips 192

Home Salons 193
    Pros 193
    Cons 194
    Tips 196

The Dollars and Sense of Microsalon Ownership 197
    Salary 197
    Local Economy 197
    Demographics 198
    Taxes 198
    Billable Hours 198
    Hourly Rate 199
    Overhead 199
    Break-even 200
    Pricing 201
    Competitors 204
    Gratuities (Tips) and Retail 206

Audit Avoidance Tactics 206
Resources for Microsalon Ownership 210
"Man Down! Call for Backup!" 212
    Desirable Substitute Attributes 213
    Tips 213

Things Your School Should Have Taught You (But Probably Didn't) 215

Your Portfolio: Your Biggest Asset 215
    Getting Started 215
    Navigating TF Collaborations 217
    Necessary Components of an Online Portfolio 220

Lies, Bullshit, and Bad Advice 223
    Bad Advice 224
    Bullshit 226

Lies 228
Build and Maintain Your Clientele 231
　　　Retain What You Obtain 231
　　　Socialize for Professional Gain 236
　　　Referral Programs: Get Others to Spread the Word 238
　　　Book Building During Downtime 238
Consult With Confidence 239
　　　Five-Step Consultation Process 240
　　　Craptastic Consulting Advice 244
Rebooking, Retailing, and Upselling 247
　　　Rebooking Techniques 247
　　　Retailing Techniques 249
　　　Upselling Techniques 251
Deep Discount Dumbassery 253
　　　The Sales Pitch 256
　　　Massive Losses 256
　　　Bad Reviews 257
　　　Poor Customer Quality 258
Salon Policies: Lay Down The Law, Sheriff 258
　　　Pros 260
　　　Cons 261
　　　Choosing Policies 261
　　　Wording, Placement, Enforcement, and Justification .. 262
Relocating: How to Inform Your Clients 265
Preserving Your Health 269
Preserving Your Wealth 273
　　　Budgeting 273
　　　Spending Habits 274
　　　Debt 277
　　　Emergency Savings 278
　　　Investments 279
　　　Retirement 280
Assess Yourself Before You Wreck Yourself 282
Achieve a Work-Life Balance 284

The Interwebs ...289

Protect Your Rep ... 289

PHASE 1: Out With The Bad—Evaluate, Scrub, and Revoke Permissions ...289
PHASE 2: In With The Good—Craft An Impressive Presence ...291

Get Social ... 293

What Social Networking Can Do For You ...294
The Issues ...294
Dos and Don'ts ...295

Respond to Reviews ... 297

Form Your Response ...297
Common Complaints ...299

Consider Your Source ... 300

Keep Smiling ...305

Empowerment and Entitlement: Know the Difference ... 305
Facts ... 308
Your Happiness Equation ... 310

Are You "That Girl?" ...310
Eliminate The People You Could Do Without ...315
What Are You Compensating For and Why? ...319
The Power, Strength, and Freedom Behind "I Don't Know" ...321
How to be Unhappy ...323

Maintain Forward Momentum ... 325
Before You Throw in the Towel... ... 327
Why You Should Quit ... 330

Raise the Bar ...339
A Note from the Author ...343
Acknowledgements ...345
Appendix ...347

"You've Been Served" ... 347

Courthouse Etiquette ...353

Moral Considerations 355
Online Resources 357
IRS Resources 357
Department of Labor Resources 358
Cosmetology Resources 358
Blogs 358

Foreword

"Inside my empty bottle I was constructing a lighthouse while all the others were making ships."
-Charles Simic

  I'm Tina Alberino; licensed cosmetologist, writer, salon and spa management consultant, independent educator, and beauty industry advocate.

  Through my blog, This Ugly Beauty Business (www.thisuglybeautybusiness.com), I break down complex legal and ethical business concepts into comprehensive articles to help salon owners, students, and licensed professionals navigate the choppy seas of our industry. I write content specific to the various beauty trades; covering everything from product reviews to management strategies and everything in between. I am a columnist for The Stylist (www.stylistnewspapers.com) and collaborate with Jaime Schrabeck on Nail Tech Reality Check (www.nailtechrealitycheck.com), a no-nonsense advice column for nail technicians.

  In addition to all the words I write, I can be found teaching at trade shows, schools, and other venues around the country.

  Throughout the years, I've met far too many licensed professionals who have been thrust into the industry without guidance and have given up several months into it. Too few schools adequately prepare their students for the realities of this business and even fewer schools teach them how to navigate the job market. As a result, these new graduates are getting taken advantage of by opportunistic salon owners, enthusiastically taking jobs at poorly managed salons, and struggling to develop their skills with little or no assistance.

  I believe that each of us experiences a different version of the beauty industry. So, before delving into this book, please understand that the advice it contains is based on the version of the industry I have experienced over my career. No advice—not even my own—is inviolable.

One of my favorite letters of recommendation says, "Tina is not an 'outside the box' thinker, she's a 'reinvent the box' thinker." My success can be credited in large part to my compulsive attention to detail, obsessive over-analyzing, and unconventional approach to business. My perspectives and strategies may not suit everyone.

I encourage you to question everything, always. Reinvent the boxes I've created in funky shapes that suit your version of the industry. Experiment. Take risks. Make mistakes. Be different. Be better.

Sometimes, lessons learned first-hand are infinitely more valuable than those imparted to you. I built this lighthouse, but I encourage you to set your own course.

Fresh Meat

Hello, potentials and current students! This section will serve as your reality check. We'll cover the honest, uncensored pros and cons of a career in the industry, how to evaluate schools, and more.

The Real Pros & Cons

"School recruiters lie. Never trust anyone who stands to gain from your acceptance of their bullshit."

The beauty industry cannot be compared to any other and the decision to pursue a career in it shouldn't be made without careful consideration. This business is an entirely different lifestyle and not one that will suit everyone.

From an outsider's point of view, our careers look glamorous and fun. It must be, right? We get to "hang out," style hair, and paint nails all day, don't we? How hard could it possibly be? Plus, the school recruiter said we make our own schedules and earn $50,000 a year, right out of school! Sounds like a dream job, doesn't it?

Although working in this field comes with many benefits, it also comes with a considerable number of drawbacks—drawbacks that school recruiters will conveniently "forget" to mention. The majority of graduates will abandon their licenses entirely in the first five years with the complaint, "I wish someone would have told me the truth about what this industry is really like." In this chapter, I'll do just that (and unlike school recruiters, I have no agenda). To make an informed decision about your future, these factors must be considered.

Pros

Significant number of diverse career options. A license gives you the ability to do whatever you want to do within the beauty industry, including teaching, managing, competing, public speaking, platform artistry, mentoring, writing, consulting, working in fashion, or touring the country as a freelancer. I'll be discussing all of these options and more in detail throughout this book. For now, know that you're not limited to a career behind a chair in a salon.

We'll never be outsourced or automated. Remember the Flowbee? Yeah, neither does anyone else. Unlike other industries, our work can't be outsourced to other countries for pennies on the dollar and we're unlikely to be replaced by machinery at any point in the near future.

Our career will survive financial apocalypse. No matter what, our skills will always be marketable. If our economy were ever to implode and send our society hurtling back to the Stone Age, we would still be capable of trading our services for goods. Even cavemen need haircuts and no cavewoman can turn down a great pedicure.

Performance-based pay. Most salons offer some form of performance-based pay or pay bonuses. (Pay structures are covered in Employee Rights.) Simply put—the harder you work, the more money you make.

Generally, these commission rates can be negotiated during employment interviews and throughout the course of your employment. If you're ready for a raise, discuss the possibility of a service price increase or a commission percentage increase. Many salons raise their prices periodically, resulting in pay raises for everyone.

For complete control over your pay, consider freelancing or microsalon ownership.

Flexible scheduling. Depending on what capacity you choose to work in, you're often able to set your availability. Some owners will allow you to change this schedule at will from week to week. Freelancers and microsalon owners have complete control over their schedules, services, the products they use, and their service protocols—and much more.

Jobs are plentiful. This also tends to be a drawback. Many salons experience high employee turnover (an indicator of poor management). Salon owners often over-staff (another indicator of poor management). The market in a lot of areas is over-saturated with salons (an indicator that the owners in the area are unemployable themselves and/or have no business sense whatsoever). Regardless, professionals often find no shortage of employment opportunities, so I suppose this qualifies as a "pro" in that sense.

Establishing a microsalon is simple. This option significantly cuts down the costs of establishing a business and comes with far less risk than moving into a full-scale salon ownership endeavor. Microsalon Ownership 101 addresses this in detail, so I won't get into it here but to say that it is a massive bonus.

This is a job—but it rarely feels like one. This may be a subjective opinion based on my own experience, but this job doesn't feel like a job. It can't compare to the average 9-5 position. We don't sit in cubicles or behind a crappy desk, cranking out mundane, repetitive work. We create all day. Every client wants something different, so we're challenged often. Our services make people feel better about themselves.

For better or worse, this industry is never boring.

Cons

Schools often under-deliver. Ask any licensed professional their opinion on the quality of their education and you're destined to hear, "Schools cover the basics. Your education begins your first day on the salon floor." They're right. Quality education can be very difficult to find. The chapter, Seek Knowledge, will provide helpful tips for screening potential institutions, but even the best schools often fail to adequately prepare their graduates. If they did, this book wouldn't exist.

Unless you're dedicated and/or talented, this job isn't particularly stable or lucrative. One of the things that make this industry so great (the non-traditional structure) also make it unpredictable. Success can't be guaranteed. Average annual incomes range from slightly below minimum wage to salaries in the six-digits. Where will you fall?

Our income is affected by multiple factors, all of which are in constant flux and only few of which we have control over. It can't be predicted or projected, so if you're sitting there trying to calculate your potential annual income, stop wasting your time. Your career will become what you make of it. I'll explain these factors and how they affect your income in the next chapter.

Employment abuses and tax fraud abound. Many salon owners have no formal business education. This wouldn't be a problem if they were willing to utilize the services of professionals like consultants, attorneys, and accountants, but most don't. Consequently, many owners are not aware of (or choose to ignore) their responsibilities as employers. Most salons are poorly managed at best, which makes navigating the industry as a job-seeker quite complicated.

Competition is fierce. Remember our little chats about jobs not being hard to find and markets being over-saturated and salons being overstaffed and pay being performance-based and most owners not having a damn clue what they're doing? This results in cutthroat competition, not just between rival salons, but between coworkers in the same salon. Salon owners sometimes engage in price wars (which will kill your paycheck) and you may have slow weeks where you'll be tempted to shank a coworker with your shears over a walk-in. This "con" can be avoided by finding a well-managed salon.

The job is extremely physically demanding. The chapter Protecting Your Health outlines the physical perils of this industry and how to prevent the breakdowns many of us experience. However, many people don't realize how hard a career in beauty can be on our bodies. Joint and muscle pain will become part of your daily life, you'll likely require surgical corrections at some point, and workplace injuries are routine.

Benefits are rare. Good luck finding a salon that offers benefits. You want a 401(k), health, dental, and paid vacations? Be prepared to obtain those things independently, because not many salon owners are willing or able to offer those luxuries in our industry. In the chapter Preserving Your Wealth, I'll tell you all about how to secure your own benefits.

People bitch. I encourage professionals to remove the questions, "How are you?" and "How have you been?" from their vocabulary entirely and keep the conversation professional, but that's not always easy or possible. Be prepared to hear people bitch all day long about their jobs, husbands, children, and weight. In addition to the complainers, you'll come across a legion of diverse, irritating individuals (some of whom will be your coworkers).

The industry attracts some weirdos, and weirdos know how to bring the drama. Alright, the industry doesn't attract "some" weirdos, it attracts a metric crapton of weirdos. Don't say I didn't warn you.

This meager list of eight "pros" and eight "cons" can only be considered a taste of what awaits those who choose to pursue a career in this field, but if you're educated, prepared, passionate, dedicated, and have a positive (but realistic) attitude, failure won't be a possibility.

Your Projections Are Worthless

"Attempting to estimate your income is a monumental waste of time."

"You'll make $50,000 a year right out of school working part-time!" the school administrator proclaims as she leads you through a tour of the campus. Unless she's some kind of psychic, do me a favor and tell that lying bitch to shut her face.

Don't let anyone deliver false expectations regarding what kind of annual salary you can expect. Your salary can't be predicted, even if every factor that influences your income were to remain stable (which it won't) and you take every one of them into account (which you can't). Here is a list of a few of the many factors that influence a salon professional's income.

Local Economy. Your area's median household income reflects your local economy. For example, the median household income in Loudoun County, Virginia is $117,876. Compare that to Clay County, Kentucky, which has a median household income of $16,000. In Loudon County, residents consider $60+ haircuts to be reasonably priced. In Clay County, that wouldn't be the case. Local economies dictate pricing.

Market Saturation. How many salons, spas, and barber shops are in your area? Market saturation directly affects the amount of traffic the salon receives.

Competitor Pricing. What do competing salons charge? While I do not ever recommend participating in a price war or setting prices based on competing businesses, be aware that what competitors offer and what they charge will affect the salon's traffic.

Your Pricing. If you're an employee on a commission compensation system, the owner dictates service pricing and may change them at her discretion. What does this mean for you? Sometimes it means a pay raise—but not always. Because of this, Groupons and similar coupon deals sparked outrage in our industry. When foolish owners chose to participate in group discount programs, they utterly destroyed their employees' (and their salon's) income. Coupons, discounts, and promotional pricing will hit your paycheck hard unless the salon has policies that dictate otherwise.

Your Pay Rate and Compensation Plan. If you're paid a flat hourly rate and enjoy a set schedule, it's easy to determine at least how much money you will earn in any given pay period. Any tips and commission can be considered a bonus on top of that rate. (I prefer to use an hourly plus commission bonus payment structure for this reason.) However, the most common compensation plans do not offer a guaranteed hourly rate. These structures (which we discuss in depth in Employee Rights) make it impossible to accurately determine your projected income.

Your Ability to Upsell and Retail. If your compensation system offers commission incentives, your ability to upsell and retail will affect your income.

Your Ability to Rebook. In high-traffic walk-in salons, rebooking won't be critical to your bottom line, but you should make a habit of securing the client's next appointment before they walk out the door. Many professionals gauge their success by their "standing" rate—the percentage of their schedule that consists of regular, recurring clients. For example, if your schedule is filled to capacity with standing appointments (assuming those clients do not move, die, or decide to leave the salon) a rough, annual income projection can be calculated. However, clients get sick and sometimes miss appointments, so this rough estimation would be just that—rough.

The Effectiveness (or Defectiveness) of the Salon's Marketing. The more aggressive/effective the salon's marketing strategy, the busier it will be. If the salon doesn't advertise or stops advertising altogether, expect to see a dip in business that will affect your paychecks.

DIY Product Advancement. What happens to your income after the release of a revolutionary new over-the-counter product? When home highlighting kits were introduced, colorists cursed the drugstores—until those DIY clients started booking color correction appointments in droves.

This factor can swing both ways, so keep an eye out for new over-the-counter products and techniques and try to anticipate how that will affect you. You never know which "hot new thing" will pull money out of your pocket—or have you sleeping on a mattress stuffed with sweet, dirty cash money.

Your Skill Level. As your technical proficiency improves your book will swell and your yearly income will increase. Never underestimate the value of continuing education.

Your Salon's Reputation. You are only as good as the establishment you work for and the people you work with. If your coworkers are not delivering great customer service and fantastic work, both you and the salon will suffer financially.

Now do you see how ridiculous those recruiters are for even thinking your income can be projected or estimated? The factors in this chapter may seem daunting, but the content in this book will teach you how to stabilize the variables that can be controlled.

Seek Knowledge

"The most unfortunate truths in this industry? Good schools and competent salon owners are incredibly rare."

The vast majority of beauty professionals feel their schools delivered an inadequate education. Many felt they were handed a text and expected to instruct themselves. Unfortunately, those common complaints are often legitimate. Good schools aren't easy to find, so thoroughly researching potential institutions before applying is vital.

Generally, when it comes to quality education, you get what you pay for. I've heard of technical schools and budget-friendly independent schools that deliver fantastic education on par with the finest academies, but these institutions are the rare exception to the rule.

Your school won't particularly matter to a salon owner if you have talent, but Aveda, Paul Mitchell, Vidal Sassoon, and Pivot Point graduates will have a huge advantage over technical school graduates in most cases. These schools have a reputation for consistently producing exceptional graduates—and salon owners know it.

Prestigious academies are harder to gain entry to. They have high tuition rates and much higher performance standards than other institutions. Most come with benefits like job placement, continuing education opportunities, and even future employment with the school itself as an instructor or guest artist.

When you've decided on a few schools to research, make an appointment for a service at the school's salon, but don't tell them you're a prospective student. It's important to see the inner workings of the school without having to hear the sales pitch from the administrator.

Pay attention to your surroundings. Is the school clean and organized? What is the student/teacher ratio? How involved are the instructors? How disciplined are the students? Does the school seem to be taking a vested interest in developing quality graduates or are the students basically left to their own devices?

Several instructors should be patrolling the floor, observing students, and guiding them as they work. The students should be dressed professionally, behaving professionally, and should be working—even if they aren't with a client. If students are behaving inappropriately or sitting around doing nothing and the instructors seem apathetic, you're not in a quality school. If the salon is clean, the students are well-dressed and well-behaved, and the instructors are attentive and involved, put that school on a list of places to tour as a prospective student.

When you've decided on schools to tour, set an appointment with an enrollment counselor, and have a list of questions prepared for them. The ones below are those I consider most important.

"Is this school accredited and if so, by which organization?" Accredited schools earn their accreditation by meeting the academic and institutional requirements required by the accrediting organization. Accrediting agencies approved by the U.S. Department of Education include the NACCAS (National Accrediting Commission of Career Arts and Sciences), the COE (Council on Occupational Education), and the ACCSC (Accrediting Commission of Career Schools and Colleges), among others. These organizations set standards for program curricula, student services, learning facilities, and multiple other factors. Schools are expected to adhere to those standards to maintain their standing.

Accreditation demonstrates that the school has been vetted and approved by an independent agency, and are viewed more favorably by salon owners because of that, but that doesn't mean an unaccredited institution wouldn't meet or exceed the same standards.

"What is the curriculum's foundation?" Currently, the most popular systems are Milady and Pivot Point (Salon Fundamentals). I attended a public school that utilized Milady's curriculum for several months before being accepted to a private, Pivot Point academy that utilized Pivot Point's Salon Fundamentals curriculum. I found the Milady curriculum to be less formal and far less detailed than the Salon Fundamentals curriculum—but the Salon Fundamentals curriculum went into a compulsive level of detail. This suited me, but not everyone learns the same way.

Professionals often criticize Milady for being more focused on the state board examinations than providing a rounded education. Others criticize Pivot Point for focusing on technical mastery, not the state board examinations. I am a Pivot Point graduate, but I purchased a Milady study guide prior to my exam after hearing that many state cosmetology exams (including mine) were drafted from Milady's texts. I strongly advise you do the same.

Find out which texts the school uses and look over their program syllabus. Purchase or borrow texts from both systems to see which approach suits you. If you're looking for an intense, detailed course, designed to prepare you as much as possible for a career in this industry, Pivot Point might be a good choice. If you think knowing every bone, muscle, and tendon in the hands, face, scalp, and feet is overkill, Milady's more relaxed, basic, to-the-test approach might be better. Just know that the Pivot Point curriculum is considered to be the most thorough available, so Pivot Point graduates are often preferred by salon owners. (If you think I'm biased on this, do an internet search on "Pivot Point vs Milady.")

"What are the pass rates, drop/transfer rates, and placement rates?" Pass rates indicate what percentage of the school's graduates pass the state board. A higher pass rate indicates that the school likely provides a solid education. However, schools that don't have rigorous standards and accept financial aid naturally attract people who don't take the program seriously, so don't put too much stock into the pass rate if the school accepts anyone willing to pay to attend.

The drop rate reflects the percentage of students who drop out and the transfer rate reflects the percentage of students that transfer to other institutions. The drop rate will be higher in schools with no admission standards since, again, these schools attract students that often don't take the program seriously. However, in private schools with admission standards, high drop and transfer percentages could indicate that the school isn't performing up to their students' expectations. Not a good sign.

Many schools have job placement programs. Ask about their placement rate. While this isn't a factor you should hinge your decision on, decent placement rates indicate that the school cares about matching its graduates with employers and that salon owners in the area actively seek out that institution's graduates.

"Do you accept student surveys and can I review them?" Many schools have students anonymously evaluate their experience with the school by completing exit surveys. Internet reviews are useful but not verifiable since anyone can submit them. Student surveys provide more accurate insight since they are written (hopefully) by actual students.

"What is the student/teacher ratio?" This factor should be taken heavily into account. The first school I attended (a public technical school), had a 30:1 student/teacher ratio. The school I transferred to (a private school) maintained a 6:1 student/teacher ratio for the first portion of the program and a 10:1 student/teacher ratio on the clinic floor for the second portion of the program. Which do you think had higher pass rates and offered a better education? (Hint: It wasn't the technical school.)

"Does the school require students to pass theory and technical exams prior to sitting for the board?" Schools that require their students to pass evaluations prior to being released to sit for the state board have higher pass rates and higher placement rates. Schools that require students to meet or exceed their own standards before going out into the world tend to have much better reputations for producing quality graduates than those that don't. If the school does require students to meet their minimum standards, find out what those standards are and consider it a great thing that they actually give a crap about preparing their students to succeed on their state exams and protecting the reputation of the institution. Go to a school you'll be proud to say you graduated from.

"What student support services does the school offer?" Some schools offer their graduates continued support, some don't. These services might include job placement, continuing education courses, future teaching opportunities, or portfolio building. These services are tremendous benefits.

You should give serious consideration to which school you attend, but ultimately, the old saying, "Your real education starts in the salon," holds true. A great education can be a fantastic starting point and might give you an edge in the job market, but a dedicated, motivated professional will excel regardless of the quality of education they receive. Don't get disheartened if the schools in your area don't meet your expectations or if the ones that do are too far outside your price range. As long as you bring your A-game and commit to rigorous practice and study, you'll be certain to do well.

Mentors: Beauty Industry Demigods

"Skilled professionals are built on the backs of patient, generous clients who are willing to be cut, burned, experimented on, and generally abused by an inexperienced professional—but skilled professionals are also built by mentors that know when to hold their hand and when to let them make mistakes."

When I started in this industry, I was blessed with a spectacular spa owner who both took me under her wing and threw me to the wolves. I strongly believe that this woman made me the professional I am today and without her, I would have burned alive during the "baptism by fire" so many recent graduates suffer through after passing their boards. This industry needs spectacular professionals and spectacular professionals need guidance.

Mentors are successful professionals who show new graduates the ropes and help them develop their skills. Mentors keep their charges on track, motivated, and passionate. They encourage their students and help build their confidence during those rough, shaky beginning years when it seems like they can't do anything right. I've done what I can by writing this book, but no amount of written words will ever be a suitable substitute for a great mentor.

A good mentor knows when to hold your hand and when to let go and throw you to the wolves. "There are some things that I can't teach you," my mentor told me, "things you have to learn on your own through trial and error." New graduates require a steady stream of patient, supportive clients and a mentor that allows them to the freedom to mess up and struggle through.

Clients would sit at my desk for four hours while I struggled to apply a truly horrendous set of nails that looked like sculpted bricks. They would leave with bleeding cuticles and ten pounds of misshapen acrylic on their fingertips. They would return the next day when all ten of those bastards popped off, happy to sit for another four-hour set.

I spent the better part of those years sweating bullets, my heart pounding, terrified to let my clients down. At the end of a rough day of apologizing profusely and replacing bad sets, when I was ready to burst into tears and hang up my brushes for good, my mentor was there to encourage me and to help me work through my mistakes.

You need this encouragement to survive those early years—and when you're ready, you need to pay that gift forward to another professional.

That trial and error period taught me far more than the videos I watched and the courses I took because it forced me to not only troubleshoot my own issues, but also to develop outstanding customer service skills to keep those clients returning, despite the fact that my work truly sucked. This experience is entirely necessary.

Learning our craft requires countless hours of hands-on experimentation on real live clients. You will make mistakes. You need to make mistakes. You will hurt clients, botch haircuts, and wreck someone's color. Clients will leave angry, demand refunds, and cry in your chair. Your mentor will be there to say, "Relax. This will pass. Learn from this and become stronger moving forward."

New professionals aren't the only ones that need mentors. I've mentored technicians whose industry careers were longer than my lifespan, teaching them new techniques. If you've been in the game for a while, don't be ashamed to ask for help from someone who skilled in a particular area, even if they have less experience overall than you do. Never feel too proud to ask someone else to help expand your skill set. A good mentor will never judge any professional who comes to them for assistance.

Because this industry is largely commission-based, I've noticed that not many professionals are interested in becoming mentors since mentoring doesn't pay much (if anything) and essentially creates a competitor. Many of the women I've talked to about this held similar attitudes, making comments like, "It's survival of the fittest. If she's dedicated, she'll learn on her own." To me, this showcases their petty insecurities.

Capable, competent professionals have no legitimate reason to keep from training someone else. They should have nothing to fear from a competitor. Successful professionals understand there are plenty of clients to go around.

So please, if you have something to offer to someone eager to learn, offer it willingly and freely, without judgment. Be patient, have fun, and help another professional better themselves.

End Your Other Life

"Career changes can be terrifying. A successful, painless transition requires advance preparation."

Are you miserably living a dual life? You're a nail technician, but you're also a waitress. You're a hairdresser, but you're also a bookkeeper. You're a makeup artist, but you're also an account manager.

You want to make your part-time passion your full-time career but you're scared of going broke, scared of the struggle, scared of failing. That fear doesn't make you weak. Any sane person would have reservations about committing to a new career, but don't let that uncertainty dictate your future or compromise your happiness.

While impulsively jumping in headfirst does effectively light a fire under your ass, you're more likely to fail. Those "do or die" situations might have a happy ending in some instances, but that road is a hard one to travel and the stress may seriously compromise your job satisfaction.

Starting out in this industry can be stressful enough, so eliminate as much of that stress as possible. To maximize the probability of success and your job satisfaction, make a plan and commit to it. This chapter will help you prepare to turn your dream career into a reality.

Build a safety net. In a perfect world, a salon owner wouldn't hire a professional without having an immediate need for them in the form of an abundance of clientele. Unfortunately, seldom ever is this the case. Calculate your living expenses (food, housing, transportation, utilities, and other necessities) for the next six months if you're a nail tech or for the next year if you're a stylist or esthetician. Save money to sustain yourself during that initial clientele-building period.

Ramp up your marketing & networking efforts. Ease into the industry slowly. Start building a clientele part-time and build your reputation on your days off. Participate in photo shoots, spew your work all over social media, create a portfolio online, and make sure everyone and their mothers know how bad ass, shin-kicking awesome you are. Generate that hype and generate it early. Hit them hard, darlings.

Give yourself a competitive edge. Thanks to the internet, no professional has an excuse to be behind the times in the latest trends and techniques. Keep updated by following beauty blogs and joining professional networking groups. Product companies post fantastic tutorial videos online. You don't have to know how to do every new technique, but be familiar with what's happening out there. Don't fall behind.

Make some raw calculations. Before accepting a full-time position, determine the bare minimum client volume you would need to service regularly at that salon's pay rate to sustain yourself.

As I've said, estimating income can be impossible in the absence of data, but if you know how fast you perform services, the salon's compensation rate, and have a general idea how busy you'll be on the slowest week imaginable, you can get a much more accurate income estimation. (Always underestimate.) If the numbers don't add up, find a salon with higher prices and better compensation. You want do better than "scrape by."

With sufficient preparation and ample savings, you can finally release the fear that holds you back and take a confident step forward into our crazy, beautiful, tumultuous world.

Salon Survival

Mind Your Manners

> *"The first time I had to reprimand an employee for dress code violations, I was seventeen-years-old. She was fifty-six. All I could think was, 'I cannot believe I need to explain why vinyl hot pants are inappropriate work attire to a woman my grandmother's age.'"*

The most important unwritten rules are the ones that will get you in the most trouble professionally if broken. Breaking these rules will hurt your ability to build a clientele and will tarnish your professional reputation.

Many of these are seemingly obvious, but many professionals aren't instructed in proper salon etiquette prior to graduation. In addition, not all salon owners hold their staff members to professional behavioral standards. Their failure to do this gives new graduates a false impression of what constitutes acceptable behavior. Don't pick up bad habits!

Professional Etiquette

Remember at all times—you are a professional and the salon is a workplace. Salons tend to be very social in nature and this rule can be easily forgotten. The salon is a business. You're a licensed professional and should be behaving like one.

Downtime at work shouldn't be spent gossiping or hanging around. There are always things to be done and to let clients see you on the salon floor, playing games on an iPad or flipping through magazines is unacceptable. Keeping busy even when you aren't with a client makes a great impression on the salon owner and the clients.

If you have somehow managed to do all the tasks that need doing (towels are clean and folded, backbar is refilled, retail is dusted and straightened, floors and chair bases are clean, mirrors are wiped down, bathrooms are clean, front desk and magazines are organized, coffee bar is stocked, inventory is accounted for) and happen to have some actual downtime, spend it in the back room promoting yourself online or researching new techniques and products.

Your work doesn't stop just because you don't have a client in your chair.

Dress appropriately and professionally. Keep it classy. Short skirts, shorts, and shirts that expose your cleavage or midsection aren't appropriate. Tank tops are unprofessional and unsanitary. (Nobody wants your armpits in their face while you're washing or cutting their hair.) I've spent exactly half my life in this industry and have encountered far too many slobs and skanks working the floor in the salon. They're an absolute embarrassment to the businesses they work for and the profession they represent.

Additionally, shoes should be closed-toed and comfortable. Closed-toed shoes are required on the cutting floors of most salons anyways, since we work with sharp objects, chemicals, and tools that can be dropped. Hair splinters (sharp pieces of cut hair that embed themselves into the skin) are also an ongoing concern for stylists, so keep your feet covered and protected.

Keep your workstation clean. A seemingly obvious rule, but you'd be surprised how many salon employees let their work spaces become a complete mess during the course of the day. No professional is "too busy" for sanitation and disinfection.

The cleanliness of your workplace gives clients an impression of how highly you value their safety. You may be diligent about disinfection, but if the salon itself looks like the inside of a dumpster, clients will assume that the filthiness of the salon translates to your disinfection protocols.

Keep the retail areas fronted, dusted, and aligned. Magazines should be organized throughout the day, not left scattered across the waiting room and the salon. The coffee bar should be tended to often. Wipe all surfaces, mirrors, shelves, and chair bases daily. Line drawers so any wayward debris can be lifted out and dumped.

Let clients see you clean. It's not enough to keep the salon tidy—let clients see your commitment to sanitation and disinfection. We've taken a lot of abuse from the media lately regarding salon cleanliness. Clients are far more informed now than they were five or ten years ago. Showing clients your process throughout the service is simple and will keep your schedule on track.

Stylists, after cutting and before styling, sweep up the hair, bring dirty towels to the hamper, wipe your shears clean, wash the combs, and put them into disinfectant to soak. Keep the station clutter-free. After using a product, cap it and return it to your shelf or to the salon's backbar.

Nail technicians, before polishing, clean the tools and put them in disinfectant, dispose of dirty files, put dirty towels into the hamper, and wipe dust from the work surface.

Estheticians, remove all of the dirty bowls, towels, brushes, and implements from the room before letting the client rise from the bed to get dressed.

Limit your conversation. After the consultation, I don't advise conversing with clients unless necessary. Clients visit the salon to enjoy a service. Our job is to perform that service. We're not their friend or their therapist. It isn't our job to entertain or amuse them. Some clients don't mind idle chat, but a good deal of them aren't interested in our opinions and aren't there to hear us yammer on throughout the appointment.

Educate the client throughout the appointment and ask for feedback periodically. ("How's the water temperature?" "Is the pressure okay?" "Are you happy with this length?") Outside of that, don't speak unless spoken to unless you're upselling or retailing.

If you have a talker in the chair, keep the content of the conversation clean and focused on the client. Never ask overly personal or inappropriate questions and under no circumstances should you answer any such questions. As the professional, it is your responsibility to direct the conversation and ensure it doesn't drift anywhere inappropriate. Remember, everyone in the salon can hear and see everything you're saying and doing.

Don't complain about personal issues or share your life story. Nobody wants to hear about your problems—least of all the clients. They aren't interested in hearing a lengthy monologue about your journey from infant to irritating, self-absorbed salon professional. Save it for the autobiography.

In addition to being annoying, speaking during the appointment will limit your focus, costing you time. In this industry, time = money. Focus on performing the service—the job you're being paid to do. You aren't getting paid to talk, so don't work for free.

Don't cross the line. Again, you are not the client's friend. Becoming overly familiar with clients is a recipe for disaster, so be sure to keep your relationships with the clients professional. Never ask for or accept favors from them. Don't put yourself in a position where you owe a client anything. Never do anything without compensation, don't fall victim to sob stories and allow clients to skip out on payment, and never perform services outside of the salon unless the client is medically homebound—even then, those appointments must be booked and billed through the salon. There are a thousand different ways to cross that professional barrier, so be vigilant about maintaining professional distance.

Becoming overly familiar will give clients the impression that your "friendship" with them can be exploited to their advantage. (Some clients will purposefully attempt to manipulate professionals into "friendships" for this purpose.) They will devalue your worth as a professional. Maintaining appropriate distance won't allow this to happen.

Set a schedule and stick to it. Clients will learn your schedule and expect you to be there. Maximize your income by maintaining consistent availability. You never know when a client will decide to drop by for a service on an impulse.

Never steal clients. Client stealing (also referred to as "client poaching") is the most deplorable, unethical crime one professional could commit against another. When one professional manipulates, encourages, coerces, or otherwise lures a client (or multiple clients) away from a coworker, they are poaching clients. If you attempt to poach clients from coworkers, expect to be fired. Salon owners take this very seriously.

Sometimes a client leaves one professional for another of their own volition. In the absence of poaching, realize that if a client left you for a coworker, you likely only have yourself to blame. Assess whether it's time to make some changes. Are you talking too much? Are your services up to par? What does your coworker do differently? Can you learn anything from her that can prevent this from happening in the future? Don't beat yourself up over it. Instead, perform a self-evaluation and see if there's room for improvement.

That being said, it may have nothing to do with you or the service quality. Every client has their reasons for switching to someone new. Those reasons are based on a need or desire they had that you weren't fulfilling. If the coworker didn't poach the client, don't blame them.

Never confront the client about it. Clients have free will and have the right to choose their service provider.

Never speak badly of another professional's work. Trying to build a clientele or inspire client loyalty by trash-talking is an insecure, unprofessional, and pathetic strategy that will only leave you looking like a fool in the end.

If the client complains about another professional or their work, apologize, sympathize, and reassure—but never remark on the work. "I'm so sorry you were dissatisfied with your last service. I promise to do my best to keep you from experiencing that disappointment again. If you have any questions about my procedures or would like me to change something, please don't hesitate to ask. Your service should meet your expectations. Your satisfaction remains my top priority, so be as picky as you need to be. You won't hurt my feelings."

In the absence of client complaints, never offer unsolicited comments on shoddy work. You could be speaking negatively about the client's newly-licensed best friend or the coworker standing beside you.

The best way to keep from putting your foot in your mouth is to keep it shut. For example, a nail technician I hired complained about a client's set. "These aren't shaped at all. The body of the nail is flat and unbalanced. If I were you, I wouldn't go back to the technician that did these. They're a mess." The client cocked her head to the side and said, "Really? Because you're the one that applied them two weeks ago. Perhaps I should take that advice and book an appointment with someone else in the future?" (I couldn't help it. I laughed.) The tech went bright red and didn't speak the rest of the appointment. Needless to say, that client never returned to her.

See what I mean about these lessons being learned the hard way? Don't embarrass yourself.

Remain courteous and professional. Always behave as if a client were present. If you wouldn't talk about inappropriate subjects in front of a client, don't do it in the back room.

This should go without saying but: no fighting, arguing, or gossiping of any kind should happen under the salon's roof. Forget what you saw on reality TV—that's not reflective of typical salon behavior. If your employer allows that atrocious behavior in the salon, get the hell out of there.

Don't talk about clients. If you spend any portion of an appointment talking badly about another client, that client will wonder if they'll be spoken about in the same manner. Don't give any clients the impression that they may be spoken negatively about.

Regardless of what abuses a client has inflicted against you, keep it quiet—especially when out in public and on social media. When I managed a salon in downtown Sarasota, we had a weekly standing reservation for a booth at a local lounge. Each Saturday after closing, the staff would walk to the lounge to decompress and network. During one of these evenings, a stylist complained loudly about a client she had to deal with that day. The client was sitting in the next booth and overheard everything.

In addition to being embarrassing for you, that behavior greatly damages your reputation and the salon's. You don't have to forgive or forget, but you do have to zip it.

No profanity. I really shouldn't have to go into detail here, but if I had a nickel for every time I've had to write an employee up for obscene language, I'd have several dollars. (That's a lot of nickels.) Just don't do it. Clients don't appreciate it.

Be honest. Never make promises you can't keep. Clients appreciate honesty. If you're not confident performing a particular service, let them know and refer them to someone skilled in that area. It's better to admit shortcomings than screw up a service. No professional can afford to have a disgruntled client trashing them to anyone who will listen—or worse, trashing them online. Don't become the target of anyone's internet smear campaign. Never be afraid to ask for a second opinion from a more experienced professional or refuse to perform a complicated service you're not confident in.

In the same vein, keep the client's expectations realistic. Don't lead them to expect a stellar outcome if they're requesting a service that may not meet their vision. If you sincerely think the service will not flatter them, refuse to do it. Let someone else compromise their professional reputation. Your professional integrity should always take priority over ego.

Avoid drama. In this book, I'll share plenty of ways to address common issues in the workplace—from settling disputes with coworkers to handling difficult clients to discussing disagreements with salon policies. None of those solutions involve fighting, arguing, bickering, or reacting outwardly in a salon full of clients. Keep your emotions in check, there's no place for them at work.

An employer's failure to enforce proper professional etiquette shouldn't influence your behavior. Adhere to a higher standard. The earlier you begin implementing these practices, the better.

Nothing is Sacred

"Keep your judgments private. In salons, ears are everywhere and nothing is sacred."

When I was a kid, my best friend's mother said to me, "Believe half of what you see and none of what you hear." She has a habit of saying profound things right at the moment you most need to hear them in a way that burns the message into your brain. Not many people have the ability to completely change someone's entire outlook by uttering a single sentence, but she does and she has done it to me numerous times. If she hadn't been in my life for the last seventeen years, I'd be an entirely different person—and not in a good way.

My mother could not be more different from my best friend's mother. My best friend's mother is very nurturing, optimistic, spiritual, laid back, understanding, and creative. My mother is emotionally isolated, distrustful, pragmatic, high strung, and a control freak perfectionist. (My mom's traits definitely aren't bad traits to have. I inherited all of them to a more severe degree and contribute my success to them; I'm just noting the differences between the two women.) When I was a kid, my mom said to me, "All people are liars whether they realize it or not."

Essentially, they both said the same thing: Perceptions are subjective, on behalf of the witness, the messenger, and the person that experienced the event being discussed or related. Your perception of their perception is also subjective, relative to your life experience, knowledge, and personal biases. Absolute truth doesn't exist. You will never know what anyone's real motivations are behind anything they say or do because you aren't them. All we can do is speculate and speculation is worthless.

We do a lot of speculating about others—often without conscious effort. Analyzing others and forming judgments are natural habits, but there's no reason to share those judgments with anyone else. Additionally, what someone speaks to you in confidence should never be uttered to another. What gets communicated to you by others about others should be absorbed, but given no weight until you witness it for yourself.

We're imperfect. I have a lot of faults. I'm an elitist, a control freak, and a compulsive perfectionist. I have extremely high expectations of myself and others that border on unrealistic. I'm brutally honest and unapologetic about it. I abuse commas like a son of a bitch and I speak profanity like it's my fucking native language. Do I form judgments? Definitely. I may leave an unpleasant exchange with a negative impression of someone, but I have no idea how they've been shaped by their experiences. Any conclusions we come to are completely uneducated guesses, so keep an open mind.

Gossiping is deplorable, detrimental, immature, and contributes nothing. Productive adults have more appropriate things to do with their valuable time than circulate rumors, speculation, and vitriol about things that do not concern them.

Believe half of what you see and none of what you hear.

Coworkers: Funky Martians, Delightful Whackadoodles, and Crazypants Predators

"Some people really should come with warning labels."

No matter where you go, there will always be one bitch (or two—three if you're really unlucky) that seems determined to make you and everyone else miserable. At the very least, there will be someone you clash with on a level that makes you seriously contemplate homicide.

Generally, I advocate handling as many issues as possible yourself before involving management. Employers and managers aren't babysitters. Our jobs are to manage the business, not referee petty employee disputes. I tell employees that unless they've already tried twice to reconcile their disputes, I don't want to hear about it unless it involves theft, violence, property damage, or something that significantly affects clients. An adult should be capable of approaching another adult with their complaints before tattling to the boss.

That being said, there are several crazies nobody should attempt handling themselves under any circumstances. This chapter will familiarize you with the most common personalities found in the beauty industry and share tips on how to deal, or not deal, with them.

Common Beauty Industry Personalities

You'll encounter many different breeds of beauty professional. Most will be enthusiastic, passionate professionals you'll be pleased to call friends and colleagues—then there are "the others." We'll start with the least threatening and work our way to the real insanos. Some professionals will fit into multiple categories.

Hobbyists. Hobbyists are usually older, semi-retired, and working in the salon for fun. They tend not to take their jobs very seriously, but aside from that are generally pleasant to work with.

Cultists. You'll find Cultists in [Insert Specific Product Line Here]-exclusive salons. Their brand isn't just a brand—it's a lifestyle.

Some Cultists come without a brand (Powwow Cultists). Powwow Cultists can be found singing, dancing, and chanting affirmations in business seminars at beauty shows.

Cultist salons tend to be very well-managed, highly organized, and focused on education, motivation, and teamwork. The professionals within cultist salons adopt those values and that lifestyle. The brand names attract a loyal clientele, particularly if the line has a great reputation and highly promoted. These salons are definitely not a bad place to be, especially if you're new to the industry—just don't drink the Kool-Aid.

Fame Whores. Fame Whores tend to be very motivated, intensely passionate about their industry, and highly charismatic. Although I don't quite understand the fascination some industry professionals have with "celebrity," I don't judge. Some professionals crave the heat of the stage lights. Their career goals generally include platform artistry, public speaking, competing, educating, or all of the above.

Artistes. You can spot an Artiste by their suffocating, ostentatious pretension and the way they stare down their nose at everyone. ("They're not scissors, they're shears, and I'm not a 'hairdresser,' I'm a hair sculptor. There is a difference, you know.") Their arrogance borders on vulgarity.

Attitude aside, many Artistes have earned the right to be pompous. They tend to be damn good at what they do, they just can't seem to shut up about it. It's a frustrating quality, but often not entirely without justification.

Although annoying, this shameless self-promotion has its value. Artistes often command higher prices and more respect from their clients and employers. If they're even half as skilled as they believe themselves to be, you might be able to learn something. Some are naturally gifted, but a good deal of them have worked incredibly hard to achieve technical mastery. Try to learn from them, just don't let their massive ego suffocate you.

Compulsive Liars. Compulsive Liars seem to have no control over the crap that flows out of their mouth and don't seem to realize how unbelievable their statements are. Ultimately, Compulsive Liars are incredibly insecure. They desire validation and approval so badly, they're willing to lie their asses off and risk being exposed to obtain it. Mostly, they're harmless. Pity them, try to be nice, and do what you can to build their confidence so they don't have to pretend to be someone they aren't.

Slobs. Sloppy behavior doesn't just affect you—it affects the entire salon. Talking to a Slob in private should suffice. Never enable her by cleaning up after her. If she doesn't improve, address it with management.

Borrowers. She "forgot" her shears, doesn't have any clips, and always needs to borrow things from you—things that you need to do your job.

Tell the Borrower you're happy to help her out when she's in a pinch, but you purchased the tools for your use and many of them are quite expensive. Let her know that it's time for her to invest in herself, then stop loaning things out.

Delusionals. Delusionals come in a staggering variety of subtypes. They can be unrealistically optimistic, naive, deranged, a toned-down version of a Drama Queen, a Compulsive Liar that truly believes their lies, or an Artiste without the skill to back up the arrogance. They generally aren't malicious; they just aren't living in reality. Try to bring them back to planet Earth.

Know-It-Alls. She knows everything about everything and she's not afraid to tell you how wrong you are—even if clients are present.

In private, tell her that the clients don't appreciate her interruptions and you'd prefer it if she would mind herself. Most Know-It-Alls just want to help and don't realize their unsolicited "assistance" might insult the recipient.

If she persists, remind her of the prior conversation. Tell her that if she doesn't stop, the next time you have the conversation, the manager or owner will be present. Advise her to bring her concerns about your performance to management.

If it continues, organize a meeting with the manager and require the Know-It-All to be present. Tell the manager that her behavior is insulting and disruptive and that you've made two attempts to speak with her privately to get her to cease, but she persists. The manager should handle it from there.

Flakes. Flakes can't be counted on for anything other than their unreliability. Flaky coworkers are obnoxious, but flaky owners are a nightmare.

Don't expect too much from Flakes and you won't be disappointed. They can't be relied upon, so don't entrust them with anything important or time-sensitive.

Greedy Exploiters. Greedy Exploiters are found in salon ownership. They nickel-and-dime every staff member and are likely to commit wage theft. Greedy Exploiters are the scum of this industry.

Don't accept jobs from them. Ethical salon owners profit off the clientele their business services, not the staff that work for them. Multiple chapters will teach you how to recognize a Greedy Exploiter, so we're not going to get into this here.

Parasitic Adulators. "You're so fantastic! I admire you! Is it cool if I latch onto you long enough to vault myself into some degree of relevancy so that I don't have to do any work myself?"

Parasitic Adulators are Fame Whores who don't want to work for the acclaim they desire. Instead, they find an industrious Fame Whore or someone with status, grip into them, and try to ride them into fame. Once a Parasitic Adulator sees a prime opportunity, they shove their chosen target under the nearest bus and use their mutilated corpse as a stepping-stone onto their own platform.

Fortunately, Parasitic Adulators are lazy and have no end-game. They have no idea what to do with relevancy once they achieve it and don't have the drive or motivation to sustain it.

If someone suddenly wants to "collaborate" or "partner" with you, despite having nothing to bring to the collaboration or partnership, that person is likely a Parasitic Adulator. They'll emulate you, claim your platform as their own, and give others the impression that they're affiliated with you.

Be wary of worshipers seeking status. Drop them. Nobody has room in their life for parasites.

Users. Users see people as tools to be used and discarded. They're good at pretending to be genuine and don't disclose their motivations. People who have nothing to covet or offer and are unwilling to share what they do have are unlikely to be targeted by a User. Don't loan or buy them anything and don't offer career assistance.

Friendship is a give and receive relationship. If you're being asked to give far more than you're receiving, that person isn't a friend—they're a User. Get rid of them.

Drama Queens. Drama Queens are exhausting and unprofessional. Personally, I don't tolerate them. I have no patience for them and no need for them in my life or in any business I manage. Avoid them. Never allow them to pull you into their personal soap opera.

"Managers." She tells you what to do, how to do it, and when to do it. She reprimands you as well. Who does she think she is? She thinks she's your boss. She's wrong.

Handle this firmly in private. Be very clear and leave no room for misinterpretation. Use constant eye contact and enunciate precisely. A lot of "senior" employees think they have leverage over newbies. They don't. Tell her, "You aren't my superior and have no right to dictate to me. Don't do it again."

If this handles the problem, great. If not, don't bother with a second warning. Arrange a meeting between you, the

Manager, and the actual owner or manager. Chances are that they won't appreciate her behavior either.

Thieves. Unlike a Borrower, Thieves "forget" to ask permission to borrow things and "forget" to return them.

Permanently mark your tools to identify them. Don't confront Thieves yourself or make unfounded accusations. Have proof and go straight to management.

Employers take theft seriously. In most salons, theft of any kind is grounds for immediate termination.

Poachers. While there are many tactics client thieves use, ultimately you're responsible for protecting your clientele. Ensure that your quality of work is such that clients wouldn't consider leaving to begin with.

Poachers know exactly what they're doing, so go straight to management. Detail instances where the coworker has blatantly attempted to lure business. If clients have complained about it, mention that also. Most owners put a stop to this immediately.

Shit Disturbers. Shit Disturbers thrive on drama, especially when they're responsible for spawning it. They often don't care if they get caught.

Teams of professional psychiatrists would have difficulty managing a Shit Disturber. Don't even attempt it. They're good at playing innocent (or worse, playing the victim). Fortunately, experienced owners see through that.

Approach management in private and tell them the beast is manipulative, malicious, and causing a host of issues between employees for her own amusement. If her behavior affects others, bring them into the meeting.

The boss will need to address this immediately. Shit Disturbers are most likely to stir up a mutiny or drive good staff away.

If she doesn't get terminated, avoid her until she does. Believe me, Shit Disturbers never last long.

Backstabbers. Backstabbers are unlikely to stop no matter what you or your employer do. Kill her with kindness and don't disclose anything that can be twisted into gossip. Ignore it, avoid her, and focus on the clients.

Incompetents. Incompetents are harmless to you—unless they come in the form of a salon owner or receptionist. There are two types of Incompetent: the Idealistic Incompetent and the Arrogant Incompetent.

The Idealistic Incompetents are characterized by their naivety and absurd optimism. Many inexperienced, first-time salon owners are Idealistic Incompetents. She doesn't have time for business plans, financial projections, or budget-setting! Everything will work itself out! She doesn't need business classes or a consultant or even any practical experience because she has passion! Her salon will be a huge success if she stays positive!

They can be frustrating at times, but Idealistic Incompetents are also amusing, fun, and inspiring. Their passion and optimism are infectious. Once all that incompetence burns away, they make great product educators, platform artists, and public speakers. Some even make fantastic owners.

Unfortunately, Idealistic Incompetent owners are very likely to fail. They neglect critical aspects of their businesses and often don't familiarize themselves with tax and employment laws. (They're too busy picking out window treatments and wallpaper to be bothered with actually running a business.)

Idealistic Incompetents soak up information and suggestions like sponges. They're eager-to-please (often to a fault). Getting and keeping them focused tends to be the greatest challenge. Private meetings are highly recommended. These owners need strong management to handle the "boring business stuff" so they can put their abundant energy into "fun" stuff.

Be warned! Arrogant Incompetents exist in vast quantities. Avoid these owners and coworkers entirely. They strongly hold the false belief that they're the ultimate authority on everything and consider themselves beyond reproach. Arrogant Incompetent coworkers will botch services, distribute bad technical advice, and never accept responsibility for anything or admit wrongdoing. Avoid them and let them destroy themselves.

Arrogant Incompetent owners don't just fail to inform themselves about federal tax and labor laws, they go a step further, making up their own and insisting their version is the law. I suspect Arrogant Incompetents bleed into the Delusional breed since seem to genuinely believe they're correct, even when confronted with irrefutable proof to the contrary.

These owners are impossible to work with and destined to fail. They're aggressive and rule through intimidation. Like the Idealistic Incompetents, they have absolutely no clue what they're doing, but unlike the Idealist Incompetents they'll never admit it. These owners are usually contemptuous of our industry and the professionals they employ.

Husband/wife ownership teams are often comprised of an Idealistic Incompetent (usually the wife) and an Arrogant Incompetent (almost always the husband) who acts as her "enforcer." Stay far away.

Psychos. One day she's your best friend—the next, she interprets every word out of your mouth as a personal attack against her and will key your car and slash your tires by the end of the shift.

Psychos are overly emotional and don't have the self-control necessary for calculated destruction. They're more likely to lash out and make a scene, but aren't capable of long-term strategy like Manipulators (our next group of crazies). They're highly sensitive people with little or no impulse control. They don't last long in the salon before being terminated, so they're more often found in booth/studio rental scenarios, which is worse because tenants have no recourse against them other than to find a new place to rent since booth renters can't be fired.

Psychos do exist outside of reality TV shows. I've personally witnessed a Psycho threaten an employee with a pair of shears before locking herself in the salon bathroom, sobbing hysterically and threatening suicide. I managed for an owner who was a Druggie Psycho. She'd down half a bottle of Xanax with a bottle of wine before 10am and spend the day alternating between being half-comatose and raging at anything that moved. One Psycho stylist pushed another down the stairs, breaking the girl's collarbone.

Psychos don't last much longer than their first outburst, so take a self-defense class, keep Mace in your station, watch your back, and wait for her to get fired.

Manipulators. Calculating, patient, ruthlessly ambitious. They're every manager's worst nightmare because they're damn near impossible to catch in the act. Good luck tracking their end game before they've accomplished it.

Fortunately, these sociopaths are rare and there aren't many of them in our industry. (We attract far more Artistes, Drama Queens, and Flakes than anything else.) You're unlikely to ever get the chance to deal with a Manipulator since the damage will be done long before you identify them for what they are. If you've been had by a Manipulator, try not to beat yourself up too much. It happens to the best of us.

I'm sure that you could identify a few people from your life outside of the beauty industry that fit into these rough personality groups. Crazies certainly aren't industry-specific. Hopefully, this random little chapter gave you a laugh and some insight into the various whack-a-doodles you may come into contact with throughout your career.

Clients: The Difficult, Toxic, and Soul-Sucking Varieties

"Choosing who to serve and who to refuse/refer elsewhere may seem incompatible with providing good customer service. But what's truly incompatible is the misguided notion that we're somehow obligated to serve/please everyone."
-Jaime Schrabeck, Ph.D. Independent Educator, Consultant, and Owner of Precision Nails, www.precisionnails.com

You won't be compatible with every person you service. Professionals who set solid policies, command respect by conducting themselves like competent, educated professionals, and refuse to book customers who present themselves as potential problem clients during their first interaction will rarely attract problem clients. Jaime Schrabeck's webinar recording, "Clients Behaving Badly," and the accompanying post on her blog (both linked in the Appendix), provide fantastic advice to help salon professionals avoid attracting difficult and toxic clients to begin with. However, even the most professional service providers with the strictest policies will periodically have to reprimand or fire a disrespectful client.

Toxic clients don't belong in your chair, but luckily, you won't often come across a client who will push you to the brink of ripping up your license and pursuing another career. This chapter will first outline the more common difficult client subtypes and provide strategies for handling them. The second portion of the chapter provides step-by-step instructions on how to dismiss a toxic client for good, when all attempts to correct the behavior fail.

Difficult Client Subtypes & Strategies

Constant Complainers & Megabitches. "My curls aren't curly enough. My cut isn't layered enough. My color isn't the perfect tone. My nails aren't the right length. My polish isn't the right color. The prices are too high. You took two hours to finish a color, highlight, and cut on my dense, waist-length hair—which was just too much time."

Lucky you. It looks like a Constant Complainer landed her unhappy ass in your chair. Nothing is (or will ever be) good enough for her.

Constant Complainers spend their appointments complaining about everything (every restaurant screws up her order, nobody does anything right, she can't depend on anyone, etc.). She's determined to be miserable. Don't let her bring you down with her.

Consult with a Constant Complainer very thoroughly. Many Constant Complainers have control issues; they feel as if they have none. To put her at ease, let her know that her words are being heard and that what she wants matters. Sit face-to-face with her and make eye contact. Constant Complainers tend to be frustrated and friendless. Show compassion and you might see a complete turnaround.

A Megabitch is an upgraded Constant Complainer. She sees each appointment as an opportunity to break you. Megabitches will degrade you, the salon, your coworkers, and will openly question your competence. They care nothing for your feelings.

Megabitches enjoy pushing your professional limits. They feed off your discomfort, stumbling attempts to regain composure, and professional inability to serve it back to them. Don't let her see you sweat and never let her bait you. The vicious little troll wants a reason to make a scene. Megabitches aren't worth taking the time to manage. They're toxic and they must go. Period.

Dependably Delayed & Last-Minute Cancelers. "Sorry I'm late! I slept in. I lost track of time. My dog was choking so I had to give it CPR. My car stalled. I was caught in traffic. I was kidnapped by terrorists."

The Dependably Delayed client always arrives late with weak excuses. The only thing about her that can be relied on is that she will never arrive on time. Fight the urge to shake this client and scream, "PLAN AHEAD!"

Last-Minute Cancelers book appointments in advance and cancel less than an hour prior. Their reasons for canceling are usually very thin and inconsiderate. "My kids and I decided to go to Disney today." "I made lunch plans with friends and won't be able to make it." "I need an oil change more than I need my highlights and color done today."

Last-Minute Cancelers leave you with huge gaps of open time and can cost thousands of dollars each year in lost productivity. (Don't total up the money you could have made in the time she's robbed. Trust me. Let it go.)

The behaviors of these clients can be brought to a halt with a tardiness/cancellation policy.

"Clients who fail to provide 24 hour notice of cancellation will be charged for the full amount of their appointment. Future appointments will have to be paid at booking. Arriving late limits the time available for your treatment, thus lessening its effectiveness and your pleasure. Clients who do not arrive within ten minutes of their scheduled appointment times will be asked to reschedule and will be charged the full amount of the scheduled appointment."

The next time a Dependably Delayed client trainwrecks your schedule or a Last-Minute Canceler suddenly decides to spend her day at the beach, it won't be a problem since you're not taking a loss. This policy may drive them away but look at the bright side: now they can be replaced with clients who actually respect your time!

Brood & Den Mothers. These clients insist on bringing their children (human or canine) to every appointment. Regardless of how well-behaved they may be, children and animals don't belong in the salon (unless the kids are there to get services and a parent stands by to supervise them). In many states, a non-service animal in the salon presents a health code violation that can result in a hefty fine.

Before anyone accuses me of being unsympathetic to the plight of a busy mother, please understand that I am one myself. I love kids (I actually can't seem to quit having them) and I love dogs (the bigger the better), but Brood & Den Mothers kill productivity, can't fully appreciate their experience, disturb other clients, and might also negatively impact their own service outcome. For example, the Brood Mother client is spending time wrangling her two-year-old twins while you struggle to get her foils in. You're trying to cut the Den Mother's hair, but the pampered, rhinestone-collared minipoo on her lap is snapping at your fingers. The worst ones allow their "babies" to run wild, ignoring them completely and expecting everyone else to supervise their cretins while they relax.

News flash, girls: You're not babysitters and the salon isn't a kennel or a daycare. Every client needs to be fully present and aware of what you're doing. She needs to observe and appreciate the service she's receiving. Take control of that situation immediately.

Pull Brood Mothers aside and tell them, "The time you've booked here is time for you and the other clients to relax and enjoy time away from your children. Next time, please arrange for a sitter. I want you to fully enjoy our services and this environment isn't safe for the kids. There are chemicals, sharp implements, heated tools, and plenty of things they can get hurt on."

That should get the hint across. If not, don't be afraid to get blunt and state things more clearly. "This is our place of business. Your children distract the staff and disrupt the other clients. The salon is hazardous and they're a liability. If you bring them in the future, we will not be able to service you."

Tell Den Mothers that non-service animals are prohibited in the salon. If she arrives again with her pooch, she'll be asked to reschedule.

Smokestacks & Cell Phone Chatters. These clients constantly interrupt their service to take phone calls or walk outside for smoke breaks. Like the Brood & Den Mothers, they are cutting into your productivity. Put a stop to it with a Cell Phone Policy and Smoking Policy.

"To ensure the comfort of all clients, all phones must be silenced or turned off while in the treatment areas. If you need to make a phone call, please do so after the appointment. Our employees are on a tight schedule and we appreciate your compliance."

"Smoking during your appointment time is strictly prohibited."

Clients rarely try to challenge these policies, but if they do, stay firm. Tell them that you do your very best to ensure that you are prompt for their appointments. Their appointment is limited to the amount of time it takes to perform the service.

There simply isn't room in the schedule for phone calls or smoke breaks.

Distraction causes much bigger problems than lost productivity. I mentioned earlier that clients need to be present and focused. There are several reasons for this.

Obviously, clients need to be focused on the service for their safety, particularly if you're a stylist. Your job also requires a small degree of cooperation from the client. (Stylists shouldn't have to remind an adult client, "Face foward, please," fifty times.) By far, the most important reason you need their attention has to do with service perception.

Clients who aren't present form false impressions of their experience because they aren't focused on what's going on. A client who spends her pedicure appointment distracted isn't going to remember a great foot massage the way a focused client will. Distracted clients aren't seeing how thoroughly their barber cross-checks their haircuts or how precisely their nail technician applies their polish. Distracted clients consider us an inconvenient distraction when we need to direct them, educate them, or even offer them a beverage. A focused client, on the other hand, requires little (if any) direction, values the knowledge we share, and appreciates our hospitality.

Pervy Creepers. These guys seem to book with you just so they have an opportunity to sexually harass you. The comments, thinly-veiled propositions, and inappropriate behaviors are unacceptable. Shut it down.

Tell the Creeper you're not interested and his behaviors are not appropriate or appreciated. If he keeps it up, have the salon owner or manager intercede. Depending on how aggressive the Creeper is, the salon owner may ask him not to return.

There's no reason to put yourself in a position where you have to confront a pervert after the initial rejection. A good boss will be happy to handle it.

Noncommittal Indecisives. "I like all of these colors. You pick." "I don't care if it's layered or blunt. You decide." "I don't know, just do whatever you think is best."

Usually, these clients are people-pleasers. They don't want to step on your toes or question your professional abilities. Sometimes, they're simply low maintenance and actually don't have preferences.

It's important to draw out a Noncommittal Indecisive's desires. Tell her you appreciate her confidence, but you want to ensure her happiness. Ask open-ended questions that require more than a yes or no answer. ("What do you think of...?" "How would you feel about...?") Encourage her to bring pictures. Extensive consulting will be required until you get to know her personal preferences.

Hagglers. "$30 for a cut and blow dry? That's too much. Is there anything we can do to lower the price?" "My roots are showing and it has only been twelve weeks. You need to redo this for free or give me a full refund!"

Hagglers have champagne tastes on a welfare budget. They know the price of everything and the value of nothing.

These clients aren't worth the time or the aggravation they cause. They will shoot down your self-esteem and criticize your competence. They want to get as much as they can for as little as possible. You're worth more than that and there are plenty of valuable clients who will recognize so.

Have refund policies in place and perform consultations that leave no room for dispute. If you live in an area where this type of behavior happens often, create detailed consultation and aftercare forms that clients must sign prior to their service. (Colorists and stylists who specialize in hair extensions, in particular, should definitely have these forms.) Give the client a copy of the form and keep the original on file for six months. These clients like to sue professionals for "mental anguish" over perceived malpractice. Protect yourself.

Never negotiate. Acquiescing will set a precedent and before you know it, you'll be working on the Haggler for free. If she's so unhappy with your work, there are plenty of other professionals she can choose from. Refer her elsewhere. Often, these clients have no legitimate complaint. They're not worth the trouble. Boot them.

IOUs & Thieves. "I forgot my wallet." "My paycheck hasn't come yet." "I'll pay you on Monday, I promise!"

IOU clients conveniently forget that they have to pay for their services. Every. Single. Appointment. When it becomes a pattern, it becomes a problem. Require IOU clients to pay in advance. No biggie. Chances are, they'll be grateful to have one less thing to remember.

Thieves outright refuse to pay. Their reasons range from "I actually don't have any money in my account right now," to "This isn't what I wanted so I'm not paying for it!"

If you provided a service, the client needs to provide immediate payment. If they refuse to pay, file a report with the police. Refusing to pay for services (or accepting services knowing that you have an inability to pay) constitutes theft. Would that client walk into a store, take something, and leave with it? Salon & microsalon owners have every right to press charges. I strongly advise prosecuting theft of any kind.

Das Boot: Toxic Client Dismissal Procedure

As a manager, I've dismissed many clients on behalf of my staff, but as a behind-the-chair professional, I have only ever shown a few clients the door. If you find yourself referencing this chapter more than two or three times in your career, you may want to reevaluate yourself and the way you do business by visiting Assess Yourself Before You Wreck Yourself. (Sometimes, it's not everyone else.)

Speak to the client in person, if possible. Do not send a letter or email. You can't text message breakup either. Discuss it face-to-face if possible, or at least over the phone.

Express gratitude for their business (even if you don't mean it). I know this client has driven you mad. She has been responsible for more than one crying fit on your part. She really does have to go—but that doesn't mean you should lower yourself. The first thing out of your mouth after, "We need to speak privately," should be, "I want to thank you so much for your business." Soften the blow that follows.

Drop the hammer. Make it clear that there is absolutely no chance of reconciliation. Stick with "I" statements.

"I feel like I'm not meeting your needs and that makes me feel terrible. I think someone else would be a better match for you. We're clearly having trouble communicating and while I do appreciate your business, I really want you to be happy."

Suggest another salon. Give her somewhere to go, either a coworker or another business entirely. The client might just not like you. She could be a pleasure to work on when paired with the right professional. So, refer her out. "I suggest you try [someone other than me]. I really think you'll prefer them."

Apologize. In all likelihood, you won't actually be sorry, but apologize anyways. "I am so sorry that this hasn't worked out and that I couldn't give you what you were looking for."

Send her on her way. Thank her for her business again and tell her to have a great day. The end.

...but what if it's not the end? What if she gets confrontational or offended?

Not all professionals and clients are compatible. If you don't feel compatible with her, let her know. Try to keep from bringing up specific incidents. Just keep it very vague and stick to the "I" statements. "I feel like I am just not capable of meeting your needs." "I am sorry if I'm mistaken, but I often get the impression that I am not performing up to your standards." "I think you suck." (That last one was a joke. Definitely don't say that.)

"But WHY?" If she presses and insists on specifics, go ahead and tell her. She might not realize what she's doing. Don't get nasty or emotional. Keep a level of cool that even the coolest cucumbers can't compete with. Bring up the most recent, most relevant event.

"I feel that you don't have confidence in my professional abilities. Today, when you seemed to become irritated, you grabbed my comb from my hands and insisted on back-combing your own hair. I don't think it's fair for you to pay me for a service that you need to correct, so I'm referring you to someone more experienced in short hair styles. I want you to be happy and it's obvious that I'm not doing that."

"Today, I felt awful that I had to re-shape your nails four times. I could see that you were upset with me. I have been doing your nails for a while now and this is a recurring problem. Clearly, I'm not understanding what you're looking for. This technician I'm referring you to might be better able to meet your needs."

For every one of those clients who make you wonder why you chose to work in this industry, a hundred others will show their appreciation and make you remember. Don't hang up your shears over that occasional bad seed.

Salon Emergencies: "Danger, Will Robinson!"

"I stepped away to sign for a product shipment and when I came back, all hell had broken loose. Nobody knows who instigated it, but something prompted Megan to hit Lauren in the face with her own blow dryer."

Periodically, drama will erupt in the salon. Although rare, when things go down in the salon, they tend to go absolutely nuclear. There doesn't seem to be a middle ground when it comes to conflict in salons—at least not in my experience.

This chapter addresses meltdowns, from disgruntled clients to enraged staff members to robberies to shootings. These things have been known to happen, and while they're extremely unlikely to ever happen to you, it's not a bad idea to have a plan in advance.

Level 1: Disgruntled, Demanding Client. She's pissed and nothing you do, say, or offer seems to be making it better—in fact, every syllable you utter seems to be the metaphorical equivalent of batting a wasp nest. She's getting loud, making a scene, and her face turns deeper shades of red with every passing second. What do you do?

Stop poking the bear, dummy! If you're not the manager or owner, get her. If she isn't there, give the client her contact information. Quit trying to apologize and stop offering the moon and stars to calm her rage. Ask her to please leave immediately and to contact the boss.

Stay polite with a disgruntled client. Don't become impatient and stoop to her level. Drop your pride. Keep your mouth shut. If she refuses to leave after one or two requests, then you can stop saying please, but not until then.

Level 2: "I'm going to…" "…sue this place!" "…smack you!" "…beat you into the ground!" "…set this place on fire!" Here come the threats. Consider this your cue to take a hard stance (from a wide distance) and tell this person to leave the premises at once. Follow up with a threat of your own. "Leave now or I'm going to call the police." If she refuses, follow through.

Level 3: "Fight! Fight! Fight!" Often, impending fights are predictable. In the salon, things brew for a few days or weeks between two people—a glare here, a snide comment there. It escalates gradually, then rapidly erupts into a screaming match. If you have two adults behaving like petulant toddlers in a slap-fight, a sharp verbal reprimand should be enough to get their heads out of their asses.

If the argument escalates into physical conflict, whether it's a coworker vs a coworker, a coworker vs a client, or a client vs another client, put an end to it immediately. No matter how sorely you're tempted, don't stand around and place bets on who the victor will be. Fights can go from zero to "Holy shit! Someone call an ambulance!" in seconds. You never know when one of those girls will decide to turn a curling iron into a lethal weapon or try to gouge someone's eye out with a pair of cuticle nippers.

I have only seen coworkers come to blows a few times. The other dozen instances where a heated argument broke out on the floor, either myself or the group as a whole were able to shut it down pretty fast. Whenever anyone in the salon seems on the verge of putting you, your coworkers, or the clients in danger, they have to go. Demand that they behave like adults and alert management. If management isn't around, the threat of law enforcement involvement should be enough to cool them both down.

In the super extremely rare instance that someone does attack another person in the salon, empty the building immediately. Don't try to pull them apart. Don't try to reason with them. Get everyone out of the building and call the police.

Level 4: "Empty the drawer." A salon I managed was robbed in mid-November of 2008. I wasn't present (an experience I'm completely fine with having missed). Luckily, our Chamber of Commerce hosted a small business safety seminar that both I and the salon owner attended after several area banks and a jewelry store were robbed in the immediate vicinity of our salon.

What do I mean by "immediate vicinity?" Like, in the same shopping center. It was a scary time.

I held a meeting the day after the class and relayed the information I learned in the class to the staff. My staff wasn't stupid, so I'm sure everything would have gone fine even without the pre-robbery briefing (especially since our "criminal mastermind" was an unarmed sixteen-year-old), but they don't teach us how to handle robberies in beauty school.

When facing a robber, keep quiet and do as you're told—and do so deliberately. No sudden movements. Robbers are nervous and a lot of them are desperate, especially around holiday season. It's a high-stress situation for them and you don't know if they're operating under the influence of drugs or alcohol. You can't control the actions of others, but you can control yourself.

Don't attempt to reason, argue, threaten, or engage the robber in any way. When the robber has left, lock the doors immediately, move the clients and staff to a safe place, and call the police.

Be hyper-vigilant during holiday season. Salons are traditionally seen as cash-intensive businesses with little security. We are easier to hit than grocery or convenience stores. We are far less secure than even the smallest independent jewelry stores. If the salon is in a questionable neighborhood and has evening hours, consider getting magnetic locks that keep others from entering without buzzing for permission first. After 5 pm, start screening those who want to enter.

When the cash drawer hits $500, make a deposit to the office safe or the bank. I recommend the bank. Office safes, unless installed in a hidden location and small enough to hold less than $2,000, are asking for trouble. You should never have that much cash on the premises at any time.

Don't assume that because the salon is in a safe neighborhood, it will never be robbed. I have always lived and work in very affluent neighborhoods. While robberies weren't a common occurrence, they did happen.

Level 5: "Tonight, on the six o'clock news…"

Florence, Montana. 2001: Two female clients and a manicurist had their throats slashed in a salon. The killer was never caught and no motive could be determined.

Chiswisk, West London. 2002: Rena Salmon entered salon Equilibrium with a double-barreled shotgun and shot her husband's pregnant mistress, salon owner Lorna Stewart.

Belleville, Illinois. 2005: Two clients and a hairdresser were stabbed to death at Cooney's Hair Salon.

Queens, New York. 2011: Denise Kenny cut her ex-husband's hair and gave him a shave at D'Galina's Salon in Midtown Manhattan, where she worked as a stylist. He stabbed her to death immediately after during a fight in the salon's bathroom, stole $800 from her purse and the salon's register, and was arrested after leading police on a five-mile chase.

Seal Beach, California. 2011: Scott Evens Dekraai entered Salon Miratage and gunned down eight people. Only one survived. His ex-wife, Michelle Marie Fournier, worked at the salon.

Casselberry, Florida. 2012: Bradford Baumet opened fire in Las Dominicanas M&M Salon, shooting his ex-girlfriend, salon owner Marcia Santiago, five times and killing three others: 28-year old stylist Noelia Gonzalez-Brito (who was five months pregnant), 52-year old client Gladys Cabrera, and 45-year old Eugenia Marte—Marcia's best friend and business partner. Despite being shot five times (once in the head), Marcia survived. Blaumet left the salon and killed himself.

Brown Deer, Wisconsin. 2012: Three days after the Casselberry shooting, Radcliffe Haughton purchased a .40-caliber semiautomatic weapon from a private seller, walked into his estranged wife's salon and opened fire. He killed her and two others, wounded four other women, and killed himself in a locked room in the salon.

Stirling, Scotland. 2013: Ahmad Yazdanparast entered Venus Hair and Beauty Salon, doused his ex-wife in gasoline, then lit her on fire. She suffered horrible burns and died shortly afterwards.

Gloucester, England. 2014: Asher Maslin entered the salon where his ex-girlfriend worked and stabbed her fourteen times with a carving knife, killing her. Staff and clients tried to protect her, but he cornered her by the salon's reception desk.

Paulding County, Georgia. 2014: Robert Steven McDaniel walked into Julia's Salon and shot his wife, Maria Nunez McDaniel, multiple times, killing her.

National-news-level insanity does happen and it does happen often. These are just the first few items that came up in a Google search. These don't include the unsuccessful murder attempts, acid attacks, near-fatal beatings, robberies, or rapes.

Not much can be done to avoid these types of unbelievable tragedies. However, recognize the common thread: domestic disputes, jealousy, and revenge. These incidents are often very personal in nature and the vast majority had serious, significant advance warning signs.

If a coworker is involved in a bitter divorce, custody battle, or abusive relationship, urge her to seek help and protection from authorities. If you're the target, don't write off the severity of the situation or underestimate the capabilities of an aggressor.

Thankfully, law enforcement agencies are taking warning signs like stalking, threats, and property damage far more seriously than they were ten years ago. Utilize the protections available to you and consider keeping non-lethal defense items (like mace or a stun gun) somewhere easily accessible. Keep alert and be ready to react if necessary.

Staff Classification

"Any salon owner who intentionally misclassifies their staff should get audited into bankruptcy and burn in Hell for eternity. Go ahead, tax-evading salon owners. Send me hate mail. I'm not sorry."

In the beauty industry there are three common classifications: renters (microsalon owners), employees, and independent contractors. In this book, each will be explained in extreme detail, but this brief overview will acquaint you with them before we continue.

Booth/Studio Renters (Microsalon Owners)

Booth/studio renters pay a fixed rent each week or month to the salon owner in exchange for space to operate their businesses. In this arrangement, the salon owner does not act as an employer, but as a landlord. They have absolutely no control over the renters in their building. They cannot tell renters what to wear, what to charge, how to behave, what services to offer, or set their schedules. They cannot force them to attend meetings, do chores, or go through any continuing education. The salon owner collects the renter's rent payments. That's it.

Booth and studio renters are microsalon owners who operate within a salon complex alongside other microsalon owners. We'll discuss more about the different types of microsalon ownership situations in Microsalon Ownership 101, but a microsalon is exactly what it sounds like: a small-scale salon operation, often owned and operated entirely by a single person.

Like any other business owner, booth and studio renters manage their own businesses entirely: advertising for themselves, providing their own tools and products, and processing their own transactions. They also carry professional liability insurance and are responsible for paying self-employment tax. They set their own schedules and are not on the salon's payroll. At the end of the year, booth renters provide the salon owner and the IRS with a 1099 for the rent they've paid. They claim that rent as a business expense on their own taxes.

The pros of rental come in the form of independence. You have control over every aspect of the business, but you also carry the entirety of the expense and responsibility. I advise only considering rental when you have established a considerable following of clients.

Only motivated, responsible professionals will succeed at microsalon ownership. I have heard the occasional success story from hard-working new graduates, but those recent graduates had several things in common: they were willing to put in the hours required to build a clientele. In addition, they found affordable spaces in high-traffic locations and had a significant amount of money to both market their businesses and carry their personal expenses through that initial building period. In short—they had detailed plans and the work ethic necessary to make those plans a reality.

Personally, I find the rental model to be frequently abused and do not recommend it.

Employees

W-2 employees are under the direct control of the salon owner. The owner controls scheduling, services offered, quality of work, pricing, policies, dress code, and products. They can assign chores and require attendance at meetings and continuing education classes. They're responsible for providing product and paying employment taxes. They're also responsible (partially) for ensuring that the staff are making money and staying productive.

I highly recommend legitimate employment. Working as part of a team is satisfying, rewarding, and low-stress. Employees don't have to handle the risks or responsibilities that accompany self-employment. They show up, do their jobs, and go home.

Certainly, employment comes with drawbacks also. Some salon owners over-staff their salons and don't advertise. Employment abuses occur frequently. Finding a well-managed salon can be difficult at best. Don't worry. In this section, I'll tell you all about how to spot exploitative salon owners, evaluate contracts like a pro, and find a great salon.

Independent Contractors

Independent contractors are self-employed freelancers and are often commissioned to work on a per-job basis. They're not exclusive to any customer or salon. (If the owner wants exclusivity, she'll have to hire the contractor as an employee.) IC's have the freedom to work wherever they want, whenever they want. They do their services their own way, without direction.

If you're considering a career as a freelancer, you might struggle to find steady work. You are responsible for your self-employment tax (15.3%) and any state income tax. (Keep this in mind when calculating service pricing.) Set your own service and/or commission rates and present these to any salon owners who express interest in your skills.

The IRS 20 Factor Test, Clarified for the Beauty Industry

"Quit accepting labor abuses under the guise of 'industry custom.' Exploitation isn't 'customary' just because many owners operate under similar self-serving delusions."

The IRS has a twenty factor test for determining employment classification status. Even a cursory examination of these determining factors makes it painfully obvious that the independent contractor classification gets abused more often than not. It's important to know what these factors are so that you fully understand why this classification is inappropriate.

First, I want to clear up some of the terminology. "The person or persons for whom the services are being performed" are not the clients—they are the salon owners. The owners are the ones "contracting" your services. The clients are the "jobs" you're being contracted to complete. As you go through these, remember that when they use that terminology, they're referring to the person that hired or contracted you, not the client in the chair.

Additionally, when the IRS refers to "services," they're often referring to the tasks you are licensed to perform. They're not always discussing the individual services you provide to clients.

Independent contractors are gypsies. They follow the money. Too many salon owners don't use this classification correctly—a subject that will be covered in exhausting depth in this section.

1.) Instructions. *A worker who is required to comply with other persons' instructions about when, where, and how he or she is to work is ordinarily an employee. The control factor is present if the* *person or persons for whom the services are performed (salon owner) have the right to require compliance with instructions.*

Working a schedule (instructed when to work), being required to perform work inside the salon (instructed where to work), following service protocols (instructed how to work), and being otherwise dictated to by an owner indicates employment, not independence.

2.) Training. *Training a worker by requiring an experienced employee to work with the worker, by corresponding with the worker, by requiring the worker to attend meetings, or by using other methods, indicates that the person or persons for whom the services are performed want the services performed in a particular method or manner.*

Being required to apprentice or assist as a condition of employment and being required to attend meetings or continuing education classes indicates employment, not independence. An IC is responsible for the satisfactory attainment of a promised result. They cannot be told how to attain that result.

3.) Integration. *Integration of the worker's services into the business operations generally shows that the worker is subject to direction and control. When the success or continuation of a business depends to an appreciable degree upon the performance of certain services, the workers who perform those services must necessarily be subject to a certain amount of control by the owner of the business.*

Salons provide beauty services. Beauty professionals perform beauty services. Without beauty services, the salon would not produce any profit and would fail. Whether or not your services are integrated into the business can't often be reasonably debated.

4.) Services Rendered Personally. *If the services must be rendered personally, presumably the person or persons for whom the* services are performed are interested in the methods used to accomplish the work as well as the results.*

If you're sick, can you call another random professional and have them cover for you? Not having the ability to delegate jobs to other professionals at your discretion indicates employment.

5.) Hiring, Supervising, and Paying Assistants. *If the person or persons for whom the services are performed hire, supervise, and pay assistants, that factor generally shows control over the workers on the job. However, if one worker hires, supervises, and pays the other assistants pursuant to a contract under which the worker agrees to provide materials and labor and under which the worker is responsible only for the attainment of a result, this factor indicates an independent contractor status.*

Can you interview and hire an assistant without the salon owner's consent? Not having the freedom to hire or manage your own assistants indicates employment.

6.) Continuing Relationship. *A continuing relationship between the worker and the person or persons for whom the services are performed indicates that an employer-employee relationship exists. A continuing relationship may exist where work is performed at frequently recurring although irregular intervals.*

Are you expected to show up to the owner's salon regularly and to remain exclusive to that salon? Independent contractors work wherever they please, whenever they please. Only employers enjoy the privilege of exclusivity.

7.) Set Hours of Work. *The establishment of set hours of work by the person or persons for whom the services are performed is a factor indicating control.*

Working a schedule dictated by a salon owner indicates employment.

8.) Full Time Required. *If the worker must devote substantially full time to the business of the person or persons for* whom the services are performed, such person or persons have control over the amount of time the worker spends working and impliedly restrict the worker from doing other gainful work. An independent contractor, on the other hand, is free to work when and for whom he or she chooses.

An owner cannot restrict an IC's ability to work freely. Being put on a full-time schedule or being required to sign a non-compete agreement indicates employment.

9.) Doing Work on Employer's Premises. *If the work is performed on the premises of the person or persons for whom the services are performed, that factor suggests control over the worker, especially if the work could be done elsewhere. Work done off the premises of the person or persons receiving the services, such as the office of the worker, indicates some freedom from control. However, this fact by itself does not mean that the worker is not an employee. The importance of this factor depends on the nature of the service involved and the extent to which an employer generally would require that employees perform such services on the employer's premises. Control over the place of work is indicated when the person or persons for whom the services are performed have the right to compel the worker to travel a designated route, to canvass a territory within a certain time, or to work at specific places as required.*

Are you free to maintain your own business location separate from that of the salon owner and take clients at that location? If the owner disallows you to perform services anywhere other than her salon, this indicates employment.

10.) Order or Sequence Set. *If a worker must perform services in the order or sequence set by the person or persons for whom the services are performed, that factor shows that the worker is not free to follow the worker's own pattern of work but must follow the established routines and schedules of the person or persons for whom the services are performed. Often, because of the nature of an occupation, the person or persons for whom the services are performed* do not set the order of the services or set the order infrequently. It is sufficient to show control, however, if such person or persons retain the right to do so.

Being expected to follow service protocols indicates employment. If the owner requires you to following a specific procedure or pattern of steps, you're not independent. Even if the salon owner gives you freedom to perform the services in your own sequence, if they retain the right to set that order, that fact sufficiently demonstrates control.

11.) Oral or Written Reports. *A requirement that the worker submit regular oral or written reports to the person or persons for whom the services are performed indicates a degree of control.*

This doesn't often apply to our industry.

12.) Payment by Hour, Week, Month. *Payment by the hour, week, or month generally points to an employer-employee relationship, provided this method of payment is not just a convenient way of paying a lump sum agreed upon as the cost of a job. Payment made by the job or on a straight commission generally indicates that the worker is an independent contractor.*

Don't let the last sentence confuse you. When the IRS refers to contractors that are paid commission or by the job, they're talking about people who come into a random business on their own schedule, do a non-integral job without any outside interference or direction, and leave with their payment and no expectation to return. Being on someone's payroll and getting paid at regular intervals indicates employee status.

13.) Payment of Business and/or Traveling Expenses. *If the person or persons for whom the services are performed ordinarily pay the worker's business and/or traveling expenses, the worker is ordinarily an employee. An employer, to be able to control expenses, generally retains the right to regulate and direct the worker's business activities.*

If the owner buys your product (or reimburses you), this indicates employee status. An independent contractor generally makes a significant investment and has a realization of profit or loss (more about that below).

14.) Furnishing of Tools and Materials. *The fact that the person or persons for whom the services are performed furnish significant tools, materials, and other equipment tends to show the existence of an employer-employee relationship.*

If the salon owner requires you to use a certain set or brands of tools (CHI blow drier, Wahl clippers, Hattori Hanzo shears), this indicates employment status. Most of us buy our own tools, but "materials" (products) are usually furnished by the salon. If the owner requires you to use a particular product line that they provide, you're not independent, even if they require you to pay them for the privilege of using the products they dictate.

15.) Significant Investment. *If the worker invests in facilities that are used by the worker in performing services and are not typically maintained by employees (such as the maintenance of an office rented at fair value from an unrelated party), that factor tends to indicate that the worker is an independent contractor. On the other hand, lack of investment in facilities indicates dependence on the person or persons for whom the services are performed for such facilities and, accordingly, the existence of an employer- employee relationship.*

Microsalon owners make a significant investment. They pay rent for their "office" and work in that space. Being dependent on an owner for use of a facility indicates employment status.

16.) Realization of Profit or Loss. *A worker who can realize a profit or suffer a loss as the result of the worker's services (in addition to the profit or loss ordinarily realized by employees) is generally an independent contractor, but the worker who cannot is an* *employee. For example if this worker is subject to a real risk of economic loss due to significant investments or a bona fide liability for expenses, such as salary payments to unrelated employees, that factor indicates that the worker is an independent contractor. The risk that a worker will not receive payment for his or her services, however, is common to both independent contractors and employees and thus does not constitute a sufficient economic risk to support treatment as an independent contractor.*

Microsalon owners can realize a profit or suffer a loss. They could spend a bunch of money on rent, product, and equipment and never recoup them. This constitutes significant investment and realization of profit or loss. If both of these factors are present in the absence of employer control and an absence of an expectation of a continuing relationship, the odds are good that you're independent.

17.) Working for More Than One Firm at a Time. *If a worker performs more than de minimis services for a multiple of unrelated persons or firms at the same time, that factor generally indicates that the worker is an independent contractor. However, a worker who performs services for more than one person may be an employee of each of the persons, especially where such persons are part of the same service arrangement.*

"De minimis" is a Latin expression meaning, "of minimal things." Trivialities. The services a salon professional provides in a salon cannot be considered de minimis. If you are prohibited from performing services at other salons (either with or without a non-compete in place), you are not independent, even if the owner gives you permission to perform de minimis services at competing businesses.

For example, let's say that you're a part-time stylist with a cleaning business on the side. If the owner says you can clean a competing salon but you can't work there as a stylist, you are being restricted from performing more than de minimis services and are therefore an employee of that salon owner.

18.) Making Service Available to the General Public. *The fact that a worker makes his or her services available to the general public on a regular and consistent basis indicates an independent contractor relationship.*

The term "general public" here translates to "competing businesses and private customers." If you're permitted to work in other salons, take clients at your home salon, and basically work for anyone willing to pay you for the privilege, you're likely self-employed. However, if the owner restricts you from performing services for anyone outside of their business, you're likely an employee.

19.) Right to Discharge. *The right to discharge a worker is a factor indicating that the worker is an employee and the person possessing the right is an employer. An employer exercises control through the threat of dismissal, which causes the worker to obey the employer's instruction. An independent contractor, on the other hand, cannot be fired so long as the independent contractor produces a result that meets the contract specifications.*

IC's can't be fired as long as they provide satisfactory results. IC's sign an agreement to perform a particular, specific, one-time job. In order to attain the result requested, they can do the job however they please, whenever they please, using whatever tools they please. They cannot be fired because they're not employees. If the owner has the ability to threaten you with termination, you're not independent.

20.) Right to Terminate. *If the worker has the right to end his or her relationship with the person for whom the services are performed at any time he or she wishes without incurring liability, that factor indicates and employer-employee relationship.*

An IC contract will have termination penalties. For example, let's pretend you hired a really sexy contractor to repair some drywall. (You may or may not have purposefully bashed a hole in that wall to lure him into your house.) As he works, you sit back, relax, and stare at him dreamily. He becomes incredibly uncomfortable with your gawking, drooling, sighing, and mouth-breathing and decides to terminate the contract and leave. The contract requires the contractor to return the deposit in full plus a $50 fee and give you a big kiss on the cheek before he goes. He's disappointed with himself for signing the contract without reading the fine print, but he pays his penalty and leaves, vowing to sue you for sexual harassment.

I may have gotten carried away there, but you get the point. IC's can't just "quit." There are penalties involved.

Proper Uses of the IC Classification

There are very few instances where the independent contractor status can be used properly in the salon. The classification gets misused 99.9% of the time, but here are some examples of the classification used properly (aside from sexy drywall contractors).

I'm a perfect example of an independent contractor in the beauty industry.

- As an independent educator and consultant, I'm not brand-specific and I'm not on anyone's payroll.
- I accept jobs at my discretion, on my own schedule.
- I'm not exclusive to anyone. I might visit twenty different salons and schools in a month and I may return to work at a few of those places again in the future, but there's no expectation of exclusivity or a continuing relationship past the fulfillment of my event or consulting contract.
- Nobody tells me where to be or when to be there. I choose when and where to host lectures, meetings, or

classes; sometimes at a salons, supply stores, schools, trade shows, or hotel conference rooms.

- Nobody tells me what to do or how to do it. They select a lecture or technical training course from my menu, or they make a consulting request. I execute those jobs the way I see fit.
- Nobody tells me what to charge or collects my money. I set my prices, collect a 50% deposit at booking, and collect payment in full by the end of the job.
- I am bound to fulfill a contract or I face consequences. If I break an agreement, my contracts require me to return the deposit and pay a penalty.
- I manage my own staff. When I require the services of an assistant, I choose, hire, and compensate that assistant myself, out of my own pocket.

Nobody owns me. I answer to no one. I'm self-employed.

IC's are freelance professionals. I call them "gypsies." Gypsies go wherever the wind blows them. They have their own websites, set their own prices, and work for whoever is willing to pay.

Most gypsies have a special edge over their competition that makes them unique and highly desirable professionals, but that "special edge" tends to be a niche specialty service that doesn't warrant their full-time employment at any one location. They often refer to themselves as "specialists" or advertise that they "specialize" in something specific. They carry their own insurance, provide their own tools and product, perform their services without any instruction, and follow the cash. Many maintain their own business locations (typically studio suites or home salons). Some high-profile nail artists are currently touring salons around the country—another good example of an independent, self-employed, beauty industry gypsy.

A salon owner can hire a gypsy professional as an IC to perform a specialty service or to work a special salon event. For example, salon owner Jasmine has several clients who are interested in getting permanent makeup, but her salon doesn't offer that service and she doesn't have enough interest to justify hiring an artist even part-time. (Also, the liability and insurance requirements of a high-risk service like permanent makeup freak her out.) However, she wants to make those clients happy and she knows of a great freelance permanent makeup artist in the area.

The owner arranges a permanent makeup party for her clients and has the artist sign a work agreement. The permanent makeup artist comes in for that event, does the permanent makeup, and leaves with her payment. If the artist broke the arrangement, she would be penalized in accordance with the contract's terms.

Working in the same salon every day, being expected to be loyal to that salon, being paid a paycheck on a biweekly basis, being told what to do and how to do it, being told what products/tools to use, being controlled through the threat of dismissal, being required to go to training or mandatory meetings, and being required to work a schedule set by the salon owner are all indicators of employment status. Nothing about that arrangement indicates self-employment, so why would you pay the entirety of your employment tax responsibility? That extra 7% is the sacrifice an independent contractor makes in exchange for the freedoms that self-employment affords them. If the owner wants to control you, they need to be paying employment tax.

The government takes a hard stance against misclassification and commits to punishing salon owners who violate classification laws. The Department of Labor, IRS, Wage & Hour Division, and State Attorney offices cooperate in these investigations and penalize offenders simultaneously. Enormous settlements have become the rule and substantial judgments adverse to salon owners have become commonplace.

Vocab Lesson: Lions, Tigers, and "Subcontractors"...Oh My.

"If you are responsible for paying the entirety of your employment tax responsibility, you are self-employed. The owner can call you 'independent,' 'contracted employee,' 'subcontractor,' or 'the goddamn supreme CEO of the unicorn fairies'—you're self-employed. Period."

As you now know, an extremely common labor abuse in our industry is the misclassification of employees as independent contractors. Unless you are a freelancer or microsalon owner, you are not "independent." I strongly advise all salon professionals to avoid these arrangements since they do not benefit you and put the owner at extreme risk. Owners who engage in this practice should be informed and advised against it for their own benefit. The only self-employed professionals who belong in the salon are booth renting sole proprietors and the occasional freelancer.

This chapter outlines some of the deceptive vocabulary some salon owners may utilize to trick salon staff into accepting illegal employment classification arrangements.

Independent contractors are considered by the IRS to be self-employed. Salon owners will try to coerce their staff to accept the IC status by telling them that the arrangement will benefit them. The owner might say, "This is better for you since no taxes will come out of your checks."

What a thoughtful, charitable soul, right?

Wrong. What they are not disclosing is that at the end of the year, you will be solely responsible for covering your employment tax since you are self-employed. At the end of the tax year, you will pay 15.3% of your total earnings to the IRS (and any applicable state employment tax). If you were a proper, W-2 employee, the owner would be responsible for paying half of that. As an independent contractor, you're also not entitled to government employment benefits like worker's compensation or unemployment, since you are not paying into them.

Clearly, this arrangement only benefits the owner. Those taxes will have to be paid eventually. It's always better to have them come out of your checks than to be stuck with a substantial IRS bill at the end of the year. It's also better to only pay what you're required to pay—half.

"Hybrid" Status. Salon owners also utilize outright deception when describing the nature of the IC classification. They refer to it as a "hybrid status," or something similarly ridiculous. You are either employed or self-employed. There is no such thing as a "hybrid status."

A lot of professionals (and owners) have an incorrect belief that an independent contractor or "subcontractor" is a special type of employee who has more freedoms than a regular employee, but not as many freedoms as a booth renter. In reality, no classification distinction exists between an independent contractor, a subcontractor, and a self-employed person.

General Contractors. A general contractor is a person who assumes responsibility for overseeing the completion of a large project and hires, supervises, and pays all subcontractors. General contractors are under contract themselves by a business entity or private employer.

An example of a general contractor in our industry would be a shoot coordinator, contracted by a company to hire and supervise the staff necessary for putting together images for an ad campaign. That coordinator would be responsible for finding a MUA, photographer, stylist, set designer, and clothing designer. She would also be responsible for making sure all of those subcontractors are producing results consistent with the company's requests; she wouldn't be telling each of them how to get the final result.

A salon owner operating in her capacity as a salon owner is not a general contractor. Owners may try to claim that they're general contractors and have the right to hire independent contractors or subcontractors to work under them because they're self-employed themselves. They're wrong. The salon owner is not under contract by anyone. They are a business entity operating independently of any outside control.

Subcontractors. A subcontractor is a self-employed person or business that contracts to provide a specialized service necessary for the performance of another's contract, under the direction of a general contractor. Unless you're hired to perform a small portion of a large project by a general contractor who is responsible for overseeing the completion of that project (like in the photoshoot example above), you are not a subcontractor.

Know what these terms mean and avoid anyone that tries to convince you that these classifications are appropriate in a traditional salon employment setting.

Freelancers: Beauty Industry Gypsies

"Freelancing can be extremely liberating, but it can also be terrifying. If you like to live on the edge and you aren't averse to subsisting on Top Ramen and canned vegetables from time to time, go for it. If the thought of financial instability gives you ulcers, freelancing would be a bad career move."

Freelancing requires dedication, self-discipline, and superior financial management skills. For professionals who possess the ability to manage themselves, freelancing can be extremely satisfying (and financially rewarding). This chapter outlines a few of the many opportunities available to industrious entrepreneurs.

Educating. Education is instruction without intent to sell—a focus on learning, not profit. Actual educating happens in classrooms, trade shows, and beauty supply stores.

As an independent educator, my opinion on educating is incredibly biased. I find it to be extremely rewarding, fun, and profitable. Educators have the freedom to go wherever they want and teach whatever they want. If they're teaching technical skills, they have the freedom to pick and choose which products to work with—no company owns them or dictates their curriculum. We can pair our classes with online supplements like videos, blogs, magazine articles, or webinars. Good educators build a following and make a name for themselves as experts in their field.

Teaching in schools as a full-time instructor also has numerous benefits, such as steady pay (and those elusive benefits we seldom see). Successful salon professionals net much more per year than salaried instructors, but teaching is definite, guaranteed regular income whereas the professional salon arena still largely operates with the unpredictable commission-only based compensation systems.

Product Marketing/"Educating." Every company has a fleet of "educators," but don't let the title confuse you. Your job as an educator isn't necessarily to educate; your job is to sell, sell, sell! You present the product and share the product's features while doing demonstrations, then close as many deals as possible before the end of the class.

Becoming an educator is usually pretty easy, depending on the company. Companies are happy to provide you with free training in how to use and effectively sell their products, which can be useful in your role as a product educator and in the salon. Most product lines have websites where links to employment opportunities can be found.

The drawbacks to these positions are: they tend not to pay particularly well, they require quite a bit of travel, and many of them require educators to pay expenses up-front and submit receipts for potential reimbursement. Notice that I said "potential" reimbursement. I have heard many complaints from educators regarding expenses that were never reimbursed. Time spent traveling also might not be compensated, depending on that company's policies. In addition, most companies classify educators as an independent contractors, so you are going to be paying your employment taxes out of your own pocket. Also, the majority of manufacturers are large corporations, and corporations often develop reputations for treating educators as expendable. (Not all of them, but a good deal are not known for treating educators as valued members of the company.) Be sure to ask veteran educators about their honest experiences with the company.

These positions usually aren't meant to serve as full-time jobs. In my experience, a class will be requested by a supply store or school. A date will be set and registration will begin. If the class doesn't meet minimum occupancy by the date of the class, it will be canceled and the educator will not receive compensation for the time lost. If you are planning on taking that particular day off anyways, you might be cool with this risky system. However, if you're booked to capacity and can't stomach the thought of booking out an entire day for a class that may not happen, this position might not be ideal.

Being an educator for a manufacturer can be fun if you're flexible, have strong sales skills, love to travel, and enjoy meeting new people. It's a great way to gain industry recognition, especially if you pair educating with competing. Some educators advance through the company and are promoted to artistic directors and platform educators; if you're interested in becoming either, a position as a product educator might be a great place to start obtaining the necessary experience and contacts.

Competing. I don't know of anyone who has made a full-time career of competing, but competing can be a great way to build your reputation. Generally, unless you have someone sponsor you to cover your entry fees, model compensation, and travel expenses, competing won't make you money.

Most competitions have an entry fee and extremely strict guidelines. If you (like me) are uncomfortable in stressful environments, working under intense time constraints under the watchful eye of judges and spectators, you might not be cut out for competition. However, if you thrive under pressure and love the energy of creating for an audience, take a shot at it!

Competitions happen at trade shows, typically. Some are also offered through trade magazines. Be sure to read the terms and conditions of entry carefully, as many of the companies sponsoring the competition will put clauses in their entry forms that give them full license to use any images you submit for any purpose, without compensating you. If you're submitting a photo entry, this clause might cause issues with your photographer or model, so be sure to have all parties involved in the project sign releases, giving you the right to distribute the work. I doubt you would run into any issues here, since trade magazines are good about crediting everyone involved in the creation of an image, but caution never hurt anyone.

Public Speaking. Public speaking often goes hand-in-hand with educating. Educators perform a wide variety of roles, including technical training, product training, mentoring, coaching, public speaking, and more. Most educators work multiple ways (for example, I do technical training, mentoring, consulting, writing, and educating/public speaking). Some prefer to focus on one area.

Public speakers make their living touring salons and trade shows, delivering speeches and lectures. Educating at trade shows can get expensive, depending on what their policies for educators are. Often times, securing a classroom requires a booth commitment or a classroom rental fee—or both. Travel fees may or may not be covered. For events that take place in salons and schools, you can set your own rates and ensure that your fees sufficiently cover travel expenses.

Public speaking as an independent educator gives you tremendous freedom to create the curriculum you want, but to get busy and stay busy, you'll have to focus on building an audience and keeping yourself relevant. For me, social media participation has practically become a second job. In addition to that, I adhere to a once-weekly blog/podcast posting schedule, write a monthly column for The Stylist, and answer reader submissions on Nail Tech Reality Check (an advice column Jaime Schrabeck and I collaborate on weekly). There's a lot more to public speaking than showing up and talking to a crowd of people.

To supplement your income as a public speaker (and offset any expenses), I recommend having some kind of merchandise or service to sell.

Writing. I love writing! Look, I'm doing it right now! Unfortunately, it doesn't pay as well as one would think. You certainly can make a decent income, but we're not just slapping words on a page and calling it "art" here.

Many trade publications in our industry take submissions from freelancers. You send in a proper query, the editor determines whether or not they want it, they send back a proposal contract, you either accept or deny. If you accept, you write the piece and collect the earnings on publication.

I have written for trade publications in the past, both inside and outside of the beauty industry. Each magazine handles its content differently. A major drawback is that writers never know if the editor assigned to their piece will be experienced or some college intern. If you're particular about the pieces that bear your name, freelance writing may not be for you.

Some publications also don't give writers much freedom or control over the piece they're writing, so it can feel very much like following a formula. If you check out the major trade magazines, you'll see that most of them (with the exception of *The Stylist*) follow a very specific formula: Intro, Facts, Quote, More Facts, Quote, Quote, More Facts, Neutral Call to Action, Conclusion. Editors will tell you how many sources they want, what they want the article to say overall, how many words you have to work with, and what information they want included. For some of us, this turns writing into a chore. It sucks.

Because of the immense freedom available, books and blogs are easier to write, but just because you have the ability to write whatever you want doesn't mean you should churn out garbage. You don't have to go to college, but your education in writing and composition never stops; read books on technique, follow blogs, and go to conferences.

Writing requires intense commitment to quality and integrity, in my opinion. If you aren't willing to spend a good deal of time composing each piece and continually improving your skills, don't bother.

Mentoring & Career Coaching. Mentoring can be an extremely rewarding experience. Mentors take new professionals under their wing and help them develop their technical and professional skills. They act as compasses, guiding their charges through the industry. Mentors that charge for their time and skills are often called "career coaches."

Platform Artistry. Lights! Camera! Tiny microphones clipped to your lapel! Standing for hours on a stage at a trade show, performing demonstrations for the writhing, shifting masses while talking about the many fantastic features your company's product line offers!

Platform artists are the product educators you see demonstrating onstage at shows. They are traditionally gifted with titles like, "Artistic Director," or "International Educator." They are product educators that get lifted into another tier by their companies thanks to their charisma, talent, and superior sales abilities.

Some of these positions are salaried, but not many from my understanding. The majority of platform artists I know also own their own salons and do performances for their respective companies during trade show season or special events.

Fashion Styling. Lights! Camera! ...but no microphones or platforms. There might be runways involved, but you won't be the one walking them. Many professionals freelance in fashion at one point or another in their careers. These jobs involve prepping models for photo shoots or runway modeling.

Many of these jobs take place on set, so you must be incredibly organized. These positions often require professionals to churn out quality work extremely fast, so you also need to possess considerable technical skill. The ability to put a mouthy model in her place will also serve you well.

These jobs can be extremely stressful, so be prepared to work under pressure.

These are only a few of the options available to you as a salon professional. Next, we'll delve into microsalon ownership—an entirely new ball game.

Employment: Working for The Man

"I find employment preferable to booth rental and freelancing because it eliminates room for conflict. If you and the salon owner share similar professional philosophies and the owner fulfills their responsibilities as an employer, the salon thrives and therefore, so do you."

What does it mean to be "employed?" A lot of beauty workers consider the freedom and independence available to us as one of the best features of our profession, but I don't feel that this independence serves us, our industry, or the businesses we work in. My experiences have made it clear to me that proper employment combined with a fair, legal compensation system creates happy employees with long-term careers in successful salons.

As an employee, you are on the salon's payroll. The salon owner pays your taxes and provides all necessary products. (Some may even provide tools, but most of us prefer to use our own.) You answer to the salon owner, work an assigned schedule, follow service protocols, attend meetings, and adhere to rules and regulations. In return for your obedience and hard work, the owner compensates you fairly in accordance with state and federal labor laws.

In this section, you'll learn about cover letters, resumes, portfolios, professional presentation, how to prepare for an interview, how to evaluate and negotiate an employment contract, and much, much more.

Your Numerous Opportunities

Many employment opportunities can be found within a salon—even if you aren't licensed yet. Here's an overview of the most common salon positions.

Assistant. Many beauty professionals get their start as an assistant. Assisting doesn't pay particularly well (often minimum wage plus tips), but the value of the knowledge you gain when assisting under someone particularly talented will certainly make up for it. Assistants are responsible for catering to the needs of the professional (or department) they're assigned to. This might mean shampooing clients, mixing color formulas, acting as a second set of hands, or all of the above.

Most state cosmetology boards outline an assistant's scope of practice and some prohibit assisting entirely unless you're licensed, so check your state guidelines before applying for a position. This should be the responsibility of the salon owner, but you're an adult—take responsibility for educating and protecting yourself. Operating outside your scope of practice can lead to hefty fines and possibly misdemeanor charges.

Do not agree to any employment arrangement that requires you to become indentured to the salon owner in exchange for "training." Some salon owners attempt to gain free labor from recent graduates by requiring them to "assist" or "train" for a period of time for free. They will often require the "trainee" to sign an agreement that makes them responsible for reimbursing the salon owner if the trainee resigns or gets fired before they meet certain conditions. Agreements like this almost always require the "trainee" to remain on staff for two or more years (working for a reduced commission rate) after the "training" ends to help the owner "recoup" these so-called "training expenses."

These salon owners often don't provide any training. Instead, they use these "trainees" as servants. I've seen owners work these naïve new graduates half to death, drive them out of the salon by being disrespectful and demanding, and then take them to court for thousands of dollars in "training expenses."

You may be inexperienced but you're not a slave. We'll talk about these "training agreements" in detail in Employment Contracts 101.

Receptionist. Clients encounter the receptionist first, whether they call or walk in. Receptionists are the face of the salon, so they're expected to present themselves accordingly. Receptionists must be organized, reliable, responsible, have considerable people skills, and capable of consistently providing stellar customer service. These positions can be very stressful, especially if you don't have experience in scheduling or reception. You'll be required to greet clients, alert staff of client arrivals, cash out clients, record tips, answer phones, set appointments, and more. Pay ranges from slightly above minimum wage to well above it, depending on the skill of the receptionist.

If the salon doesn't have computerized software, you will also require a solid memory or great recordkeeping skills. Because receptionists are responsible for scheduling appointments, they need to know each service provider's time requirements for each service the salon offers. They also have to remember each individual client's needs. (For example, clients with long hair will require more time than clients with shorter lengths.)

Don't panic. Thankfully, most salons utilize computerized booking software. This software allows owners to program these service times and client histories, so you're unlikely to have to commit this information to memory.

Guest Coordinator. Guest coordinators are often found in upscale spas. They're a combination between concierge, janitor, receptionist, and assistant. Guest coordinators make sure towels and linens are clean and stocked, escort clients to locker rooms and treatment areas, keep the salon orderly, greet clients at the desk when necessary, and restock backbar products. In some businesses, they may also be required to breakdown treatment rooms after services; it really just depends on what the owner's needs are.

These positions are hard work and require initiative. Pay ranges widely, depending on the spa and the duties the coordinator is required to perform.

Salon Professional. The vast majority of states require salon professionals to be educated and licensed before you can perform beauty services of any kind in any environment for compensation. Unlicensed activity (or worse, presenting yourself as a licensed professional when you aren't) often comes with large fines and serious penalties. Some states even consider it a misdemeanor offense. It is in your best interest to ensure that you are compliant with all applicable state regulations.

In the salon, your duties will vary, but generally, your job requires you to provide beauty services to clients. Salon professionals may also be expected to perform salon upkeep duties also, such as towel washing and folding, sweeping, and other chores.

Manager. As someone who has spent the majority of their career working in this field, let me assure you that only the strong survive this position. You must be extremely organized, professional, prompt, diplomatic, educated, and prepared to take swift action when necessary. You need to be pragmatic, proactive, and patient. You must be able to work well under intense pressure. Positions in management also require considerable people skills.

Floor managers are charged with overseeing operations on the salon floor while general managers are tasked with running the entire salon overall, so duties vary depending on the needs of the owner and their level of involvement in the business. Salon owners who are involved in their businesses don't require much from a manager while owners who prefer to work behind a chair and let the manager oversee operations will require much more from a manager. Therefore, manager salaries vary widely. Experienced managers can command salaries as high as $50,000 a year or more, depending on the size and type of salon or spa they're charged with and their responsibilities.

Personally, unless you're inexperienced and getting your toes wet, I don't recommend taking on a floor management position for less than $15 an hour or a general management position for less than $20 an hour.

Owner. If you are reading this book as a potential student, recent graduate, or inexperienced professional, you aren't ready to even consider ownership. I don't care if you have an MBA, until you've spent time in this industry working it from multiple angles (or unless you're willing to shell out the money for a quality consultant), don't even entertain this idea.

A salon owner's job is to keep the staff busy, motivated, and on-track. They keep the salon visible by dedicating a considerable amount of time to marketing, new service development, social media engagement, and community involvement. A salon owner ensures that all employees are doing their jobs—and somehow completes the five-hundred other tasks necessary to keep a business thriving and growing exponentially. A general manager assumes these same responsibilities if working for an owner who works behind the chair instead of actively managing their salon.

Owner responsibilities vary widely, as do their salaries. Absentee owners who set up shop and walk away, assuming their salons will "run themselves," are destined to fail in short order. Incompetent owners who don't structure their businesses appropriately or manage it correctly make very little money and are unlikely to make it through their first five years.

Competent owners who commit to growing their business and structure their compensation and service pricing appropriately will reap the benefits of those efforts. Their businesses often thrive for decades and many expand into multiple locations.

Because so many factors influence salon performance, attempting to provide you with a range of salaries is impossible. Don't believe the Bureau of Labor Statistics' figures—they're bullshit. You get out of the salon what you put into it.

Extensive education and experience are necessary requirements. The reason so many salons are so poorly run can be attributed to owners stubbornly failing to acknowledge that you can't just "wing it." Many fail to plan, build their businesses on credit, and refuse to hire the necessary support professionals that a successful business requires (like attorneys, accountants, or consultants). They start their endeavors asking themselves, "How hard could it possibly be?" when they should be asking, "Am I prepared? Am I educated enough about this business?" Because of their failure to plan and educate themselves, the vast majority of these salons fail within a very short time period—usually as soon as the salon owner's credit runs out.

When most aspiring owners fully understand what salon ownership requires and entails, they no longer want move forward. They all like to think that they own the business, but the sad truth is that the salon owns them—they become slaves to a monster they created. Many owners open their salons for the wrong reasons. They want to craft the perfect working environment for themselves, without realizing that ownership requires full-time commitment.

Simply put: you can't be a successful salon owner if you're working on the floor with your staff.

I have spent my entire career running the businesses of talented stylists. They opened their shops, struggled to juggle the duties of salon owner and salon professional, and ultimately realized that one person can't perform both functions well.

So, before considering a career in ownership, think long and hard about what you want to spend your days doing. If you can't handle the fact that you'll spend the vast majority of the week behind a desk, on the phone, running errands, or at networking events and that you'll only have enough time to take clients two days out of the week (if you're lucky), then either plan on hiring a general manager or consider microsalon ownership instead.

Employee Rights

"You don't need a federal law to tell you what you deserve. Simply refuse to take jobs from owners who can't afford to pay their staff."

One of the most frequent questions I get asked by my subscribers is, "How do owners get away with [insert common violation]?"

My answer: Because you let them.

I've had many owners contact me for advice, horrified to discover that they unintentionally violated state and federal laws. Part of the blame can be placed on them for not putting forth the effort to research for themselves, but a bit of blame can also be placed on schools for not making it a priority to include this vital content in their curriculum.

Few schools teach their students how to identify exploitative salon owners or abusive labor practices and that can be attributed to the fact that schools are businesses. They want students in and out as fast as possible. Many teach the bare minimum required. Consequently, a lot of graduates enter the industry without knowing their rights. Everything they learn about salon management and employment practices, they learn from their employers, most of whom are doing things wrong.

Unfortunately, I have no control over the monkeys in that circus.

Aside from the ignorant, a great deal of owners willfully violate federal tax and labor laws. For example, one of my readers reported that her employer requires her to purchase product from her "backbar boutique," takes 50% of her income, 20% of her tips, $30 out monthly, and $5.75 out each paycheck for "advertising fees" and deducts even more for use of the credit card machine. This owner classifies the stylist as an "independent contractor," making the stylist responsible for paying the entirety of her self-employment tax and state income tax. Those tax figures combined drop her 50% service commission down to 29%. In addition, she's paying the owner at least $35.75 every month for "fees" and must purchase all products from the owner. I don't even want to think about how much the owner rakes in by taking 20% of her tips or that arbitrary "credit card processing fee."

These violations happen often. Around the country, salon owners violate tax and labor laws at their staff's expense claiming "that's how it has always been done." Salon employees believe this wage theft and tax fraud are "industry custom." Employment abuses are not a "custom" in any industry—at least not in America. Just because these crimes are commonly committed and often go unpunished doesn't mean they're permissible or acceptable.

Every single day, I hear unbelievable stories of exploitation and abuse. Rarely do victims hold salon owners accountable for their crimes. Many salon employees naively believe their boss "know best." This needs to stop now. Get informed and inform others. If something doesn't sound right, don't just shrug and accept it. Question it. Stand up and put an end to these asinine employment practices.

Compensation, Overtime, and Benefits

"If the salon owner couldn't afford to meet their minimum wage responsibilities, they had no business opening a salon to begin with."

Compensation Structures

Salon owners utilize many different compensation methods. These structures include commission, hourly, hourly plus commission, hourly versus commission, and hourly plus tiered commission bonuses.

Hourly compensation is straightforward. The employer pays a set rate for each hour you work. You know exactly how much money you'll make each pay period and you're guaranteed to go home with something. Hourly compensation doesn't get utilized in our industry often because it doesn't serve anyone's interests.

The primary complication this compensation system presents is that it attracts the wrong employees. Hourly employees have no incentive to upsell or work harder than they have to. If a service provider earns the same amount per hour regardless of what they're doing, an empty book won't bother them. They won't attempt upselling because their pay won't change either way. They won't care if clients are satisfied with their services or if they return. Hourly employees don't care because they're getting paid regardless.

I don't like this pay structure. If you're looking to work at a salon where the staff values its clientele, avoid hourly salons. Nobody is more committed to meeting the needs of a client than an employee whose financial success hinges on their clients' continued satisfaction. Employees who have financial incentive to perform are more attentive, hard-working, and motivated professionals than those who are being paid to be present. Employees who are happy to bring in a minimum hourly wage instead of commission either aren't very experienced or aren't very good at what they do.

Commission-Only Pay currently predominates the industry. Staff members are paid a percentage of their gross sales (average ranges from 30%-60%, with the majority of salons offering 50%). Some owners include retail sales with service sales, but most offer lower commission rates on retail (typically 10%). Employees may also be permitted to accept tips.

Many professionals and salon owners don't realize that unless the owner requires their staff members to clock-in and clock-out and audits their hours against their commission every pay period, the owner may not be in compliance with the Fair Labor Standards Act (federal labor laws we'll discuss further throughout this book), making the legality of "commission-only" dependent on each employee's performance from one pay period to the next. Many owners do not track hours or perform the minimum wage comparison—which means that if you aren't performing services, you aren't making any money. This puts the owner at risk for labor investigations, IRS audits, and/or civil lawsuits.

I dislike commission-only for multiple reasons; the circumstantial legality being one of them. While these commission percentages seem great on the surface, they don't serve the owner, the salon, or the employees and equate to a bad arrangement for everyone involved.

Owners of commission-only salons will often over-staff because they're not honoring the minimum-wage requirement. Because these employers aren't paying their staff hourly, they have little incentive to ensure their employees are busy, instead shirking that responsibility entirely and telling their employees, "You have to market yourself." (We'll discuss this and more infuriating lies perpetuated throughout the industry in Lies, Bullshit, and Bad Advice.) These salon owners assume no payroll expenses, so they have no problem filling their salons with bodies and telling them to "sit and wait." Employees in overstaffed salons often don't make enough money to live on, so commission-only salons tend to experience high employee turnover and frequent mutinies (entire staff walkouts).

Under this compensation model, staff are at the mercy of the owner's whims regarding promotional pricing. If the owner chooses to discount a service or run a Groupon, employees are expected to honor it. This results in significant pay cuts for the duration of the promotion, as most owners don't make up the difference.

Commission-only works for nobody when you do the math, especially the business itself. Owners rarely make enough money on the split for it to be sustainable. Slim profit margins often force them to resort to committing labor abuses—specifically wage theft and tax evasion. Motivating staff to work a schedule or perform salon duties can be challenging when staff aren't getting compensated for performing those tasks.

Federal minimum wage requirements effectively light a fire under the asses of business owners, forcing them to actually manage their businesses. Owners who adhere to the prevailing wage laws manage their salons more attentively to ensure the staff are making enough money to cover payroll and overhead. These owners only hire the amount of staff their business can sustain. Their staff earn more money and happily perform necessary chores because they are being compensated for their time. Staff are still expected to honor discounted pricing (which does affect their paychecks), but the compensation system still guarantees them their hourly pay. These businesses experience significantly lower turnover rates.

Additionally, traditional commission rates give staff the false impression that they deserve to make as much or more than the business itself. In no other industry do employees have this delusional expectation. You deserve to be paid (and paid well) for your time, not just your services. You deserve the reassurance of a steady paycheck. You deserve the same things other employees have available to them, like healthcare, a retirement package, sick days, and paid vacation time. You can't have any of those things if you're working on commission. In order for a salon owner to afford to provide these things, you need to understand that you are an employee. You do not carry the financial burden that the salon owner does.

Salon owners are not in business to break even. They're in it to make a profit which can then be re-invested into the business or put aside to sustain it (and the staff) through slow periods. If they're smart, they're also setting aside a chunk for themselves to retire on. Owners deserve to profit and shouldn't be faced with committing wage theft and labor crimes to keep the doors open.

I do not recommend working on a commission-only basis and I strongly discourage salon owners from utilizing it. Just because commission-only is "the way things have always been done" doesn't mean that it's right or working for us. It isn't. Not anymore.

Hourly pay vs commission offers the employee a base hourly pay (usually minimum wage) vs a commission percentage. At the end of the pay period, the owner compares the total hourly pay to the commission amount and the employee receives the higher wages. This system ensures FLSA compliance, gives staff the reassurance of knowing at least how much they'll be making each pay period, and motivates staff to upsell. As opposed to commission-only, staff can't complain about being required to perform chores. They'll be getting compensated for washing and folding towels, cleaning the floors, and answering phones.

This compensation method can also be used to evaluate under-performing employees for possible termination. Many salons that utilize this system have policies in place that make continued employment conditional on whether or not the employee's commission consistently meets or exceeds their base pay. For example, if an employee's commission does not exceed their base pay for three pay cycles in a six month period, their employment will come under review to determine the problem, whether it can be corrected, or whether the employee needs to find work elsewhere.

This is my second-favorite system. Salons that utilize it thrive and the owners are protected from labor disputes. It ensures that you will be fairly compensated and that the salon will be well-managed.

My favorite compensation system, **hourly plus tiered commission bonuses,** differs slightly from the the hourly vs commission pay scale. Instead of a set commission, employees are rewarded with different commission bonuses based on whether or not they hit performance goals. For example, staff will get a set base pay, but if they exceed the first goal amount, they earn an additional small bonus. If they exceed the second goal, they earn a higher bonus. If they exceed the highest goal, they earn a massive bonus. If you hit none of the goals, you suck and should shred your license—just kidding, but repeated failure to hit these goals would likely lead to termination.

I prefer this compensation model above all others. Staff are motivated to make more money since their bonuses significantly increase their paychecks. It promotes a team environment and encourages owner participation. Owners who use this model are less likely to over-staff, more likely to advertise, and more inclined to keep on top of employee performance. In the end, salons that utilize this compensation model are more successful and far less likely to fail. Everyone wins with this model.

Overtime

The FLSA classifies salons as "retail and service establishments" since 75% of their annual dollar volume of sales are not for resale and are recognized as retail sales or services in the particular industry. As a retail and service establishment, salons can be considered exempt from overtime requirements only if all three conditions are met:

1.) the employee must be employed by a retail or service establishment (salon owners often intentionally misclassify employees as independent contractors to skirt minimum wage and overtime requirements), and

2.) the employee's regular rate of pay must exceed one and one-half times the applicable minimum wage for every hour worked in a workweek in which overtime hours are worked, and

3.) more than half the employee's total earnings in a representative period must consist of commissions.

Unless all three conditions are met, the exemption isn't applicable and overtime premium must be paid for all hours worked over forty in a workweek at time and one-half the regular rate of pay. Tips paid to service employees by customers may never be considered commissions for the purposes of the exemption.

Benefits

Many salons don't offer benefits. No health. No dental. No PTO. No vacation time. No maternity leave. No 401k plans. If you want benefits, you can attempt to negotiate for them, but the vast majority of salons operate under the commission-only model and can't afford to offer them.

Finding a competent owner is hard enough. If you find an owner who adheres to all applicable federal, state, and city labor and tax laws, consider yourself lucky. If you find an owner who does things right and gives you benefits, count your blessings and do a jig—you've found a damn unicorn.

The FLSA, Free Services, and Being "Engaged To Wait"

"If you are being engaged to wait, the employer should be required to pay. No exceptions. If they're unwilling to pay someone to perform a task and they're unwilling to do it themselves, they must not want it done that badly."

Are you wondering what you're entitled to in terms of service or retail commission?

None. You're entitled to none. Yes, really.

The owner determines whether or not you get commission and how big of a percentage you get. Unless you have a contract, they can change that amount at will. As long as your pay at the end of a pay period equals or exceeds what you would have made in minimum wage for the hours worked, owners can do as they please. Employers retain the right to dictate the salaries of their employees. As a free citizen, you retain the right to either accept that salary or leave in search of a larger one.

The Department of Labor's Fair Labor Standards Act establishes minimum wage, overtime pay, recordkeeping, and child labor/youth employment standards. Those laws protect employees from mistreatment (misclassification, abuse, wrongful termination, discrimination, etc), but no law in

America requires an employer to pay anything in excess of the prevailing minimum wage, excluding overtime compensation.

In the next section (Wage Theft), I explain the importance of tracking your hours and sales totals to protect yourself against wage theft. Part of the reason to keep your own records also has to do with the FLSA. In order for a salon owner to be in compliance, they must be auditing hourly minimum wage earnings against commissions and paying their staff the higher amount. In reality, owners seldom do this.

For example, let's say you're just starting out in a new area. The owner scheduled you to work eighty hours this pay period, but you only had six clients over the course of those two weeks. You made $120 in commission and $30 in tips. That equates to $1.50 an hour. In this instance, the owner would have to pay $580 ($7.25 an hour for the eighty hours you worked). You worked her schedule. You sat in her empty salon, folded towels, cleaned floors, answered phones—or maybe you just sat on your ass reading Fifty Shades of Garbage—regardless, you were "engaged to wait" and must be compensated appropriately. The FLSA doesn't care what you're doing at work. If you're there at the request of the employer, you need to be getting paid.

Lunch Breaks

You are free to leave the salon during break periods—otherwise you are being engaged to wait and must be compensated.

Promotional Services

Salon owners often encourage staff to perform complimentary services to "promote" themselves or "build clientele." I'm not going to get into what a terrible business idea it is to offer free services until Deep Discount Dumbassery, but it is a bad business decision and an amateur one that shows a clear lack of experience and foresight. If your deluded employer complies with the FLSA and pays the prevailing hourly wage, go ahead and humor her foolishly optimistic "business strategy." However, if you are working on "commission-only" for a salon owner who doesn't meet her minimum wage responsibilities, you are not obligated to perform any service or task.

If you want to devalue yourself and offer complementary services to "build" a clientele or gain proficiency in a particular technique, that's a stupid decision you need to make for yourself—not one that a non-compliant so-called "employer" can force on you.

"Test" Services

Salon owners often require job applicants to perform test services on which their employment will hinge. As long as the owner doesn't collect compensation in excess of any applicable product cost in exchange for the test service, this practice is legal. (However, I find this unacceptable and compensate potential hires for test services.)

This is an industry, not a charity. Don't work for free. In no other industry are employees expected to "sit and wait" or perform tasks without compensation. Too many professionals allow themselves to be treated like slaves. They're told, "pitch in" and "do your share" and "be part of the team." It's one thing to clean up after yourself and help out your coworkers, it's an entirely different thing to work for free. You cannot be expected to work for free under any circumstances, nor can you be fired for refusing to work for free.

The Wage and Hour Division of the Department of Labor conducts investigations of alleged FLSA violations. When, pursuant to such an investigation, the Department of Labor

decides a company is not in compliance with FLSA, there are several ways back wages can be recovered:
- The Wage and Hour Division may supervise payment of back wages.
- The Secretary of Labor may bring suit for back wages and an equal amount as liquidated damages.
- An employee may file a private suit for back pay and an equal amount as liquidated damages, plus attorney's fees and court costs.
- The Secretary of Labor may obtain an injunction to restrain any person from violating FLSA, including the unlawful withholding of proper minimum wage and overtime pay.

When it comes to recovery of back pay, there is a two-year statute of limitations, except in the case of a willful violation, where the statute of limitations is three years.

When salon owners are found to willfully violate FLSA, they can also face criminal prosecution and fines up to $10,000. Upon a second conviction, salon owners could face imprisonment. In addition to all this, the IRS joins forces with the DOL and local labor divisions to hit owners on multiple fronts and really maximize the damage.

I find it hard to believe salon owners are genuinely ignorant of FLSA requirements. To expect licensed professionals to sit in a business for hours on end without compensation is inconsiderate, disrespectful, and completely ridiculous. That gross lack of common sense and common courtesy indicates serious psychological deficiency, in my opinion.

Wage Theft

"Owners who thieve from their staff do not deserve to have staff."

Wage theft is the illegal withholding of wages or the denial of benefits that are rightfully owed to an employee. Wage theft is a huge problem in the United States and alarmingly common in salons. Theft of wages can be committed through various means: unpaid overtime, minimum wage violations, employee misclassification, illegal pay deductions, working off the clock, and refusal to provide payment at all. Since 2010, the federal Labor Department's WHD (Wage & Hour Division) has recovered nearly $1 billion in stolen wages. Even big businesses like WalMart, FedEx, DirecTV, and McDonald's have been busted for altering time sheets, intentionally misclassifying staff, and withholding income illegally.

Wage theft continues to be a serious, ongoing issue because most salon owners believe they have little chance of being caught. Luckily, a huge movement is taking place in each state right now to stop wage theft and labor abuses. Laws are being passed that increase the penalties for committing this crime against American workers. This chapter will tell you what paycheck deductions are permissible, how to avoid becoming a victim of wage theft, and what recourse you have if a salon owner steals from you.

Legal Wage Garnishment

There are only a few legal instances (outside of employee payroll taxes) where an employer can withhold or deduct an employee's wages. The legality of the practice will depend on the individual circumstances and any applicable state legislation, but outside of these circumstances, an employer cannot withhold any portion of an employee's wages without their consent.

Income Withholding Orders. If an employer is served with an income withholding order, they're legally required to provide the employee with notice of the order and divert that employee's pay to whatever authority the order dictates. Often, these are issued by Child Support Enforcement (for unpaid support) and the IRS (for unpaid taxes). Title III of the Consumer Credit Protection Act regulates wage garnishments, limiting the amount of earnings that are subject to garnishment and offering discharge protections to employees whose pay is subject to garnishment.

Advance & Loan Repayment. If an employer advances wages or loans money, they can deduct principle from wages and those deductions can drop an employee below minimum wage without violating the FLSA. However, if the employer charges interest, the amount of interest deducted can't drop the employee's wages below minimum wage.

Special rules apply during overtime weeks. If you worked overtime during the week that the employer wants to make a deduction, the deduction must be in accordance with a very specific agreement you reach (before you perform any work that week) that outlines what will be deducted. The overtime must be determined using your regular pay rate prior to the deduction. (So, if your base pay is $9/hr but the deduction would reduce you to $8/hr, your overtime compensation will still be based on $9/hr.)

Uniform Deductions. The FLSA doesn't allow uniforms or other items which are considered to be primarily for the benefit or convenience of the employer to be included as wages. An employer can't take credit for such items in meeting their minimum wage or overtime obligations. If the employer requires uniforms, the cost and maintenance of that uniform is considered a business expense of the employer. If the employer requires the employee to bear that cost, it cannot cut into that employee's overtime compensation or reduce that employee's wage below the prevailing minimum wage.

Questionable & Illegal Wage Garnishment

"Redo" Penalties. If you make a mistake, who pays for it? Without a solid employment contract that forbids it, you might have to absorb that cost. In some states, an employer can deduct damages or shortages from a worker's paycheck if they suffered a loss due to the employee's negligence, dishonesty, or intentional misconduct. The FLSA doesn't prohibit deductions of this nature as long as you're being paid the prevailing minimum wage. Many state laws require employers to get written employee consent before they can deduct the cost of breakages or shortages and some states only allow these deductions when employees assume responsibility for the employer's loss.

In my opinion, penalizing staff like this just isn't a wise or productive practice. In my experience, this disciplinary tactic has proven to be ineffective and leads to unhappy staff. Positive reinforcement is a more reliable tool than punishment. A good employer or manager will use the mistake as an opportunity to educate their staff and help them develop their skills.

Product Fees. Many owners remove "product fees" prior to calculating commissions, a legal practice as long as they're FLSA compliant and the employee was made aware of their actual pay rate prior to accepting their position—but a good deal of owners don't follow proper protocol (which is why employment contracts are so important for both staff and employers). Too frequently, employers offer their staff 50% of gross sales without mentioning that 10-12% (or more) will be deducted for product. Some owners go a step further and pull the product cost out of the employee's cut. This puts the owner in very dangerous wage theft territory.

Remember, the FLSA prohibits deductions for items that are primarily for the benefit or convenience of the employer.

Like uniforms, employers cannot deduct these expenses or take credit for them in meeting their minimum wage or overtime obligations. Product is a CODB (cost-of-doing-business) expense, and employers are expected to absorb those expenses. CODB expenses include supplies necessary to perform the employee's job. In addition, salon owners often cannot accurately quantify product when each client requires a variable amount per service.

The practice of charging CODB fees to employees remains legally questionable. (Can you think of any other business in any other industry that employs these deductions? I can't.) I don't advise my consulting clients to utilize this practice and I don't advise you to work for anyone who thinks deducting arbitrary fees from their staff's pay is a rational, convenient, or acceptable practice (because it is none of those things). Charging service fees complicates payroll unnecessarily. Those expenses should be deferred to the clients, which can be easily done by properly structuring service pricing. An employer's inability to do this basic business calculation indicates to me that they're not very experienced. In the event the employer made an intentional decision to make their job more difficult by implementing product fees, I highly suspect wage theft.

Tip Theft. Some owners try to claim (steal) a portion of their staff's tip income. The most common manifestation of this involves diverting tip income to support staff, like receptionists and assistants (tip pooling). You can't be required to pool tips with support staff that don't normally receive tips (so the shampooers and assistants can be part of the pool, but the receptionists can't). Even if the salon owner works behind the chair and receives tips, they are prohibited by law from being able to receive tips from a tip pool because they are the business owner. Unless your state specifically allows it, managers also cannot be part of the tip pool.

The FLSA prohibits any arrangement between the employer and the tipped employee whereby any part of the tip received becomes the property of the employer. For example, even where a tipped employee receives at least the prevailing minimum wage directly from the employer, the employee may not be required to turn over his or her tips to the employer.

Deducting credit card processing fees from tips might permissible in your state, but only for the processing fee amount on the tip, not the entire bill.

In any arrangement, tip deductions that drop an employee below the prevailing minimum wage are not legal.

Punishment Withholding. Wage withholding as punishment is expressly prohibited by federal and state laws. When and how often an employer is obligated to pay employees varies from state to state. Many states have strictly outlined payment requirements (New York, for example requires employers pay their employees at least bi-monthly and in recurring intervals such as every two weeks). Withholding pay from an employee can result in legal consequences for the salon owner, including civil suits, investigation, and/or criminal violations.

Not a single state or federal law permits an employer to retain a paycheck due to "disrespect" or "tardiness" or any of the other bullshit excuses some employers try to use.

Protect Yourself

To avoid becoming a victim of wage theft, take responsibility for your pay and hold employers accountable for any discrepancies.

Demand detailed wage statements. Theft of wages can be deterred by demanding detailed earnings statements. Many states have legislation in place that requires a business owner to provide detailed pay stubs upon request, so check the statutes. Whatever your state's laws, you're an adult professional. You don't need legislation to set employment terms.

When you interview with an employer, make these wage statements a condition of your acceptance of their offer. The statements should detail each service performed, tip income, product sales totals, the commission rate for both retail and services, and the amount of hours worked. You also need to see how much went to FICA (that bastard). Every penny must be accounted for.

Explain to the owner that you keep your own records and expect to be provided with detailed pay stubs every pay period so you can make comparisons. Make certain that the employment contract details the commission rate being offered—this prevents salon owners from hiring you with promises of high commissions and then shorting you later, claiming they "never promised that percentage" or "forgot."

At this point, most owners utilize salon software that tracks hours, sales, and tips. These programs come with a plethora of reports and most calculate payroll automatically. Owners who use salon software have no valid excuse to refuse their staff detailed wage reports, since doing so is often as simple as printing off an automatically generated report.

Whether or not the owner uses software, refusal to provide detailed wage statements indicates dishonesty. An owner who isn't stealing from you will have no problem providing a detailed wage statement. It's not reasonable for any employer to expect any staff member to "trust" them with their money.

Never accept an employer's excuses for why they can't provide detailed wage statements—some will try to pass off lame excuses in the form of Salon Bafflegab and IJD Technology.

Bafflegab: overly-complicated language intended to confuse the listener.

IJD Technology: "It Just Does" technology. For example: "How does faster-than-light travel work?" It Just Does. In this case, we have the opposite of IJD Technology; "It Just Doesn't" Technology.

"The system isn't capable of generating those kinds of reports."

"I keep all of that on file. Don't worry about it."

and my current favorite: "That is confidential and proprietary business information."

An owner who resorts to deceptive avoidance tactics of any variety can't be trusted. If you're not an hourly employee, your commission earnings are not "confidential" and they certainly aren't "proprietary." Unless you're an hourly-only employee, you need to be able to see those sales figures. (If you are hourly-only, the owner needs to provide your hours and hourly rate each pay period since hourly income isn't based on sales.)

Don't accept cash or personal check payments. Never accept payment in cash or personal checks. You need a payroll check from a legitimate business banking account (or payroll company) and a detailed wage statement. Nothing else will do.

Track your hours. Either use your phone to record the time you enter and leave the salon or write it in a small notebook. I highly suggest using your phone and a password protected document app that automatically backs up the data online. Free and secure, Google Drive integrates with your Gmail account, backs up automatically, and synchronizes across all apps and platforms.

Track your sales & tips. If a portion of your paycheck is commission-based, find time after each appointment to track your sales and tips. Again, Google Drive is a fantastic tool for this. Even the most honest owners make mistakes. Take responsibility for tracking hours and sales so you can check your math against the owner's. In a perfect world, all employers would be trustworthy, upstanding, law-abiding citizens, incapable of making mathematical errors. Unfortunately, we do not reside in a perfect world. (...and a lot of us absolutely suck at math.)

Hold your employer accountable for discrepancies. If your own figures and the paycheck don't add up, schedule a meeting with the owner to rectify it. Show the owner your math and ask to see hers. An owner who isn't thieving will appreciate that you noticed the issue and will figure out where the missing pay went. A thieving owner will likely get defensive and refuse to help (many will start spouting some of that Bafflegab I mentioned).

Don't kick the door down and automatically assume you're being robbed. Give the owner the benefit of the doubt because mistakes happen—a lot. I've used software to calculate payroll for many moons. Roughly three or four times a year, part of my system breaks down due to user error.

Here are some common reasons for payroll discrepancies:
- A receptionist accidentally checks out a client under the wrong service provider's name.
- A service or upgrade does not get put into the system at all—which means the client doesn't get charged and neither the service nor the payment are reflected in the EOD (End Of Day) reports.
- A service provider forgets to clock in or out.

- A service gets canceled or isn't performed but the client gets charged anyway.

As you can see, the majority of payroll discrepancies I've had to correct were caused by receptionist error during booking or checkout, a service provider's mistake, or miscommunication between the service provider and receptionist.

If you have been stolen from, hold the thief accountable. If an employer illegally deducted wages that rightfully belong to you, no matter what excuse they use, they have committed theft. Plain and simple. Would you let someone reach into your purse and pull out $20 or $50 and walk away with it? No? Then why the hell would you let an employer steal your wages? If the owner has committed wage theft, take action. Laws are written to protect you, but they only work if you use them.

Recovering Back Pay

"Back pay" is the difference between what you were paid and the amount you were owed. (If you were owed $220, but the owner only paid you $50, you are due $170 in back pay.) Your records are crucial for when wage disputes occur. Without them, you will have an uphill battle to fight.

To recap, the FLSA provides four methods for recovering unpaid wages: the Wage & Hour Division may supervise the payment of back wages, the Secretary of Labor may bring suit for back wages and an equal amount as liquidated damages, employees may file private lawsuits for back pay and an equal amount as liquidated damages (plus attorney's fees and court costs), and the Secretary of Labor may obtain an injunction to restrain the employer from violating the FLSA—including the unlawful withholding of proper minimum wage and overtime pay. You may not bring suit under the FLSA if you have been paid back wages under the supervision of the WHD or the

Secretary of Labor or if either have already filed suit on your behalf for those back wages.

Generally, a two-year statute of limitations applies to the recovery of back pay. In the case of willful violations (and many of these violations are intentional, willful theft), that statute of limitations extends to three years.

Diplomatic Dispute Resolution

"Letting employers commit crimes against you and walk away from them without penalty sends the message that their behavior is permissible. It isn't."

Sometimes, employers will implement questionable new policies that the staff won't find acceptable. Instead of orchestrating a mutiny or ganging up on the owner, approach the owner or manager like a rational, reasonable, helpful adult. Handle the issue with sensitivity, professionalism, understanding, patience, and confidence.

All employers respond differently. You will know how best to approach yours and what reaction you're likely to receive. This chapter serves as a guideline to help you prepare for that discussion. Use your own discretion during yours.

Expect the best but prepare for the worst. Prepare for the owner to turn hostile. Prepare to be terminated. You don't have to go so far as to find a new job, but updating your resume might not be a bad idea. Exploitative owners will terminate employees who catch on to their tactics 99.9% of the time. (I made that statistic up, but I have yet to come across a single professional who wasn't fired by an obviously exploitative owner.)

Compile evidence and plan out the discussion. Fully understand every relevant statute you plan on quoting. Have the statutes listed and the appropriate website for each organized so the employer can check them.

"Plan out the discussion," doesn't translate to "plan your attack." You are not attacking your employer. Flesh out your reasoning for approaching them about the issues you're bringing up and prepare to defend those reasons with supporting evidence when questioned.

For example, if the owner has you classified as an independent contractor but you want to be an employee, show her your projected income after self-employment taxes. Show her why the current system doesn't benefit you with cold, hard numbers. Supplement this reasoning with the relevant statutes regarding the independent contractor model and explain why it isn't appropriate.

Don't get caught off guard. Gather more supporting documentation than you'll need. With knowledge comes confidence.

Arrange for a private meeting. Don't bring this up during a staff meeting. If your employer has violated federal tax or labor laws, give her the benefit of the doubt and assume she didn't have a clue. Don't put her on blast in front of her staff. That is disrespectful, cruel, and unprofessional. No owner in their right mind would put up with that treatment. You never want to make the owner feel cornered. Extend professional courtesy.

Show the owner what you've found and assume that her error was exactly that—an error. Never make the owner feel like you're attacking, accusing, or berating them. You're sharing knowledge. This information may be entirely new to her. Operate under that assumption and keep the dialog civil. Your attitude needs to be, "I've learned this and I thought it was important to share with you. I'd really like to see some changes made because ____. I have some ideas about how we can do this together."

Be constructive. This meeting shouldn't be all negative. Tell the owner about the things she does right—the things that motivate you to show up every day. You could have jumped ship and left her to sink or swim on her own. Instead, you want to work with her and help her business thrive. That shows integrity, and loyalty—qualities that aren't easily found.

Have solutions prepared. Don't dump a bunch of information in her lap and expect her to know what to do from there. If you spent time and energy forming a legitimate complaint, you better have spent some time and energy thinking of at least two ways to rectify it, otherwise you're just bitching at the owner to correct something. Nobody likes that. If you had time to research what she did wrong, it's reasonable to assume you had time to research how to make it right.

Even if the owner doesn't want help, extend the offer. Taking that extra step displays initiative, great teamwork, and a positive attitude. It shows that you're invested in the business. Any owner who doesn't appreciate an employee who offers solutions or constructive criticism needs to reevaluate themselves immediately.

Not-So-Diplomatic Dispute Resolution

Do not be surprised if the owner gets defensive or argumentative. You'll see that with owners who knew damn well they were doing something illegal. Clueless owners and intentionally abusive owners exist in nearly equal number.

A clueless owner with good intentions will respond with wide eyes, a dropped jaw, and the common, "Oh my god! I had no idea! How do I fix this?" An intentionally abusive owner will get hostile, defensive, and sometimes even verbally abusive. You'll see narrowed eyes, pursed lips, crossed arms, and hear the extremely common, "My lawyer said this was just fine and I'm going to do what he suggests. Are you calling my attorney a liar?" or "My accountant says it's legal."

Call their bluffs. If you've done the necessary homework and provided statutes, there shouldn't be room for argument, but some owners will attempt to intimidate you by putting words in their "attorney's" mouth.

No skilled, ethical attorney or CPA will endorse a contract or practice that violates federal or state laws. Ever. If the owner claims her illegal business practices were advised by her attorney or CPA, either she's lying to your face or she took advice from bad counsel. Any reasonable person that suspects they were misled by a legal representative will want to call that representative to task immediately. An unethical owner will turn on you, not the representative that supposedly provided the advice.

If the owner becomes defensive and starts making claims about what her "attorney" or "CPA" said, immediately ask for that attorney's contact information. Exploitative employers lie and don't expect to be called out.

I can't believe I even have to say this, but in the extremely unlikely event that the owner provides a name and number, run an internet search to verify that they belong to an actual attorney. I have heard of owners who had their friends pose as legal counsel to intimidate staff members into accepting their illegal employment conditions. That level of insanity shouldn't surprise you. If the salon owner was desperate enough to intentionally break the law, the odds are pretty good that she's also willing to recruit a friend to pose as legal representation to cover her ass.

Follow through. Have a plan of action prepared in case the owner refuses to address your concerns. If these are issues with completely legal business policies that you don't agree with to the point that you're willing to resign, have written resignation notice prepared. If these issues pertain to illegal labor practices that you plan to take action on if the owner refuses to rectify them, explain to her that you will be reporting it and bringing her to civil court if necessary.

If you speak it, be prepared to act. Don't waste your breath making empty threats. Be ready to file suit if the issues aren't addressed. Don't embarrass yourself or your profession. Walk your talk.

Do your part. Things will change only if we each do our part. Your part may be as small as filing an SS-8 with the IRS and having an exploitative salon owner audited. Salon owners will have no choice but to change the way they do business and the way they treat their staff if we send a clear message that we will not accept these employment practices any longer by holding them accountable for employee abuses and labor law violations; report tax evasion, sue them when they violate contracts, and question them when they propose illegal policies.

Punish the Wicked

Getting a law drafted and adopted into legislature is a lengthy, complicated process, even on a state level. They need to be written, introduced, recommended, lobbied, voted on, lobbied again, approved, and finally (hopefully) passed. They're written to protect you and provide the means to hold others accountable for the wrongs they commit against you. Use them.

When you report a bad business owner for wage and labor abuses, you aren't just standing up for yourself, you are standing up for everyone in this industry. You're setting an example and making a firm statement that we deserve better.

You don't deserve to be stolen from. You don't deserve to be overworked without compensation. You don't deserve to be treated like a second-class citizen. You don't deserve to be taken advantage of in any capacity.

You deserve fair, living wages. You deserve reasonable contract terms. You deserve employment benefits. You deserve to be classified appropriately. You deserve overtime pay.

All of these things are guaranteed to you by federal (and in some instances, state) laws.

Massive change will correct this industry, but these changes happen gradually. We must fight for it together a little bit at a time. Spread information. Refuse positions that don't honor the laws of this country or the working citizens those laws protect. Walk away from exploitative owners. Question authority. Most importantly, report and enforce.

Get actively involved in changing this industry for the better by influencing legislation and aggressively pushing for changes (instead of passively responding to proposed changes). Fight for yourself, fight for our industry, and fight for fair treatment. We deserve it.

Intentional Misclassification

If you discover the salon owner intentionally misclassified you following your diplomatic dispute, file an SS-8 form with the IRS. This form can find them on their website (www.IRS.gov) and at any local IRS office.

Filing this form will cause the IRS to launch an investigation into the employer's business practices. If the IRS determines that you were misclassified, that owner will get flagged and the status of all other employees (past and present) will be evaluated. If they determine that the owner intentionally misclassified them, the owner will be fined and will be held responsible for paying all of that employment tax back (7% of each employee's total earnings per year—it adds up).

Wage Theft

If the owner illegally withheld your wages, quit immediately. No pay. No work.

Then, gather evidence. Were you keeping records like I told you to? You'll need them. You'll also need your pay stubs, service tickets, employment contracts, emails, and texts—whatever you have that shows when you worked and what you were promised. Without evidence, it will be nearly impossible to win your case.

Next, demand the unpaid wages in writing. Edit the template below to suit your situation. Keep a copy and send it certified.

[TODAY'S DATE]
[FORMER EMPLOYER'S ADDRESS]
RE: Wage Claim for [YOUR NAME].
Dear [FORMER EMPLOYER'S NAME]:
This letter is a formal demand for the payment of my unpaid wages pursuant to [YOUR STATE'S RELEVANT STATUTE].

My unpaid wages include work which was performed for [BUSINESS NAME] between [STARTING DATE] and [END DATE]. I was employed as a [POSITION], and am owed [PERCENTAGE OF SERVICE COMMISSION] of my gross service sales and [PERCENTAGE OF RETAIL COMMISSION] of my gross retail sales for this pay period, as per our signed employment contract (see attached) [ATTACH EMPLOYMENT CONTRACT].

My ticket sales equal [GROSS SERVICE SALES] and my retail sales equal [GROSS RETAIL SALES]. This equates to [TOTAL OWED]. Please send payment to me by [DATE] to the address provided below.

Please be advised that under [RELEVANT STATE STATUTE], an employer is required to pay employees wages promptly. The statute reads in part:

[RELEVANT STATUTE PORTION].

If I have not received all the wages owed to me by the date above, I will be left with no choice but to report this theft of wages to the Federal Department of Labor and bring this matter to conciliation court.

Sincerely,
[YOUR NAME]
[YOUR ADDRESS]

If the owner doesn't remit payment, follow through on those threats. Don't let this go. You earned that money. Do not let anyone steal your income.

Contract Violations

Contract violations are tricky business. Before you can file suit for a contract breach, you have to be able to prove that the breach caused tangible monetary or material damages. Monetary damages result in loss of money; material damages are significant and often defined by your state's statutes. I recommend retaining an attorney to deal with breaches. They're far too complicated to even attempt addressing in general.

Finding a Job

"Don't take a job based on your emotions or out of desperation. A lot of factors go into picking a place that will ensure your long-term happiness, and none of them have to do with the beautifully decorated interior or the product line the salon utilizes."

Finding employment at a salon will be simple with a spectacular application packet, but finding the right salon is not as simple.

The first hurdle is finding salons that appear to share your style, professional values, and work ethic. Before walking into the interview, you need to understand your role and responsibilities as an employee.

Your job is to show up on time, keep on schedule, behave professionally, deliver services to the best of your abilities, and make positive contributions to help the salon continually improve.

It's not your job to suffer financial loss due to an owner's incompetence or to waste your time, talents, and efforts on people who don't appreciate them. Your job also isn't to "market yourself" outside of the salon. If you would like to, you certainly can. Marketing never hurt anyone. However, you're an employee. The owner's job is to put asses in the chairs; it's your job to keep the clients attached to those asses happy.

To be fair, I consistently performed duties that weren't my responsibility. Don't feel bad if you're the kind of staff member that can't help but to take initiative and carry the slack of others. Some of us are programmed that way. Just remember that the choice to take initiative and perform extra tasks should remain your decision, not one imposed upon you.

You need to find the place that suits you; a place that you're excited to be every day. You deserve to work at a salon that appreciates you and encourages you to grow and be the best, most successful professional you can be.

Don't settle. Every day in the salon, you make contacts. You'll meet clients and perform services on them. They will return to their jobs, their families, and their lives with your signature on their head, hands, or face. They're a walking work of art and you're the artist. Your name will come up. People will remember you when they're ready for their next cut, color, fill, or facial. Every day, your reputation grows and your book builds. Clients are walking advertisements, investments you may not see returns on for weeks or months after they've left the salon. What happens when you spend six months or a year building a book at a salon and then decide that the salon doesn't suit you? Leaving will displace that clientele and make it impossible for those word-of-mouth investments to find you. If you move to a local salon, some clients may follow, but don't rely on that. This is why the initial process of selecting the right salon is so important.

Step 1: Your Professional Packet

Walking into an establishment and asking for an application is tacky, pathetic, and reeks of poor planning. You aren't a high school student looking for a part-time job at the mall. Take a few hours to put together a professional packet, even if you don't have much industry experience.

A professional packet contains your cover letter, resume, contact card, and any letters of recommendation you may have. It should also contain copies of your beauty diploma, professional license, and continuing education certificates.

Cover Letter Composition

There are two types of cover letter: the application letter (when you're responding to a job posting) and the prospecting letter (when you're inquiring about possible positions). In the sample letter below, I'll illustrate the differences between them.

Compose a unique cover letter for each salon owner. Cover letters are your first introduction to these employers, so give them a personal touch by addressing the owner by name and mentioning something specific about their salon. Run a spell-check, proofread it several times, and have some friends read it and provide feedback.

When writing your cover letter, keep it to-the-point. You're looking for a job, not sharing your life story. Keep personal details personal. Do not go on about how fantastic you are ("passionate," "detail oriented," "prompt," etc.). Employers see these generic, meaningless lists all the time. Anyone can slap self-aggrandizing personality traits on a paper. Actions speak louder, so show your best traits—don't tell them. Your portfolio and qualifications show you're passionate. Your beautiful cover letter and resume show you're detail oriented. Arriving at your interview ten minutes early shows you're prompt.

SAMPLE COVER LETTER:
[Your Name]
[Your Address]
[Your City, State, Zip Code]
[Your Phone Number]
[Your Email]

Date
Owner's Name
Job Title
Company
Street
City, State, Zip

Salutation:
Dear Mrs. Biscuitsnatcher:(If you don't have the salon owner's name, substitute "To Whom It May Concern:")
Prospecting Introductory Paragraph:

While researching salons in the area, I came across the Fancy Pantaloons Salon & Spa website. I believe we share similar professional philosophies and I would like to inquire about the possibility of any openings.

Application Introductory Paragraph:

I saw your employment ad in [place where you saw the ad] and would love to be considered for the position. I researched Fancy Pantaloons Salon & Spa and am thrilled that we both hold sanitation and disinfection in such high regard.

Body Paragraph (Suitable for Both):

I am a licensed [cosmetologist, nail technician, full specialist, monkey wrangler] and am interested in a career as a [stylist, nail technician, boot licker]. I graduated from Snobby Private Beauty Academy in [year] and have extensive experience in all aspects of salon operations. In addition, I have completed [multiple super impressive continuing education courses] and hold certifications in [hair extensions, e-file safety, erotic earlobe massage].

Prospecting Closing Paragraph:

The enclosed resume contains additional information on my experience and skills. I would love to discuss the possibility of employment with you further. I can be reached anytime via [phone number] and would appreciate the opportunity to schedule an interview at your convenience. In the event that you are not currently hiring, please keep my information on file for future consideration.

Application Closing Paragraph:

The enclosed resume contains additional information on my experience and skills. I am available for interviews any time this week. You can reach me anytime via [phone number].

Say Thank You and Bye-Bye:

Thank you for your time and consideration!
Sincerely,
[Your Signature]
[Your Typed Name]

If you're spending longer than thirty minutes on a cover letter, you're putting way too much thought into it. It shouldn't be long enough to require a significant time investment. Redirect that time into constructing a great resume!

Resume Construction

Resume writing is a science and an art form. This brief chapter serves as a quick overview, so I highly suggest researching the best way to communicate and format yours utilizing the various methods available to you (specifically, the miraculous Googlesphere inside The Webanet Machine). While the examples online can provide valuable insight into template options (fonts, page dividers, layouts), the sample resume content may not be useful. Unfortunately, most sample resumes are created for traditional industries that are nothing like ours.

There are three resume formats: the chronological (listing your previous jobs in chronological order), the functional (highlighting your skills and achievements and listing your job history in the lower portion of the resume), and the combo (a mix of both). Many resume sites claim that employers prefer a chronological format. I completely disagree with this. For our industry, functional resumes are king.

If you're new to the profession, the chronological format is unlikely to work since you won't have much relevant job experience or education. So, I'll share with you the way I have formatted mine throughout my career and what I like to see from applicants.

Your resume should include the following:

Your first and last name: Put it at the top of the resume, in the header.

Your contact information: Include your physical home address (no PO boxes), phone number, and an appropriate email address. Sexxxybunni22@gmail.com isn't appropriate; neither is hairgurl69@aol.com or catsrmypassion@yahoo.com. Use your real name or first initial and last name. Those email addresses are easy to remember, professional, and don't lead others to form opinions on the kind of person you are.

Your education: Salon owners don't care what middle school you went to; they want to know what cosmetology school you graduated from, what cosmetology-related continuing education courses you've taken, and what cosmetology-related certifications/awards you've received.

Relevant experience: Salon owners don't care that you worked at the photo center at Walgreens for six years, that you're a certified karate instructor, or that you have a side job as a promotional model. We want to see relevant experience. Include any positions you've held in a salon or beauty-related field. If you haven't held any yet, say so in the cover letter. Unless the owner specifically seeks an experienced professional, this shouldn't count against you. We all started somewhere!

A list of professional references and letters of recommendation: Don't list family or friends as references. They don't know you on a professional level and an employer will not bother contacting them because we know they're just going to sing your praises. List prior employers (inside or outside of the beauty industry), beauty academy instructors, coworkers and fellow students, and maybe throw in a loyal client or two. Include five references if possible. Get permission from each person before using them as a reference. Provide their full name, your relationship to them, and their phone number.

Some people recommend only providing references upon request. I hold the opposite opinion. As an employer, I shouldn't have to "request" your references. If your references are "available upon request," why not just make them "available upon application?" Don't waste our time, Applicant. If you want the job, provide references up front with the cover letter and resume.

Your career objectives: This does not have to be an outline of your five or ten-year plan; it can be a current goal. For most of you, the goal is to gain employment in a stable establishment where you can focus on expanding your skill set and building a clientele.

If you want to eventually be a salon or spa owner, that's an excellent goal to have but not one that needs to be mentioned to a potential employer, who may or may not like the idea of training and supplying clientele to an employee who may become a future competitor. Honesty is important, but remember: omission is not lying. So, keep those dreams of ownership to yourself.

The technical areas you're strong in (Technical Skills) and the areas you're working on (Developing Skills): Career advisers might hold a different opinion on this, but I think it's appropriate in our industry to put your cards on the table. Don't just list your strong points, list your weak ones as well. That question will come up in the interview, so beat them to it and address it on paper. Present it in a positive way by titling the list of shortcomings as, "Developing Skills." This communicates to the interviewer that you're working on mastering these skills, but aren't as confident in them as the skills listed under "Technical Skills."

A list of service times: At some point, this will come up. Beat them to it by providing a list of approximate service times on a separate page. How long does it take you to do a traditional manicure? How about a routine color retouch? For services with variable times, specify a range. (Full set of nail enhancements: 45-90 minutes. Foil highlights: 35-60 minutes.)

I recommend not including a list of personality traits. Employers see those lists on every resume they receive. We're sure that you're very reliable, responsible, respectful, prompt, polite, and professional, but we're more interested in knowing what services you excel at. Besides that, those traits are just words on paper. They mean nothing. Let your references tell us how great you are.

Remember that attitude and work ethic are of the utmost importance, everything else can be taught. Employers want to see professionalism, dedication, honesty, and a strong desire to learn.

Presentation

"You could have the most impressive resume and cover letter of any applicant, but poor presentation of that information will kill it completely. The ink should be crisp and consistent, not running or smeared. The paper should be a heavy enough weight to keep the ink from bleeding through the other side. These little details make a big difference."

It sounds superficial, but a great presentation impresses. How you present yourself to a potential employer matters. The overall look of the documents in the application packet communicates just as much about you as your resume and cover letter.

Your resume and cover letter should have identical margins and matching font types and sizes. Fonts should be readable and professional, preferably Times New Roman, Arial, or Helvetica. Your name and header information can be typed in a more decorative font, but stay away from script or handwritten fonts. For decorative header fonts that are classy and professional, I recommend Caviar Dreams, Trajan Pro, or Optimus Princeps. All can be found for free online (I use www.dafont.com and www.1001fonts.com). Decorative fonts must be clean, readable, and crisp and should give the impression of professionalism, reliability, and attention to detail.

Utilize page dividers, typefaces, and bullet points to organize your information. You can find tons of sample resumes and cover letters online. Whole books are written on the subject of resume formatting. There are tons of different ways to make your resume unique.

Print your documents on white or off-white card stock. Spring a couple extra bucks at the printing store for nice paper. If the type is visible through the back side, it isn't heavy enough. Get paper with a nice weight to it.

Include two contact cards. Contact cards are business cards without company information on them. They should complement the resume and cover letter in style and color—no tacky graphics or stock photos. The contact card will have your name, license type, license number, phone number, mailing address, email address, and portfolio URL. (I'll teach you everything about creating a portfolio in Your Portfolio, don't worry.) Since your portfolio will have all of your social media links in the headers and footers, they won't need to be listed on the contact cards.

If you have letters of recommendation, include them. If you don't have letters of recommendation, consider asking for one from your professional peers, clients, or school instructors. Do not solicit them from family members or friends.

Include copies of your credentials. Your certificate of completion, professional license, and continuing education certifications must be included.

All of these components are things that 99.9% of salon applicants do not provide. Many applicants show up to a salon, ask for an application, fill it out, and leave. A lot of them don't even bother to dress professionally—or worse, go out of their way to dress "trendy." They don't research the salon prior to applying.

For the most part, that behavior was tolerated by salon owners. No longer. As the industry continues to shift to one that values professionalism, this half-assed laziness won't be accepted. Most upscale salons would immediately shred the application of a "professional" in jeans and a t-shirt who showed up without a resume. If you want to work for the best, you have to be the best. Stand apart by researching the salon prior to applying, dressing professionally, and delivering a spectacular application packet with a customized cover letter.

To this day, I have never been denied any job I have applied for, and neither will you if you bring that level of awesome to an employer who has dealt with an endless stream of mediocre applicants.

Step 2: Prep

"Success depends on previous preparation, and without such preparation there is sure to be failure."
-Confucius

Why do applicants fail to secure positions? Why do salon employees get taken advantage of by opportunistic employers? Why do professionals hop from salon to salon, looking for their ideal workplace?

They don't prepare.

You're different. You're going to research salons extensively before applying. When you apply, you're going to be the most impressive applicant that salon owner has ever met. You're going to be damn ready for the interview and the evaluation and you're going to nail both of those sons of bitches because you're a professional. You might be green, but your impressive presence will command the respect of a veteran.

Technical Proficiency. Most salon owners will require applicants to perform a test service on a model, which they will observe and analyze. An extremely picky employer (like me) will select the model and the service themselves to test how well the applicant works under pressure. So if you think you're going to walk into an interview with a model you're familiar with and do a cut that you have down to a science, you may be in for a shock. Be especially prepared for this if you're applying at an upscale establishment. If you aren't 100% confident or feel you could benefit from a confidence boost, consider working with a more experienced mentor to have your technique evaluated.

Impressive Presentation. In Step 1, I taught you how to put an application packet together. Have it ready for action.

Interview Preparation. In Step 6, you'll get a taste of an Interview From Hell. Prepare to meet with a complete bitch that has interviewed a seemingly endless parade of lazy, unprofessional drama queens in search of employment. She can and will see right through you if you slip up—and she'll say something about it. I perform Interviews From Hell on a regular basis (it's how I separate actual professionals from the trash that carry cosmetology licenses and call themselves professionals). I highly doubt you'll face an owner or manager that formidable, but be prepared. You never know what you're walking into. You'll need to hold your composure against an intimidating owner and have the confidence to flip the interview on her when it's your turn to ask the questions. (We'll cover that process in Step 7.)

Portfolio. The last thing you want is to bring a physical portfolio into an interview only to discover that it's missing images, pages are stuck together with some mysterious gunk, or that your cat has pissed all over the binding. Even if you've kept it locked in a safe protected by ninjas—check over it. Make certain that nothing is ripped, missing, bent, or creased.

If you have a web portfolio, check over every page. Remember, that portfolio demonstrates your attention to detail. Everything should be properly aligned and grammatically correct. Contact information should be current, links should all point where they need to, and the images should showcase your best work. Look over it as if you're the most selective salon owner out there.

Web Presence. It doesn't matter if you do everything right, if a potential employer does a web search on you and finds anything unprofessional or less than flattering, you are screwed. Don't be a dum-dum. (Managing your web presence will be discussed more in the Interwebs chapter.)

Step 3: Research

"This research might take a few hours, but by eliminating the salons that will obviously not suit you, you'll save precious time later."

No portion of your job search will be as important as your research and recon. These steps allow you to evaluate potential salons prior to making contact as an applicant, giving you the opportunity to objectively consider the business before having it presented by an eager employer.

Check out the salons in your area. View their websites, social media pages, and reviews to get a feel for the salon's style and reputation. Consider them from a client's perspective, as well as that of a potential employee. Make a list of the salons you're interested in visiting. Include the salon names, addresses, websites, and phone numbers. If you can get the owner's name, write that down also.

Does the salon advertise? Where do you see their advertisements and how frequently do you see them? Most salons need to advertise regularly. With so many salons saturating the market, owners and managers have to remain diligent about maintaining visibility. However, there are a few exceptions to this. Salons that are fully-booked with standing clients, for example, do not need to advertise often. If they're enjoying a high-traffic location or a lucrative referral relationship with another business and they have superior retention skills, they may not have to advertise at all. Smaller operations with a smaller staff of talented, established, experienced staff members often have their reputations perpetuated through word-of-mouth entirely. So, consider their advertising efforts, but don't place a whole lot of weight on it if the business is obviously thriving.

Does the salon website have any employment opportunities posted? Don't be discouraged if they don't; not all salons post their open positions. Check job listings in your local paper and on job posting sites like Craigslist, Monster, or Indeed. Highlight any salons on your list that have ads up and notate the type of position. For these salons, you'll compose an application cover letter instead of a prospecting letter.

The highlighted salons with open positions won't get special priority because you won't be limiting your search to salons that are actively seeking staff. It never hurts to schedule an appointment with the owner and present yourself for consideration, just remember that a prospecting cover letter will be required as opposed to an application letter.

Analyzing Employment Ads

Ads should clearly list the business. If the salon's name isn't listed, run the contact number through Google and try to find it that way. I don't recommend going into an interview blind under any circumstances. Think about this: if the salon owner doesn't have the foresight or the extra money to drop on a proper employment ad that includes their business name, what does that communicate to you?

I might read too far into these things, but to me, an owner who doesn't bother to name their business in their employment ad says several things.

- They don't want applicants to research their business. Nothing about that possibility indicates anything good. An owner who doesn't want you research them either has something to hide (like a poor reputation), knows they're not a desirable business to work for, or has no respect for your time or what you're looking for in an employer.
- The owner is either cheap or of questionable competence. Either they "forgot" to include the business name (incompetent), thought it "wasn't important" (disrespectful and incompetent), didn't have the extra money to spend on the extra characters in the ad (doesn't actually need another employee), or didn't want to spend the extra money (disrespectful and cheap). I don't know about you, but I would want nothing to do with any of this.
- The owner seems to have no interest in pre-screening applicants. You don't want to work for an owner who will hire whoever applies. You want a selective owner. A selective owner will list their salon's name and website so potential employees can check them out prior to applying.

Applicants deserve the ability to research the business and see if their professional philosophies mesh with the prospective employer's. If you're a trendy, tattooed, spunky stylist with multicolored hair looking for a fun salon that matches your work ethic and personal style, you don't want to walk into an interview at some snooty ass, upscale spa full of snobs like me. Selective owners will minimize the risk of that happening by giving an applicant the ability to do some preliminary research.

Ultimately, not providing the salon name is inconsiderate at best and disrespectful at worst. Whether intentional or unintentional, it says, "I don't really care about your time, what you want, or whether or not my salon is a good fit for you. If you want to know more, you'll have to seek me out and spend time asking me questions." Don't waste time on inconsiderate or incompetent owners. Skip those ads that don't list the business name.

The ad should never say, "Must have clientele." For a job offer to be legitimate, there must be actual, compensable work to be done. Simply put: the owner must actually have clients who require servicing. If a salon owner truly had need of another professional, they wouldn't require that professional to bring a clientele with them. If the salon were busy enough to justify hiring another staff member, the owner would be seeking someone without a clientele so that they could ensure their overabundance of clientele could be serviced.

When you see an ad that reads, "Must have clientele," you aren't reading a job offer, you're reading a "bring your clients to my struggling salon and let me collect a portion of your income" offer. It basically screams, "poor management." Save yourself the aggravation and skip these ads.

If the owner felt the need to describe their salon as "drama-free," you can bet your ass that it isn't. First of all, no salon (no matter how well-managed) is "drama-free." No workplace in any industry goes without some form of drama periodically. A mature, experienced salon owner will not feel the need—nor will they find it appropriate—to put this terminology in an employment ad. These ads communicate unprofessional, childish management. "Drama-free" isn't an achievement; it's expected from a professional establishment.

Do not respond to ads posted by owners who don't understand the difference between an employee, booth renter, or independent contractor. I don't think I need to elaborate too much on my reasoning on this topic at this point, but this indicates gross incompetence at best and intentional exploitation at worst.

Consider "flexible schedule" a warning. An employer with genuine need for an employee is unlikely to be "flexible." Flexibility indicates to me that the owner doesn't actually need someone. They might have enough business to justify hiring someone in some capacity, but if they were experiencing real need, "flexible" wouldn't be in their vocabulary—they would know exactly where they require coverage and would be hiring for those specific days and times.

That being said, some owners are cool with turning away business if necessary. For example, I would rather turn away a thousand dollars' worth of service sales a day than hastily hire someone out of desperation. Also, my staff take lunch breaks and they don't work holidays. We walk out the door promptly at closing time—I don't care if clients are lined up out the door and down the street; we have families and lives outside of the salon. I refuse to compromise my staff's break time or their family time for any client or any amount of money.

Employment with me isn't "flexible" by any means, but a lot of owners are more laid back than I am. So don't discount this wording entirely, but take note of it and be sure to evaluate whether the salon actually has enough business to require another employee.

Beware of high commissions. Unless their pricing and overhead are meticulously balanced, salons that offer high commissions (50% or more) are operating with an extremely slim profit margin. (I could run all kinds of math to point this out, but I'm saving that aggravation for my next book on salon ownership.)

Although higher commissions sound great, they often come with massive downsides in the form of misclassification, wage theft, questionably legal fees, and other employment abuses. Salon owners who pay high commissions are also unlikely to be able to afford advertising or provide benefits to their staff. You would be better off working at a salon that offers a base pay and a reasonable commission that leaves the owner with enough profit to re-invest in the business.

Remember: a business exists to generate a profit. Employees facilitate that purpose. You aren't there to bleed the business dry; you're there to ensure it continues to thrive. You deserve fair pay for your labor, but you do not deserve to make more money than the business itself. Businesses do not survive like that, which is why you don't see that kind of backwards compensation in any other industry.

Step 4: Recon

Now you're going to go undercover and experience the salon through the eyes of a client while evaluating it as a potential employee. Book an appointment at the salon and arrive early. Pay very close attention to everything happening around you.

What is going on at the front desk? While you wait for the appointment, take note of how you're greeted. Are you offered a beverage? Is the receptionist behaving professionally? Is the waiting room orderly and clean? Is your first impression a good one? How about the retail area? It should be stocked, dusted, and orderly.

How busy is the salon? Are a lot of people checking in and out? Are people walking by outside? What kind of clients does the salon attract and do they seem to fit your target demographic?

Remember, a lot of salon owners make grand claims about the volume of clients they service. In commission-only salons (most of which don't concern themselves with FLSA compliance), it costs a salon owner nothing to hire you and have you sit around and wait. I can't tell you how many spa owners have tried to lure me to work for them with the promise of "more clients than you can handle." When I ask to view their scheduling books or drop in on their spa for a random visit, those promises turn out to be false. Don't get lured into a dead spa.

Are the employees busy? Are staff members sitting around in their chairs, flipping through magazines, or screwing around on their computers? Are they eating on the cutting floor?

Where is the manager? A well-run salon has either an owner or manager supervising daily operations, making sure the staff members are actually working—folding towels, sweeping floors, and cleaning/disinfecting tools. A well-run salon with a strong manager will not allow staff to be sitting around the salon floor like a bunch of lumps. In the rare event that the chores are done, those employees should be out of sight unless they're with clients.

Is the salon clean? Are the stations orderly and wiped down? Are jars of disinfectant on the stations? Does the liquid inside appear clean or is there a ton of filth and clippings inside? This indicates improper, lax disinfection. Do you want to be associated with that?

How do the employees interact? Are they behaving professionally or are they being loud and rowdy? As much as I hate it, some salons have more casual atmospheres. Evaluate that atmosphere from a client's perspective. Do the staff seem to get along well, or can you sense tension?

Do you see why this initial evaluation has value when you're researching potential salons to work at? The way a salon or spa looks and the way the professionals dress and behave dictates the kind of clientele that will frequent that establishment. If you walk into a salon with casual decor, stylists wearing jeans and t-shirts, the clients all seem to know one another, they're playing a country radio station on a boom box, and kids are running around—you've probably walked into a mom-and-pop family shop. If you entered a salon with fresh and funky decor, stylists wearing all black, younger clients with avant garde styles, and dance remixes of the current top 40 hits playing on the surround sound speakers—you've walked into a trendy salon. If you walk into a salon with dim lighting, lit candles, clients shuffling around in robes, weird zen music playing, and everyone leaves looking half-asleep and $200 poorer than when they arrived—you've found an upscale spa.

Choose an environment that suits you and attracts the clientele you prefer. If loud, cozy, casual environments, reasonable prices, and clients who seem more like family appeal to you, aim for the mom-and-pop. If you want to rock out to techno while you trim blue mohawks and work with other professionals who take their art seriously, consider the trendy salons. If you're a snobby elitist like me and prefer the calm, quiet, intimate atmosphere of an upscale spa (and the impressive paychecks), find one.

Be sure to update your list when you get home. Eliminate the salons that aren't a good fit and put the salons in order, listing your favorites at the top. Compose your cover letters and put together those application packets.

Step 5: Making Contact

Finally, it's time to apply. Your next step is to make contact. When you call, ask to speak with a manager or the owner. If they aren't available, leave a message with the receptionist with your name and phone number. Do not tell the receptionist what you are calling in regards to unless she asks. Try to keep it vague if she does ("I just had a few questions I wanted to ask her. Can you have her contact me at her convenience?")

Why so secretive? Simple. Receptionists make friends with the staff members. The industry remains largely commission-based. If that receptionist thinks you are going to compete with her friends, she may choose not to pass your message to the owner. I have seen this happen multiple times and have actually fired two receptionists for withholding applicant information and lying to potential applicants by telling them we already filled open positions.

If you'd like, you can leave your specific reason for calling, but make sure to mention that you will be following up so the receptionist doesn't get any bright ideas.

If you do not receive a call back within a day or two, call back. If you still can't reach the owner or the manager, put the application packet (unfolded) into a manila clasp envelope, seal it and tape it shut, and send it to the salon by mail. If you choose to drop it off in person, do so prepared to interview. You might get lucky and be seen right away.

Step 6: The Interview

These interview tips might seem like common sense, but it would be foolish to presume that all schools properly educate their students on how to behave during an interview. (I have seen too many applicants show up late, completely unprepared, and dressed inappropriately to omit this brief chapter.) Sorry if this information seems superfluous, but apparently people still need to be taught these things.

Have your paperwork ready. If you haven't already given the owner the application packet, bring it to the interview.

Pull up to the salon twenty minutes early. Give yourself plenty of time to get through traffic and find parking. Plan to be in a parking space, collecting your paperwork twenty minutes prior to the interview appointment.

Leave your phone in the car. Don't put it on vibrate or silence it. Leave it. Until you know the owner's policy regarding cell phones, don't bring it into her business. Besides, you never want a potential employer to see you screwing with your phone while you're waiting and you certainly don't want it to ring or vibrate during your appointment. Be fully present and leave the device behind.

Walk into the salon ten minutes early. Not fifteen minutes early, not right on time, not five minutes late—ten minutes early. This shows that you are reliable, respectful, and prompt. It gives you time to check-in at the front desk and wait for reception to notify the owner that you have arrived without infringing on the appointment time or on the salon owner's time. You never, ever want to keep an owner waiting, but you don't want to show up too early either.

Present yourself professionally. Dress as well as or better than the owner. Don't wear clothing in loud neons or patterns—especially animal print. Freshly ironed black dress pants, a nice black blouse, well-fitted blazer, and clean, black, closed-toed shoes are excellent. Keep accessories unobtrusive, classy, and to a minimum. One pair of earrings, a simple bracelet, and a simple necklace are perfect.

Have your hair, makeup, and nails done. You're representing the beauty industry. Don't show up with raggedy nails, tacky nail art, messy hair, and loud cosmetics. Your makeup should look natural, your nails should look well-maintained, and your hair should be styled nicely. Trendy salons tend to encourage more outrageous hairstyles and colors, but when you're looking for a job, keep your hair a natural color. Avoid nail art altogether for interviews. Stick to classic polish colors (reds, browns, deep bronze, light pinks, French).

Until you get a feel for the owner, keep them focused on your qualifications and what you can bring to the salon, not wondering whether or not your propensity to dress like a hooker is going to cause a problem for them.

Remember this: You are a valuable professional. You're not desperate. It might be an employer's job market, but you have standards and expectations as well. You're seeking a place that suits you and respects you as a professional. You're interviewing the salon as well.

Interview Questions From the Desk of Satan

Don't be surprised if you find yourself facing an interviewer who seems less-than-enthused to be dealing with yet another potential employee. For a lot of employers, especially in this job market, interviewing has become a tedious, frustrating chore. Convince this cynical beast-person that you are exactly what they've been waiting for.

To help you prepare for the worst, here is a list of questions I ask every potential new hire:

Why did you chose a career in the beauty industry? Are you following your passion? Do you love making people feel better about themselves? Preach it. Do not spit out some bullshit your school administrator filled your head with or some idiotic comment that shows how little you know about the industry or the job you're applying for. These are some of the answers I've heard in response to this question:

"I want to make $50,000 a year working part-time." Then become a prostitute.

"I want to set my own schedule." Then go freelance. Employees work the schedule we give them.

"I want to get paid to hang out all day." You're at a job interview—at a business. While many salons do allow their staff to "hang out" all day, a profitable, well-managed one will certainly not.

Where do you want to be in three years? In my opinion, no wrong answer to this question exists, but I'm a rare person. Most salon owners believe that one answer is very clearly wrong and won't hire anyone who utters it. The answer you never respond with is: "I want to own my own salon." For every salon owner who isn't named Tina Alberino, that response will very likely immediately disqualify you from employment.

What are your pet peeves? One applicant blurted out to me, "When my husband doesn't flush the toilet!" Sure, it was funny and honest, but it wasn't quite what I was looking for. Other answers I've heard include: "Old ladies that can't drive," "Rude bank tellers," and "Pineapple body spray." None of those answers help any manager. Give us something we can work with: "Gossip," "No-shows," "Clients who use cell phones during their service." These are great because they let us know how we can make your work life easier.

What would your worst enemy say about you? Be honest, but keep it relevant and appropriate. I once had an applicant answer, "That I'm a slut because I slept with her husband on accident." Of course, I burst into laughter—but not all owners will find that as funny as I did. Are you impatient? Critical? Too easily stressed when under pressure? Confess. How you answer will tell a manager how to manage you best.

What do most people often criticize about you? Are you impatient? Stubborn? Hot-tempered? We all have shortcomings. For example, I'm a perfectionist. I hold myself and others to impossibly high standards. I have no patience for excuses and I don't tolerate unprofessional, immature behavior at work. I have poor delegation skills because I'm very particular about things being done right and being done well. Yeah, these are all negative traits, but they make me a great manager. Your negative traits might be interpreted as positive traits also, depending on what they are.

Be honest when sharing your negative traits so the owner or manager has a clear picture of what they're working with. The answer to this question won't necessarily disqualify you, unless the answer involves drug use or something similarly reprehensible.

What is your idea of a strong work ethic? Let the interviewer know you're a hard worker during your scheduled hours but that you value your private time also. Don't tell them what you think they want to hear if you don't plan on delivering. "I believe I possess a strong work ethic. I am dedicated to building my clientele and retaining them. I perform all of my services to the best of my ability and really focus on making sure every guest has a great experience. I strive to be as accommodating and hospitable as possible. When I set a schedule, I stick to it. I also help around the spa, doing laundry and light cleaning when necessary. However, I do believe in moderation. I do not work outside of my schedule and when I'm off for the day, I'm off. I take a lunch every afternoon at a set time and spend time with my family on the days I'm not in the spa. I find that this keeps me from getting burnt out and contributes to my professional happiness overall."

That is a winning statement. You're telling the interviewer that you work hard but you're also making it clear that you have boundaries. You're entitled to a lunch break. You should not be expected to work after hours. Employees who burn themselves out get sick more frequently and tend to be unhappy at their place of employment. No smart employer wants that. If an employer isn't satisfied with that answer, you're interviewing at the wrong business.

Have you ever worked with someone you didn't like? If you answer with, "No! Never! I've loved everyone I've ever worked with!" I'm going to stand up, rip your resume in half, and say, "We have no room for liars here. Good day, sir."

...alright, I probably won't actually do that, but you'll definitely get an eye roll and an audible groan.

Everyone has worked with someone they didn't like. To answer this question honestly and well, pick a coworker that exhibited a trait or behavior you didn't agree with. Tell the interviewer what that coworker did and why you found it offensive. Don't name names, but be real and take this opportunity to contrast that coworker's behavior with your own. This communicates your values, which helps the interviewer determine whether or not you're likely to have problems with any of the existing staff. This answer helps them learn more about how you like to work and gives them insight on how best to manage you.

"Another nail technician I worked with refused to properly disinfect and store her tools. She also didn't take pride in her work and rushed through services. Because I value sanitation and hold the reputation of my workplace in high regard, I found this behavior unacceptable."

"One of my coworkers enjoyed spreading gossip and stirring up conflict in the salon. I don't think that is appropriate in any setting, let alone a professional one."

"An esthetician I worked with was very unreliable. She often missed work and when she actually showed up, she was usually late. The owner and I would have to call her clients and try to rearrange their appointments and work them into my schedule. While I appreciated the extra business, I couldn't tolerate this and felt she was a poor representation of the salon."

What would you change about your last job? It's a trap! Don't speak negatively about your last place of employment. A lot of applicants will take this question as an invitation to bash their former boss and coworkers. Instead, pick one thing that you found inefficient or inappropriate. "I would implement a dress code or assign a uniform to keep the staff looking professional." "I would design a more efficient inventory system so that we could keep on top of product orders better."

What didn't you like about your last boss? It's another trap! Be honest here, but don't bash your old boss. Tactfully point out something she did that wasn't working for you professionally. Step lightly. You never know if the interviewer is friends with the ex-boss. Start off with a disclaimer. "I don't want to speak badly about her. On a personal level she's fantastic. However, I found that her laid-back management style didn't suit me. Our professional philosophies weren't in sync." Keep it professional (not personal) and relevant to work.

If the interviewer pushes you to reveal more, just say, "I'd prefer not to talk badly about them. I appreciated the opportunity they gave me, but it just didn't work out. If you'd like to call them to inquire about me, please feel free. They might not have nice things to say about me, but I won't disparage other professionals." Refusal to participate in a bashing session shows integrity. Even if the interviewer calls and the ex-employer talks her ear off for an hour about what a terrible person you are, you're going to come out on top for the way you handled it.

Why are you changing jobs? The interviewer wants to know what trespass drove you from the previous salon. They want to know whether or not your reasons for leaving are logical and make sure that you're unlikely to encounter the same problem in their salon. Answer honestly, but remember, no trash talking.

Why do you appear to change workplaces so frequently? Most salon managers know how poorly competing salons are managed, but we're hesitant to hire someone who switches jobs every six months. Deliver an honest answer but keep it vague. "I've been having a hard time finding the right place for me. I believe this had to with me not asking enough questions during the interviewing process and impulsively choosing jobs on the spot. I've since realized that my prior method was not a great strategy for promoting professional longevity and have committed myself to being more inquisitive and more selective. I've also discovered that finding the right fit in this industry can be a bit of a trial and error process if you aren't diligent in screening potential employers. I'm hoping this salon will turn out to be a place I can build a career at."

Some interviewers ask exactly why you left each place on your resume. Put forth truth. The answers help them determine what you're looking for and what you value.

"I left X Salon because it wasn't very busy and the owner didn't invest in advertising."

"I left Y Salon because my coworkers were unprofessional and management wouldn't rectify it, even though it was affecting our clients' experience at the business."

"I left Z Salon because the owner implemented a new policy requiring all staff to pay product fees, which I didn't consider to be fair or reasonable."

Those are great answers that communicate your expectations and values.

Why were you fired from your last position? Be honest, because some interviewers will call and ask. If you made a mistake, own it. Show humility and growth. If the problem was a lack of experience, say so, but express a strong desire to learn and list the efforts you're making to improve independently. If you were terminated for bucking authority, explain why you disagreed with a particular policy or practice.

Depending on the circumstance, getting fired from your last position might not disqualify you. One applicant told me she was fired for insisting on detailed pay stubs from her boss. She tracked her totals and they weren't matching up with her pay. When she requested the pay stubs, the owner became defensive and fired her. Her honest answer gave me the opportunity to tell her that I didn't feel her termination was fair or appropriate. I was also able to reassure her that we provide incredibly detailed wage statements each pay period, all of which were tied in with our scheduling system and accessible to her at any time.

Tell the truth, even if it isn't pretty.

Why is there a gap in your employment? If you've been out of the business for a while but worked in other fields, offer to provide the details to the unrelated jobs you've held; just tell the interviewer that you felt the experience wasn't relevant to the position. If you spent a long time looking for employment or caring for family, state that. Be honest, but don't go into detail if you aren't asked to.

Why do you want to work here? Bad answers to this question include: "I need money," "I need a job," and "It's pretty inside." Stay away from superficial, self-serving answers.

Good answers show that you've done research. "I've looked through your website and I think this salon might be a good fit for me: the marketing seems geared towards the demographic I like to serve, we share a commitment to client safety, and the atmosphere appeals to me."

Having a service done earns massive bonus points because it shows that you really want to see the spa from the perspective of a client. Mention that you are looking for long-term employment in a business that will ensure your continued success in the industry and you've got a slam dunk.

Why should I hire you? Answer this with, "I don't know," and a smart interviewer will respond with, "Neither do I. Thanks for coming in." You'll be sent on your way and won't get a call back.

You should know exactly why a salon could benefit from having you on staff. This is your opportunity to tell the interviewer what you have to offer. Avoid saying generic things that are obvious to the interviewer, like, "I'm friendly," "I'm trustworthy," or "I'm professional." Stick with what can be proven: you have a lot of great marketing ideas (have some examples prepared), you love to network (mention what networking groups you're involved in and what events you attend), and you are dedicated to furthering your professional education (if you have completed certificate programs and are planning on attending any in the future, mention them).

What is your least favorite service to perform? What don't you like doing and why? Don't lie and claim to love every service. Nobody loves every part of their job. However, you should express an interest in learning and improving.

One nail technician I interviewed responded, "I don't do pedicures." Explain to me: what use do I have for a nail technician that refuses to do pedicures? (Spoiler alert: None. None at all.) This told me that the applicant wasn't a good fit for our business—a spa where 80% of the nail department's revenue was generated through pedicure services. Unless you have a medical reason for refusing to perform a service—like a product allergy or asthma that's triggered by chemical inhalation—there's no legitimate reason to outright refuse to perform a service.

Tell me about the technical areas you feel you need improvement on. Tell the truth, the whole truth, and nothing but the truth here. This question gets asked so often in salon interviews that you really should include it on the resume. (Remember our "Technical Skills" and "Developing Skills" lists?)

Notice how this isn't formed as a question. Many interviewers will tell you to talk about the areas you need improvement on rather than ask you if there are areas you need improvement on. Do not say you're "great at everything." That's crap. Everyone has something they struggle with. Besides, you will eventually get busted if you lie.

When answering, add that you have been working on your weak points in your spare time, but that you could benefit from hands-on training. Instead of saying, "I can't do it," say "I'm excited to learn how to do it better."

Tell me about a time that you botched a service and how you handled it. We have all screwed up services in our careers, so don't lie and claim you have never made a mistake. Recount a failure that happened in school if it makes you feel better, but emphasize the way you handled the situation, not the details of how you screwed up. Employers want to see how you approach a situation where you have clearly made a mistake. We want to see humility, honesty, integrity, and improvement.

"I was so nervous during my first perm at school, I accidentally squirted neutralizer in a client's eye. I helped rinse her eyes out with cool water. I was so embarrassed and apologized profusely. Now, I make certain that the clients' eyes are protected before I even cut the cap off the bottle. The experience made me a more cautious professional."

What do you expect from a salon owner?/What do you believe a salon owner's responsibilities are? The answers to these questions accomplish two things: the first communicates what you're looking for in a boss and the second communicates how well you understand their position. Even if a career in management doesn't appeal to you, it's important to understand the position's responsibilities.

Your expectations should be realistic but honest. Do you want a salon owner who properly classifies employees and holds coworkers accountable for bad behavior? Do you want an owner who invests in the salon by utilizing an advertising budget? Do you want an owner who understands the importance of continuing education? Speak up.

How do you feel about working under a younger manager? This question helps young owners and managers determine how big of a pain in the ass you plan on being.

I was teaching one of the owners I worked for how I screen applicants. She asked questions from my list while I evaluated her and took notes. When she asked this question, an older applicant said, "I've been in this business for fifteen years. I don't answer to children." I put the pen down, stood up and said, "Thank you for your time. I'll show you to the door." She balked.

I'm not sure who she thought I was, but she definitely didn't realize I was the general manager and that I was coordinating the owner's management training. This applicant's fifteen years of experience meant jack shit because I could tell that she had no idea how the industry actually works.

In this industry, age does not equate to competence or experience. Sometimes, even experience doesn't equate to managerial competence. If you are being interviewed by a younger manager or salon owner, treat them with the respect their position commands. Ignore their age. Your answer needs to be, "Age is not a measure of ability."

We do require a full drug screening as part of our interviewing process. Would you be able to stop at the testing center today? Drugs should never be a problem for you. You should be able to happily agree to an immediate drug test. As an employer, I've had issues with staff members and cocaine, meth, and pills. No spa owner wants a user in their building. If you're a recreational user or an addict, handle that before stepping into any interview.

Do you have any questions? You always have questions. We'll get into the cross-interview next. This question is your opportunity to turn the tables and interview the employer—and you need to take advantage of it.

Step 7: Turn the Tables

"Never blindly agree to everything just to get hired and don't make a decision based on immediate need (or you'll pay for it later)."

A lot of applicants (particularly recent graduates) see job interviews as personal obstacles. They walk into the interview believing that they have to prove themselves and sell themselves to the owner. These beliefs are partially correct, but you should be entering interviews with expectations of your own.

Employers meet with applicants because they are interested in possibly hiring them. If they weren't, the applicant wouldn't have an interview to begin with. As an applicant, you are at the interview to present your qualifications and experience and communicate your expectations. The owner needs to present their requirements and expectations of you. The two of you then decide whether the arrangement will be suitable. If your mutual terms, conditions, and expectations do not match, move on.

The interview process moves both ways. You aren't the only person proving yourself, so meet the owner on equal ground. Interview them and their way of doing business. It's not unreasonable to bring up any concerns you have or inquire further about policies or conditions that seem unfair or questionable.

Evaluation Point 1: The Boss

Was the owner on time or late? Does she focus on you or does she allow other things to distract her during the interview? Owners and managers are busy people, but when you set an appointment, you deserve their full attention.

Disrespectful owners will get around to you when it's convenient for them, regardless of the appointment time, and may allow other things to preoccupy them. They may also cut your responses short and show other signs of superiority. Disrespectful owners won't ask if you have questions. If you do ask any questions, they may become defensive. Do not overlook this behavior. Some owners are just assholes, but some intentionally do this to exercise their control over you and test your boundaries. They want to send a message that they are the authority and you are a peon. Do not work for an owner like that.

Competent owners thoroughly evaluate applicants and take interviews seriously. They are courteous, prompt, and allow applicants to respond to questions without cutting them short. They have no problem answering questions and they do so without an attitude.

Evaluation Point 2: The Tour

During the tour, the owner walks an applicant through their facility, acquainting them with the space and the staff. If you have already done your recon, the tour shouldn't yield any new information, but since you are being presented as a potential employee, observe the reactions from the staff. Are they welcoming and kind or are they closed off and defensive? Welcoming staff that seem genuinely happy to have another staff member on board are either a.) so busy that they're confident that another coworker isn't going to cut into their paychecks or b.) trust their spa owner's management decisions, which means the owner is doing something right.

If you're being introduced to the staff, ask them how long they've worked in the salon. If the staff members have been there for three or more years, you've likely found a great management team.

Remember during your tour that some salon professionals (stylists in particular) can be incredibly hard to keep happy. If a few of the staff members seem less-than-thrilled at your presence, remember that this industry can be competitive and that some professionals are never satisfied. Don't let a few bad seeds taint you against the salon.

Evaluation Point 3: The Boss' Office

When you enter the owner's office for the interview, take note of your surroundings. If the owner's desk looks like someone emptied a garbage can on it and she's hoarding piles of miscellaneous crap that reaches the ceiling tiles: beware. Clutter and filth point to an owner or manager that doesn't have their shit together. They either can't manage their own time properly or can't delegate effectively. That kind of physical disorganization often translates to their business operations. Giant, massive red flag. Keep it in mind as the interview proceeds.

Evaluation Point 4: The Boss' Questions

Pay attention to the questions the interviewer asks. Are they predominantly focused on your experience, your professional philosophies, or your personal life? The type of questions the interviewer asks clues you in to what's important to them and provides insight into their management style. Owners who ask more about your professional desires and philosophies want to evaluate how well the salon would suit you. Owners who ask more about your skills and experience place heavy importance on proficiency and competency. Owners who want to know more about your personal life are gauging how you'll fit in with the existing staff.

Evaluation Point 5: "Do you have any questions for me?"

Yes, you really do. Lots of them.

"How do you classify staff for tax purposes?" The answer to this question may determine whether or not the interview continues. If the owner classifies her staff as "independent contractors," get out of there.

"How is your compensation structured?" If the salon is commission-based, find out what percentage they offer. Your next question to a commission-based salon owner needs to be, "So, you must track hours then and weigh the minimum wage against the commission to ensure FLSA compliance, right?" If they give you a blank stare, get defensive, or offer up some bullshit, end the interview and find an owner who knows what they're doing.

"Do you provide detailed pay stubs?" Asking this question helps to gauge whether or not the salon owner values transparency. Remember, owners have no reason to withhold this information, as they a.) presumably calculate these totals when they do payroll and b.) are required to have copies of their records on file for the IRS and DOL for at least 3-4 years.

"Do you charge product fees?" Unless you are a booth renter or freelancer, the owner supplies product. However, many owners try to justify this practice by deducting the expense of product prior to calculating the commission. I strongly advise avoiding any owner who engages in this practice.

"Do you participate in group discount deals and if so, what is your policy regarding payment for those services?" By now, most salon owners know better than to participate in Groupons, but ask this question up front. You don't want to show up to work on the first day to find out that the owner ran a Groupon for your services, sold 1,500 of them already, and only pays 50% of the take after Groupon's fees. (Yes, this happens—a lot.)

If the owner does participate in group coupon deals, explain that you will not participate in them unless you are compensated for the full service value, not the discounted value. Any policy that requires you to take a huge pay cut in exchange for "exposure" like that should be an immediate deal-breaker. We work for money, not "exposure." I have many, many reasons why Groupons and similar "marketing opportunities" are absolutely awful, but we'll discuss those in Deep Discount Dumbassery.

"Can I see the job description?" Any owner worth their title will have detailed job descriptions prepared for all positions. Be leery of an owner who doesn't, as this indicates weak management. Job descriptions deliver a clear understanding of what the owner expects of you.

"Do you have an employee handbook I can read through?" The owner should have no problem giving you a handbook so you can review their rules and policies.

"Can I review your employment contract?" Most owners utilize employment contracts at this point, but if the interviewer doesn't, request a written job offer or employment agreement. This request is not unreasonable. Be wary of any owner who refuses to put their promises to paper. If they do require you to sign an agreement, ask if you can bring it home to look it over and make certain you'll be provided with a signed copy if you choose to take the job. We'll cover employment contracts in detail in the next chapter.

"Are any benefits offered?" How many sick days or vacation days are you allotted? Do they offer medical insurance or retirement plans? Not a lot of salons offer benefits, but some do. It never hurts to ask.

"Do you offer continuing education?" Again, some salons do and some don't. Salons that regularly schedule continuing education workshops are the ones that deserve serious consideration.

"Do you advertise regularly?" Find out how this owner maintains their visibility.

"Does the salon have enough business to justify hiring me?" You should already have a decent hypothesis based on your research, but ask anyway. Let the owner know that you are motivated to build, but you do have bills to pay. If they don't have enough traffic to ensure you'll be receiving a solid paycheck, you aren't interested.

"How is the salon's client retention rate?" The salon's client retention rate provides insight into how good the salon and the staff are at keeping the new clients they obtain. If you're applying for a position at a touristy hotel, resort spa, or on a cruise ship, don't bother asking this question. The numbers will be bad, but that will have nothing to do with the customer service. (In those cases, the online reviews will provide better insight.)

"How do the staff get along?"/"How do you handle staff conflicts?" Not a question you would ask in any other industry, but one that needs to be asked during a salon interview. Explain to the owner who you are making a career decision. You do not want to waste their time or yours by working in a salon plagued with conflict. You are a professional and expect others to behave accordingly. Clients don't want to visit a hostile, toxic salon, so this factor is crucial to your bottom line.

Don't settle. Shop around. This first interview will not be the last. Never accept an offer immediately. Take time to consider your options. If an owner asks, "When can you start?" Reply with, "When I've wrapped up the other interviews I have scheduled, I'll let you know my decision." Set a date to follow up before leaving. This communicates to the potential employer that you aren't desperate, you don't jump into employment impulsively, and that you're looking for a long-term position.

This list serves as a general guideline. Ask every question you need answered. The more you know in advance about the salon you're considering employment with, the less likely you are to be confronted with nasty, deal-breaking surprises on the first day. You're also less likely to end up jumping from salon to salon. Salon hopping like that makes it impossible to build a book and you don't want to develop a reputation for taking and leaving jobs impulsively. Doing your research, asking thorough questions, and giving each opportunity serious consideration makes it more likely that you'll land in a long-term position with a competent employer who you're compatible with.

Employment Contracts 101

"Contract law is essentially a defensive scorched-earth battleground where the constant question is, 'if my business partner was possessed by a brain-eating monster from beyond spacetime tomorrow, what is the worst thing they could do to me?'"
-Charles Stross

Don't tempt fate. Never assume "nothing will go wrong." Just because the potential employer seems amazing and the two of you really hit it off does not mean that you have found a professional home for life. People change. First impressions are rarely ever accurate. Remember this when evaluating a proposed employment contract. If it doesn't sound right or seem fair, it isn't. Look out for your own best interests.

Too often, I'm contacted by people who signed their names on agreements they actually didn't agree with, desperate for a way out. If you sign something, you are agreeing to comply with whatever the terms are, regardless of how unreasonable they may be. If you don't agree with those terms or have no intentions to following through with what is expected of you, don't sign.

Unlawful agreements will never hold up in court, but unreasonable ones might, depending on the state's legislature. For example, an owner who requires an employee to sign a non-compete that restricts them from working in any beauty-related field within a 50 mile radius of her salon for a period of three years will have that agreement struck down by a judge. It is overly restricting and unreasonable. However, the employee can expect to be blasted by opposing council (or the judge, or both) for being stupid enough to sign the agreement to begin with.

Nobody is holding a gun to your head or threatening physical harm against you for not signing the documents presented during an employment negotiation. In the worst case scenario you may not get the job, but if you have to sell your soul for the position it's unlikely to be worth the trouble anyways. Ask yourself: Are the terms reasonable? Will I be able to comply with the terms of the agreement? Am I 100% comfortable signing this?

Never permit a verbal agreement. If the owner can speak it with their lips, they can put it on paper and sign their name to it. Verbal agreements are incredibly difficult to enforce. Any owner unwilling to put their promises in writing can't be trusted. Never, ever forget this. It applies to your "friends" who own salons also. Business is business.

Negotiate. All contracts are negotiable. You don't need to accept the terms as they are. When a potential employer presents a contract, take it home, bust out a red pen, and make changes where you see fit. Arrange a meeting with the owner and present your terms. Lay out what you will and won't accept from the owner at this meeting. If they don't accept, find employment elsewhere.

Protect your copy. Ensure that you are given correct copies of every document you sign. Keep them safe at home—not at the salon. Any changes made to them during negotiations must be kept as well.

The following chapters will tell you everything you need to know about common employment contract terms.

Non-Solicitation & Non-Disclosure Agreements

Non-disclosure agreements and non-solicitation agreements are restrictive covenants, designed to protect the salon and its property.

A non-disclosure agreement (NDA) is a confidentiality agreement that protects proprietary business information and trade secrets from third parties. These are sometimes used in place of (or in addition to) non-solicitation agreements to secure client contact information. Some salons use them to protect innovative, unique service protocols also.

A non-solicitation agreement (NSA) revokes an employee's right to solicit clients of the salon if they resign or are terminated and may also restrict their ability to solicit their coworkers to work for them if they decide to open a competing business. Mutinies happen often, so don't be surprised to see this in a contract. (It only takes one mutiny for an owner to realize how necessary that clause is.)

These clauses often also prohibit salon employees from copying, downloading, or otherwise transferring client information for any purpose. Salon owners include these clauses to protect client information and their own marketing investments. However, these clauses often don't exclude the clients that a new hire brings with them to the business, so the vast majority of them require amendment to make them fair to both parties.

They're People, Not Cattle

In the event of a termination or resignation, oftentimes both the service provider and the salon owner scramble to claim the clients for themselves. I often get asked, "Who do the clients belong to?"

Clients aren't property. They don't "belong" to anyone. They have free will and the ability to choose where and with whom they spend their money. Generally, client loyalty tends to lie with individual professionals rather than the salons that employ them. It's my personal belief that clients deserve to be given their preferred professional's contact information if they ask for it, but not all owners are as considerate of their clients. It's rare to find an owner with integrity who will honor an agreement to provide forwarding contact information to clients that inquire.

The Importance of a Portfolio

Online portfolios are great for not only attracting new clients, but also for giving existing clientele an easy way to find you if the worst should come to pass. For example, let's say your boss sells the salon and the new owner fires everyone to bring in her own staff—but before she does so, she has everyone sign non-solicitation agreements which legally keep all of you from contacting those clients you've been caring for the last fifteen years.

Normally, you would race to the computer and bash out an email to me, attaching frantically scanned copies of that contract, begging me to find some kind of loophole. With an online portfolio, all you'll have to do is take about five minutes putting up a notice, letting clients know that you are no longer at the old salon and to contact you via phone or email. No biggie.

Some professionals resort to data theft—an absolutely deplorable, inexcusable practice. Clients provide their contact information to the business—not to you. Taking this information for the purposes of solicitation is an unethical, presumptuous violation that infuriates me as a consumer and a business owner. I would never abide an employee who violated the trust my clients place in my salon's ability to protect their privacy. Many clients do not appreciate it when professionals do this and will bitch out the owner or manager (I speak from experience). Many owners (including myself) will litigate over data theft.

Never steal client contact information under any circumstance. Instead, maintain that online portfolio and let the clients come to you. A portfolio is the best insurance policy any professional could have.

Protect Your Existing Clientele

If you're bringing a following to a new salon, you need to ensure the contract protects the business you built. That clientele is your livelihood. Don't surrender the rights to contact clients you've gained through your own efforts to a new employer.

A lot of employers post job offers with the statement, "Must have clientele." If you're bringing clients to their business, they have no right to claim those clients for their own. Their concern should be protecting the clients their business brings in and the future clients who are earned through their own marketing efforts, not the acquisition and retention of clients who were never theirs to begin with. In this industry, your following is everything. Don't put yourself in a position where an owner could take your following and sue you for a contract violation. Always consider the worst-case scenario and prepare for it.

The clients you bring to the business should be listed in the contract. The clause should state that you obtained the clients prior to your employment at that particular salon. You will retain their contact information and the right to contact and solicit them freely.

Be Reasonable

Be understanding of the owner's desire to protect their business. Any restrictive clauses present in the contract should be fair to you both. Some owners spend a good deal of money on advertising and rent in high-profile locations that attract a lot of traffic, so it's only fair that they protect that investment and the clients who have provided them with their contact information. For example, my contracts prohibited data theft or data collection of any kind. Staff were not permitted to collect client data or steal the data provided to the salon. The only clients they could retain information on or solicit were the ones listed in their contract—the ones they brought with them. I take my responsibility to secure client privacy very seriously. Any clients obtained during the course of their employment were protected by those clauses.

If You Don't Agree—Don't Sign

Some professionals don't like to sign restrictive covenants under any circumstances. If you're not comfortable signing it, don't do it. Personally, I have no problem with restrictive clauses if they're written to protect both the professional and the salon. Both sides have reasonable, valid concerns that deserve contractual protections.

Non-Compete Agreements

Many salon owners try to protect their business by having their staff members sign contracts containing non-compete agreements (NCA)—an agreement on the part of the employee to not enter into or start a similar profession or trade in competition against the owner within a particular distance for a specified period of time. Salon owners create these clauses to protect their client lists, believing that if an employee leaves the salon, clients won't follow them if they're are forced to work too far from the business. States vary in their laws regarding the enforceability of non-competes, but overall, unreasonable contracts will be seen as such by a judge and will not stand. NCAs are very rarely enforced in our industry, even if they are reasonable.

Components of a Valid Non-Compete Agreement

A non-compete has to be reasonable, extremely detailed, applicable to properly classified employees, and compliant with the laws in your jurisdiction regarding non-competes.

What makes a non-compete "reasonable?" Distance and dates. The agreement must specify a reasonable distance within which the employee cannot work and specify a foreseeable end date. A non-compete that states: "Employees agree not to work in any beauty industry profession in [CITY] for the rest of their lives," isn't reasonable. The "beauty industry" covers many different professions, the entire city is too broad of an area, and the rest of the employee's life is too long. That clause restricts the employee from working in anything beauty-related for the rest of their lives unless they work in another city. A judge will declare that unenforceable.

In our industry, a reasonable distance is 1-3 miles from the salon. A reasonable time period is six months. Even then, judges tend not to like any clauses that bar employment, and the vast majority of non-competes in our industry do get struck down.

I don't advise owners to include NCAs in their contracts and I don't advise professionals to sign them. They're ridiculous and inappropriate for our industry—which is probably why they're so rarely enforced. It's not appropriate for an employer in our industry to attempt to restrict anyone's right to work, particularly in this economy. I'd see this clause as an indication of the owner's insecurity and outright refuse the position. The way to protect the salon's clientele is through providing stellar services, protecting data through fair non-solicitation/non-disclosure agreements, and continually exceeding client expectations, not requiring potential employees to sign overly-restrictive non-compete agreements.

Binding Arbitration

"Would you ever sign a contract that waived your Constitutional right to a jury trial if you ever suffered some kind of injury or wrongdoing at the hands of a business owner? If you have a credit card, a mortgage, a car, or a cell phone plan—you already have."

An arbitration clause requires the parties involved to resolve a dispute through an arbitration process. Arbitration is an out-of-court proceeding in which a neutral third party (the arbitrator) hears evidence and then makes a ruling. Arbitration is the most commonly used method of alternative dispute resolution and you'll find arbitration clauses in the fine print of many contracts these days—including employment contracts. Arbitration can be non-binding as well (allowing you to challenge the ruling before a judge), but this is the exception rather than the rule. The majority of arbitration contract clauses are binding, which means they cannot be challenged.

Companies use arbitration clauses to keep their employees or customers from bringing them before a jury. Many arbitration groups actively market their services to companies, casting doubt on their objectivity. In our case (as salon employees), we don't particularly have to worry about this bias when employed by a private or small-scale employer.

However, when working for a much larger corporate chain, the objectivity of an arbitrator may be a concern.

Arbitration keeps the company from having to deal with the PR fallout of a scandalous lawsuit. Unlike court proceedings, arbitration prohibits public records and requires that the proceedings be kept confidential. They almost always prohibit class action. If you and ten thousand other professionals are shafted by a corporate chain salon, you cannot band together as a united front against them. Companies know that individuals often do not have the resources to fight them. They don't want you to form a mob because mobs have the ability to bring them to task.

Here is an example of a simple arbitration clause:

Arbitration. *All claims and disputes arising under or relating to this Agreement are to be settled by binding arbitration in the state of [insert state]. Any decision or award as a result of any such arbitration proceeding shall be in writing and shall provide an explanation for all conclusions of law and fact and shall include the assessment of costs, expenses, and reasonable attorneys' fees.*

Remember never to tempt fate. Never say, "What's the worst that could happen?" Nobody knows what could happen. What we do know—and this is because it's sitting in front of your face in black and white on the contract—is that if anything does happen, you're required to comply with the arbitrator's decision. The ruling you get may not be fair or rational and there's nothing at all you could do to appeal it.

Don't sign contracts that contain these clauses. They're designed to benefit the ownership exclusively. If you're presented with this clause in an employment contract, refuse it. Ask that it be amended to a mediation clause which requires both parties to attempt to come to a private resolution in mediation before filing suit in court. Mediation has many of the benefits of arbitration (less hostile than court and faster) and none of the drawbacks (high expense, potentially biased arbitrator, no right to appeal).

The goal of mediation is to reach a mutually acceptable arrangement to avoid litigation. In mediation, you and your attorney negotiate a mutually agreeable deal with the company's legal team. If you don't agree, you go to court. Nobody decides for you in mediation. You retain that control until it can be determined that a satisfactory arrangement just won't happen. If you think you could get a better deal with a judge and jury, then you retain the right to try your luck in court.

"Training" Agreements

A work agreement is a contract written up by the owner of a salon to ensure that she sees a return on her training investment in a new employee. These contracts generally give a specified date or length of employment in order to "repay" the expense/value of the training. If the contract is broken for any reason, the employee is typically required to repay huge sums of money to the owner.

For example, a clause of this nature might state,

"Employee agrees to work for Chop Shopz Nail Studio for a period no less than two (2) years. If Employee is terminated or resigns from Chop Shopz for any reason, Employee will be required to reimburse the owner of Chop Shopz two thousand dollars ($2,000) within seven (7) business days."

A lot of times, these contracts also contain binding arbitration clauses as well.

Standard Employment Training vs Professional Training

Business owners cannot charge their employees for standard employment training, which covers things like how to answer the phone, how to wipe down the mirrors, salon service protocols, or how to take inventory of backbar. Those are business-specific operational procedures that business owners have no right to charge for. They compensate you to perform those duties. It's their responsibility to provide instruction on how to perform those tasks to their standards.

Professional training covers things like advanced coloring techniques, new trend cuts, and other industry-specific skills that are not typically taught in schools or at basic levels. For this, the owner absolutely can charge, but they have to go about it the right way.

Advanced Professional Training as a Prerequisite for Employment

Owners can require applicants to have undergone advanced training as a prerequisite for employment. Salon owners are responsible for ensuring the safety of their clients so it's reasonable for them to hold applicants to a higher standard.

The Thirteenth Amendment: Debt Bondage, Indentured Servitude, and Slavery

Owners can require an applicant to complete advanced training and they can charge for it—but they don't have a right to hold anyone in debt bondage. Owners who offer advanced training expect to see a return on that training investment. They've donated their time, skill, and expertise, all of which have real monetary value. However, they need to remember the Thirteenth Amendment, which states, *"Neither slavery nor servitude, except as punishment for a crime whereof the party shall have been duly convicted, shall exist within the United States, or any place subject to their jurisdiction."*

Contractually obligating any professional to remain under their employ for any period of time (or face legal or financial consequences for not doing so) is unconstitutional and unenforceable. The Thirteenth Amendment prohibits the holding of a person in a condition of slavery, involuntary servitude, or debt bondage of any kind. The term "involuntary servitude" means: a condition of servitude in which the victim is forced to work for the defendant by the use of threat of physical restraint, physical injury, or by the use or threat of coercion through law or the legal process. When you are threatened with hefty fines for exiting employment, you are being coerced into compulsory service. Compulsory service of any kind is unconstitutional.

Conditional servitude by which the worker is compelled to labor against his will in liquidation of some debt or obligation, either real or pretended, is "debt-bondage." Whenever a person is required to make a pledge of their labor or services as security for the repayment of a debt or other obligation, they are being enslaved and their civil rights are being violated.

Don't be stupid. By signing work agreements like this, you're becoming a peon in a very literal way. (A "peon" is a slave indebted to a master.) Never, ever sign these work agreements.

Proper Training Arrangements

If an employer wants you to complete their professional training as a prerequisite for employment, ask them to set a price for that training and pay for it up front. Have the penalty clauses removed entirely from the employment contract. Legitimate owners who are truly interested in turning you into a better professional (not using you as a servant for six months and charging you for the privilege), will prefer to have you pay for their expertise at once instead of indenturing you to them.

Make sure that you're clear on what you will be getting for your money and get it all in writing. If the owner violates that contract by failing or refusing to deliver what was promised, you will have the means to sue them in civil court to recoup your losses.

If you're compensating someone for providing training, you are their employer during that training period. They are on your dime so you call the shots. You're paying to be trained in advanced techniques, not to fetch their color, wash their towels, answer their phones, or sweep up their hair. Don't be afraid to correct a "trainer" that forgets exactly what your role is when you're paying them for training.

"Take This Job and Shove It"

"We spend 99,117 hours of our lives working. Do not commit that time to an unfulfilling position...but don't be an idiot either. You still have bills to pay."

At multiple points in your career, you will have to assess your current employment situation and decide whether or not you're in the best salon for your career goals. Sometimes, the decision will be obvious, but not all situations are clear. Coming to a conclusive decision might be difficult. You don't want to make a rash decision you'll end up regretting later but you don't want to stay in a toxic workplace either. This chapter will help you decide if you need to wait it out, approach the owner about making changes, or leave.

Do you wake up excited about your workplace and coworkers? Few people jump out of bed every day thrilled about going to work, but if you consistently wake up dreading the time you're going to spend in the salon, then it's time to consider other options.

Are the salon's professional values (or your own) drifting in conflicting directions? Let's say you're employed at a family salon. When you began working there, the dress code dictated that everyone wore black and conducted themselves professionally, but over the last few years, things have changed and those values are slipping. Eventually, the dress code no longer applies. The employees are behaving inappropriately at work. The clients aren't happy about these changes and you start losing business.

Your professional values no longer mesh with the salon's. Consider whether or not you want to allow the salon to affect your reputation in the area. Approach the owner and propose a solution. If the owner is unwilling to compromise, hit the classifieds.

Are the clients complaining? You work in the service industry. If the people you are servicing express that they're unhappy, you have two options: address their complaints and keep their business or ignore their complaints and lose those clients to a competitor. If clients are unsatisfied with your coworkers and your work environment, get out.

Does the salon help facilitate your professional growth? Plenty of salons offer continuing education and opportunities for advancement. Some even offer portfolio building assistance and participate in fashion shows and photoshoots for local fashion magazines. If you want to gain exposure, advance, or get more education and the salon is unwilling or unable to offer those opportunities, it may be time to resign and find another salon.

Are you making enough money? If you're not getting enough business to build a decent book or the prices are set so low that you're barely making enough to get by, move on. Once the cash flow dries up, there's no reason for you to be there.

I recommend setting a benchmark and a deadline. You'll quickly learn what you're capable of in terms of building a clientele. If you're not seeing sufficient growth after this probationary period, you'll know you're in the wrong salon.

Are your coworkers making you miserable? Hopefully, you're in a properly managed salon and those problem coworkers we discussed get dealt with accordingly, but if you're enduring constant bullying and mind games that are going unacknowledged by management, resign. You shouldn't be forced to put up with it and the clients shouldn't be exposed to it.

Leaving a toxic workplace can be hard. Although the problems might be costing you clients and compromising your professional happiness, you may be close with the owner or some of your coworkers. Don't forget that business is business. Nobody deserves to be miserable at their place of employment or suffer abuse at the hands of malicious coworkers. You shouldn't be struggling financially. Don't let some false sense of loyalty keep you chained to a salon that doesn't meet your needs.

Resign Without Burning Bridges

Despite all your planning, it may take a few attempts before you find that ideal salon. All professionals must master the art of gracefully resigning from positions that aren't quite right. How do you make your exit? How do you bring it up with the boss? What do you do about your clientele? This chapter will help get you out of there without burning bridges or starting a war. The ultimate goal is to leave on good terms so your ex-employer will serve as a reference. If you're lucky, they might also leave the door open in case you discover that those greener pastures aren't quite as green as they seemed. (You never know, right?)

In this industry, resignations can be complicated. You don't want to burn bridges and there are multiple bridges that must be tended to; one that connects you to your ex-employer and dozens that connect you to your clientele. To sever ties with honesty and professionalism, several issues need to be handled tactfully: the distribution of clientele, your resignation letter, and your exit interview.

Make sure you're ready to walk. You're going to give written notice in a proper resignation letter, but be prepared for the owner to decline it and send you packing as soon as they read it. Secure a new job before tendering your resignation.

Read over your contract. Does it restrict you from soliciting clients or removing their records from the salon? Is a non-compete clause included?

If you signed a contract, you must abide by it. Breaching that contract could lead to some nasty litigation for both you and your new employer, particularly where theft of client information is concerned.

Refusing to comply with the terms of an employment contract is the equivalent of strapping explosives to the bridge that leads from you to your ex-employer and mashing the detonator. If word circulates that you've willfully violated your contract, you could develop an unfavorable reputation among the salon owners in the area and have a hard time finding future employment.

Compose your resignation letter. It doesn't have to be lengthy or detailed, but it should be typed.

"Dear [owner],

Please accept this letter as my notice of resignation. My last day of work will be [date]. I have been very satisfied at [salon] but have decided to make this move to advance my career. I have enjoyed working with you and appreciate the opportunities you have given me.

Sincerely, [name]"

Schedule a meeting with your employer to deliver the letter and discuss it. Don't just drop the letter on their desk and leave or use it to ignite the Molotov cocktail you toss in the salon window.

Be constructive during the exit interview. Many salon owners will schedule resigning employees for an exit interview at the end of their last day. They do this to learn more about why you're leaving. Don't be afraid to be honest during this meeting. Owners and managers want feedback to become better at their jobs. They deserve to know where they went wrong so they can have the opportunity to improve in the future. Be honest during this meeting, but keep it civil, friendly, constructive, and don't let it turn into an argument.

Keeping bridges intact during a resignation requires showing consideration where you're not expected or legally obligated to. Remember, you're a professional. Don't be the silent ninja that slips out and never returns or the walking embarrassment that makes a scene and rage quits. Always take the high road.

Microsalon Ownership 101

"Microsalons are one-man shows. You wear all the hats—owner, service provider, receptionist, janitor. It's all on you, kid."

If you haven't heard the word "microsalon" before, that's because it's a very new word for which no formal definition exists. Here's my informal one:

Microsalon (n): *a small, independent salon business, owned and operated entirely by a single service provider. Booth renters, studio operators, home salon owners, mobile operators, and on-site freelance professionals can all be considered microsalon owners if they are both the owner and sole operator of the salon.*

Microsalons can come in many different forms. This chapter will familiarize you with all of them.

Booth/Studio Salons

Booths and studios are the most common type of microsalon. These microsalon owners rent out space (a booth or a studio, usually located in a complex with multiple other microsalon owners) and operate their business from that space. Generally, the salon owner carries the establishment license and ensures the establishment meets state board standards, but each renter assumes responsibility for their own insurance policies and any fines they may incur for violating state board regulations.

On-Location/On-Site

On-location or on-site services occur outside of approved salon facilities. Almost all states have heavy regulations against offering on-location services. Professionals who pack up their supplies and perform services at people's homes or hotel rooms are working "on-location" or "on-site."

Mobile Salons

A mobile salon is an approved salon facility that isn't fixed to a particular location. It can be a bus, an RV, a trailer, or one of those awesome tiny houses that are gaining popularity right now. States that allow mobile salon businesses often regulate them in the same way they regulate traditional fixed salons.

To facilitate periodic inspections of mobile cosmetology salons, many states require mobile salon owners to file a written monthly itinerary prior to the beginning of the month—so you won't be able to fire up your bus and take last-minute appointments at different locations. Your business will operate like a bloodmobile. You submit the itinerary every month and go to the locations on the itinerary.

Many states also require each mobile salon owner to maintain a permanent business address in the inspection area of the local district office at which records of appointments, itineraries, license numbers of employees, and vehicle identification numbers of the mobile unit shall be kept and made available for verification purposes.

State boards also tend to have strict plumbing and water requirements, as well as provisions for the handicapped. You'll definitely want to look into that as well.

Home Salons

Home salons are legal in most states as long as they are properly inspected and licensed. Check with your state board to find out what their specific requirements are. Also check with your county and homeowner's association (if you have one). Almost all states require home salons to be completely isolated from the living quarters by a permanent wall and have their own separate entrance. Aside from that, the home salon will often have to comply with the same state regulations that standard salons do.

Recommendations for Microsalon Owners

If you are motivated, have an established clientele, and possess the ability to self-manage, you will likely succeed at microsalon ownership (providing you can keep your overhead reasonable and your prices balanced). Microsalon owners nearly always make more money than commissioned employees.

These are the recommendations I make to anyone considering microsalon ownership:

Wait until you're at least 75% booked. Don't even entertain the idea of self-employment until you have a significant following. Without that following (or a considerable amount of income reserved for advertising), you are incredibly likely to fail.

Ensure that you fully understand your responsibilities. This section will help immensely with this, but you need to know what your licensing, insurance, and tax reporting responsibilities are before you get started.

Do the math required to determine if microsalon ownership will be more or less profitable than employment. What will your initial investment be? What will your advertising budget be? How much money will you have to make each hour to break even? Can you balance your service times and pricing to ensure microsalon ownership makes financial sense? The chapter, The Dollars and Sense of Microsalon Ownership, will tell you how to figure all this out.

Understand the risks and know how to protect yourself. In Booth/Studio Rental, I'll impart my wisdom on commercial leases to you, but you need to understand right now that the vast majority of states do not have any legislative protections for commercial tenants. It is up to you to ensure your lease is properly written.

Determine whether the benefits of self-employment outweigh the aggravation. Once you fully comprehend what microsalon ownership entails and the risks associated, use your judgment to determine whether or not the endeavor will be worth the less desirable factors.

Booth/Studio Rental

Before we get into this further, I want to clarify some terminology I'll be using when discussing this topic. I use the term "salon owner" to refer to a person who owns and often manages a salon with properly classified employees. In salon with renters, I refer to the person who collects the rent from the renters as the "landlord." People who operate rental salon complexes (salon suites or booth rental salons) are not salon owners; they are landlords who sublet space to microsalon owners. The building itself may have a different owner, and thus, the building owner and the salon landlord have their own lease agreement. The building owner likely has a property manager to work directly with tenants and maintain the building and property (parking lot, landscaping, etc.).

I don't try to hide it. I hate the rental salon model. Every pro comes with at least two cons, so this chapter will serve as an overview of the factors you need to consider.

Clients don't understand the business model. You know what a client sees when she walks into a rental salon? A salon. She doesn't understand that every professional in that salon runs their own business. Since they often don't differentiate the renter from the establishment, disgruntled clients tend to trash talk the business as opposed to the responsible party. If your fellow tenants behave unprofessionally or produce garbage work, the salon earns a bad reputation, not the individual stylist-owned business. If you don't care what kind of reputation the salon you work in develops, go ahead and rent a space in a rental salon.

A lot of booth renters don't understand the business model. Many renters falsely believe they're owed services and amenities from the landlord. They aren't. Self-employed means self-employed.

Many landlords also do not fully understand the business model. That's right. Nobody in the arrangement has a damn clue how the arrangement works. Many landlords falsely believe they have the right to dictate to their tenants. They make rules up as they go, so this system gets abused very frequently.

Landlords have no control. Both a blessing and a curse. On one hand, you can't be evicted for blowing a service and you can't be told how to run your business. On the other, if a client brings a complaint regarding service quality or unprofessional behavior to the landlord (the person they see as the salon owner), the landlord cannot rectify it because it's not their responsibility to do so.

For example, I briefly rented a table in a booth salon. The tech working adjacent to me was a slob, accepted pain pills as payment, and would broadcast her many sexual exploits to the entire salon (including how she paid a man to tint the windows of her van with sexual services delivered in the back of the aforementioned van, loudly proclaiming to my horrified client, "I'm not a slut, I'm sexually liberated!"). You have no protection against that kind of insanity. The landlord cannot intervene on your behalf. That unprofessional behavior can (and would) affect your business.

Theft of product and tools is also an issue the landlord has no control over.

Heightened potential for conflict between renters. Unless the tenants have separate rooms, there are going to be issues between renters. Having multiple owners operating similar businesses under the same roof is a terrible idea. If no new client distribution system is in place, conflicts occur regarding who gets walk-in or call-in clients.

Rental salons don't promote a team environment. The salon as a whole suffers with this "survival of the fittest" way of doing business. When a salon is staffed with employees, all working towards the same goal of producing quality work, creating a specific atmosphere for the clients, and working for the long-term success of that business, everyone wins. Salon owners have the opportunity to control the quality of work, provide continuing education, and keep the staff motivated by taking them to shows or bringing in guest educators. Clients and staff understand the traditional employment model—sometimes employers do too.

Perhaps I'm biased, but I'll always prefer employment over the booth/studio rental model. I see booth rental as a complete free-for-all. It doesn't mesh with my professional values in the least, it invites abuse and conflict, and it doesn't make sense to me why anyone would willingly subject themselves to such a truly ridiculous arrangement.

Renters: Know Your Role

"If you want to be your own boss, then commit to being your own boss. Accept the responsibilities and expenses of small business ownership

like all other small business owners. Aside from a space to work in, your landlord owes you nothing."

Some employers and salon owners out there want to have their cake and eat it too. That's old news.

We're going to talk about renters who also like having and eating cake. They want their landlords to pay for product. They want to take advantage of walk-in or phone business. They want their rent waived for two weeks so they can take vacation. They want to use the receptionist and the salon software system.

Renters—you're called "self-employed" for a reason. You run your own business. The person who collects your rent checks is just your landlord.

Walk-Ins

A lot of salons are "blended." In them, you'll find renters working alongside commissioned employees. I often get emails from salon owners who are frustrated that the renters within their salon expect to be put on rotation with their employees for walk-in or phone business. Let's make this clear: as a renter, you're paying for space, not business. You don't pay for any advertising the salon owner may be investing in so you aren't entitled to profit from it. You only have a right to clients who call the salon phone or walk in the salon door when they specifically request you. If the commissioned employees are too busy to take a walk-in, your landlord may give you the client—but a smart landlord will charge you a fee.

Salon owners who have employees also have a responsibility to make sure that those employees are earning a livable wage. Renters generally enter lease agreements because they have already established a strong following and have no problem maintaining and building independently. Harsh truth time, renters: if you need walk-in or phone business, you weren't ready for rental to begin with. Self-employment requires you to accept responsibility for all aspects of your business, including client acquisition and retention.

Vacation Time

Renters are considered "commercial tenants." No commercial landlord offers their tenants annual periods of "free rent" so they can take a vacation. One of my favorite Italian restaurants shuts down so the family that owns it can flee the Florida heat and visit their family in Jersey from July to September. Does their landlord waive their rent while they're gone? Absolutely not. That space remains occupied by them, even though the business does not operate during their vacation. That landlord still has a mortgage, property taxes, and maintenance fees to pay.

Why on earth would you think that your landlord should take a loss so you can have two weeks of vacation time? You're a business owner now. If you want time off but don't want to lose your space, pay your rent like every other business owner in the world.

Product and Back Bar

When you decided you wanted to be your own boss, you said goodbye to those days of having your backbar provided for you. You're not the landlord's employee. They're not setting your prices to accommodate for your product overhead. Restaurant owners don't approach the property manager of the building they're in and ask them to pay for their food and ingredients, so why would you ask your landlord to cover your business expenses?

Reception Services

In blended salons, receptionists are employed by salon owners. They cater to the salon owner's business, seat the salon employees' clients, and collect payment from clients. The salon owner pays for that receptionist with the money they make from the employees the receptionist serves.

Your rent covers your space. It doesn't cover any support staff. You cannot utilize the assistants or the receptionist because you don't pay for them. If you want a receptionist or assistant, hire one and pay for them yourself. The salon owner doesn't have time to waste helping you manage your business; she has her own to worry about.

Booth rental is small-scale business ownership. It allows you to see exactly what business ownership entails before you open up an actual salon. Here are some indicators that you may not be ready for booth rental:
- If you have to poach clients from your landlord, you aren't ready for rental.
- If you can't afford to purchase your own products, you aren't ready for rental.
- If you can't handle answering your own phone, doing your own booking, collecting your own money, paying your own taxes, or cleaning up after yourself, you aren't ready for booth rental.

I want to clarify that although I supremely dislike booth rental (particularly these asinine "blended" salons), I don't have a problem with renters. I have a problem with people in general—whether they're landlords, employers, employees, or renters—trying to take more than they're owed at someone else's expense due to some false sense of entitlement. If you want to enjoy the freedom that comes with booth or studio rental, be ready to shoulder the responsibilities that accompany it.

Commercial Leases 101

"Signing a contract that hasn't been approved by an attorney is a level of idiocy on par with walking across a busy freeway blindfolded, allowing the one person who stands to benefit most from your failure instruct you on how to safely reach the other side."

I'm going to be very harsh in this chapter. I need you to understand the seriousness of this subject. Negotiating a lease will be the biggest responsibility you will have as a microsalon owner. The security of your business rides on this document.

Remember how I said, "Blah blah, my advice isn't gospel, no advice is inviolable?" Disregard that here. This advice is definitely gospel. Deviate from it at your own extreme risk.

Do your research. Check your state statutes to see what protections (if any) your state offers commercial tenants. If you can't read legalese, schedule an appointment with an experienced attorney who specializes in commercial landlord-tenant law to get educated about your rights. If you aren't ready to make this a priority and spend the time/money necessary to protect yourself, you aren't ready for microsalon ownership.

Leave your emotions at the door. Don't become emotionally attached to a space. If the numbers or the lease don't make sense, move on.

Only dumbasses accept verbal contracts. Are you a dumbass? No? Good. Because here's the thing: the vast majority of states don't offer legislative protections to commercial tenants. Your contract will be your shield. Without one, you are a fleshy mass of meaty vulnerability. Never trust a landlord who claims to operate on verbal agreements. They could be your best friend or your dear old granny—that landlord is either criminally naive or a wolf waiting for an opportunity to swallow you whole. You both need a contract. Spoken words aren't worth a damn. Have that landlord put their promises in legally-binding black and white.

Commercial leases are highly customized, rarely written by a professional, and almost always favor the landlord. Repeat after me, "Are the lease terms negotiable?" You will ask this question of every landlord you consider renting from.

All landlords wish tenants would sign their lease as written (since the document is designed to serve the landlord's interests), but educated tenants know that the lease must be negotiated to balance it. Experienced landlords expect tenants to request several alterations, so instead of seeing the lease as a document written in stone, consider it an invitation to negotiate.

Never sign a lease that doesn't suit you. No excuses. No bullshit. If you can't come to an agreement during negotiations or if you aren't comfortable with the terms on a non-negotiable lease, walk away.

Get comfortable saying, "I'll get back with you once my attorney reviews this." Have money set aside for a lease review by an experienced commercial real estate attorney (and not the one the landlord uses, dummy). If you want to play ball with the big kids, then put on your big girl panties and behave like a knowledgeable business owner. Walk away from any landlord who refuses to allow you to have their lease reviewed by a professional. I don't think I need to explain why those landlords should be avoided.

Things To Look For in a Lease

Lease Term. Where microsalons are concerned, shorter terms are better. There are too many unstable variables to even consider signing a long-term commitment. What if your clients don't like the space? What if your fellow renters are disrespectful, unprofessional, and cause you issues? What if you find out the landlord has a significant drug problem? (Been there.) If things work out, you can always renew the lease. If they don't, you don't want to be tied to a five-year commitment.

Option to Renew. If the lease doesn't include one, negotiate it. You want a short lease with an option to renew that gives you the ability to remain at the location by notifying the landlord in writing within a certain time period before the lease expires. If you've been a good tenant, it's likely that the landlord will want you to renew, but having this option in your lease will ensure that they extend the offer your way before leasing your space to someone else. You retain the right to accept or decline.

Rent Increase/Escalation Protections. Many booth/studio landlords will not negotiate rent, but might offer incentives like reduced rent for a period of time to encourage new renters to come aboard. Ask if the landlord will be willing to make that arrangement and if so, get it in writing.

Most landlords will raise rent from time to time (as they should, since their commercial leases and fees are subject to increases). The rent increases should be capped and communicated in writing well in advance of your renewal. This way, you will be protected against random, arbitrary increases. You'll be provided with plenty of warning before an increase and will have the option to move to a more affordable space without penalty if you can't swing the increase. The landlord will also have time to find a new tenant to replace you. Everyone wins.

Never sign a lease that gives the landlord carte blanche to raise rent without notice. If you omit these provisions and no laws exist to prohibit it, you have no protections against it whatsoever.

Inclusions. Some landlords like to nickel and dime their renters to increase their bottom line. I don't disagree with this practice when utilized properly. I do disagree with it when the landlord misrepresents what they include and doesn't outline these fees in the lease. Your lease should specify whether or not utilities, phone, cleaning services, insurance, bathroom supplies, waste disposal, landscaping, and other amenities are included or charged separately. If they are charged separately, those expenses (typically referred to as CAM, Common Area Maintenance fees) need to be listed and detailed to the penny. Make certain the lease clarifies that the amount stated is fixed. You will not be paying anything additional for any random, arbitrary "services" or "fees" that may come up during your lease term.

Restrictions. Does the landlord understand her role as a landlord? Anything in the contract that indicates that the landlord will try to overstep her bounds must be stricken and replaced with clear verbiage that effectively communicates her role. Her job is to collect your rent check. You choose and provide your products. You set your prices. You handle your own payments. You retain your own client information. You are an entirely separate business operating under her roof. Remove anything in that lease that gives the landlord an inappropriate degree of control over you or your business operations. You do not pay rent and self-employment tax to be dictated to like an employee.

Assignment Clause. Would the landlord be willing to discuss the possibility of an assignment clause that would allow you to waive termination provisions? If you need to move out, you should be able to find another tenant to assume your lease. Since the landlord wouldn't be losing rental income, you would not be responsible for paying any lease termination penalties.

Security Deposit and Conditions for Return. I recommend that all rental complex landlords require deposits and rent payments a month in advance to protect against defaults. These aren't unreasonable landlord protections. Generally, a landlord will require a security deposit that will equal your first month's rent and your final month's rent. The conditions under which the deposit gets returned will vary, but make certain that they're outlined in the lease.

Advertising Practices. In no other industry does this verbiage need to be outlined in a lease agreement, but because so many salon landlords don't fully understand what they can and can't do as landlords, you need to get this on paper. When you pay for advertising, you advertise using your business name and logo—not the landlord's.

A good deal of landlords will try to restrict microsalon owners from advertising their own businesses, requiring them to place the landlord's business name and logo in all of their advertisements. Some landlords may attempt to require you to participate in collaborative advertising, by either contributing money to a fund or honoring deals offered by the salon. If you find these conditions on your lease, have them stricken and replaced with a clause that allows you to advertise as you please. Don't ever pay to advertise someone else's brand. You do not work for the salon; you operate within the salon.

Modifications and Equipment. When you rent a booth in a salon, your rent usually covers the use of a station. However, when you rent a studio, you're often given a bare room. Some studios have the space outfitted with shampoo sinks and stations, but many require you to furnish the space yourself. If you're furnishing the space, make sure the lease specifies who the improvements and fixtures will belong to after the lease ends. If the space you're leasing requires heavy modification (like plumbing or ventilation), try and negotiate to have the landlord pay for that or reduce your rent for a period to compensate for those expenses.

It's not unusual for the landlord to retain control over approving your choices regarding flooring, paint, or other modifications. Remember that unless they are the building owner, they also have lease terms to abide by.

Repairs. I will never forget the day I received three emails from three renters within the same studio complex who claimed their landlord billed them each $300 for repairs to the salon's septic system. Guess what? Their leases didn't have protections disallowing those maintenance fees and their state offered no legislative protections.

Don't let anything similar happen to you. Your landlord sublets the complex from the building owner or property manager, so they are responsible for maintaining the building. In most cases, the building owner will be responsible for those repairs, but make sure the lease clarifies this.

Neither your landlord nor the building owner maintain your equipment. If you break your station, get a hair clog in your U-pipe, or spill color on the wood flooring, you fix that yourself.

Termination and Eviction Provisions. Smart landlords will have conditions in the lease that allow them to evict you if you default on rent. Expect that and don't try to negotiate it away. However, ensure that the termination and eviction provisions are clearly spelled out. Some landlords will try to put bogus, obscene termination fees in their leases. Have those fees removed completely. Your contract will ideally allow you to give the landlord thirty day (or six week) written notice of termination with no termination fees of any kind. Extend it both ways and give them the ability to evict you only with thirty day (or six week) written notice, no questions asked.

In the event of a default, many landlords will "lockout" tenants. Yes, it's exactly what it sounds like. The landlord will lock you out and sell your equipment and products. I consider this theft and do not recommend that landlords do this to renters. Ensure that lockouts and property seizures are prohibited in your contract.

If you miss rent, the landlord should serve you with a written, seven day notice to remit payment or vacate. If you fail to remit payment, you forfeit your security deposit and will be out on your ass. Any tools, equipment, product, or personal belongings left behind will be held for a nominal storage fee for fourteen days until payment is remitted in full. If you fail to claim those items, the landlord can sell them and keep the money.

Proof of License and Insurance. Expect to be asked for proof of professional liability insurance and your state cosmetology license. In addition to being asked to provide proof of these things, your lease may also contain a condition that requires you to maintain both documents in good standing. Failure to do so will invalidate your lease, giving the landlord justification for terminating your tenancy immediately. Some landlords may also request that you list them as "additional insured" on your policy to keep clients from pursuing them if you injure the client. It is not unreasonable to ask the landlord to provide proof of general liability insurance and request a similar covenant that requires them to maintain that policy.

Deal-breakers

You're halfway through your client's updo when suddenly the power shuts off. You discover the landlord hasn't paid the bill in months. What do you do?

You show up to the studio complex but find a lockbox on the door and an eviction notice—turns out the landlord has been blowing the rent on her Vicodin addiction and the building owner wants all of you out. You're fully booked and your tools, products, and equipment are inside. What do you do?

The toilet has backed up and rancid sewage floods the hallways. The landlord says, "It's not my problem," and refuses to pay to have it repaired. What do you do?

You whip out your awesome lease that includes termination provisions and tell that landlord to rot in hell, because you planned for this ridiculousness in advance like a smart person.

Make sure your lease allows you to terminate without penalty if the landlord fails to meet their responsibilities. Their responsibilities are to keep the lights on, the rent paid, and the facilities in proper working order. If they fall short of those responsibilities, you should be able to terminate without penalty.

Arbitration Clauses. In Employment Contracts 101, I discuss this in detail, so I won't get into it too much here. Never waive your right to a proper hearing. Do not sign arbitration clauses. Have them stricken from the lease.

ADA Compliance. The Americans with Disabilities Act requires all businesses that are open to the public to have premises that are accessible to disabled people. If the salon doesn't have a ramp or wide enough doorways to accommodate wheelchairs (most do, but some older buildings may not), ask the landlord if they're aware that their compliance with the ADA is mandatory and if they'll be making the necessary alterations. You don't want to get sued by a disabled client for discrimination because your building isn't ADA compliant.

Fixed Rent—No Percentage Agreements! If I could pound this into your skull or tattoo it in beautiful script across your forehead, I would. Never, ever agree to a percentage lease or profit-share lease arrangement. These arrangements require you to pay a minimum rent plus a share of your gross sales. This arrangement does not benefit you or the landlord. It invites conflict and begs to be abused by either or both of you. For example, you could lie about your gross sales, work one day a week, or set your pricing extremely low to spite your landlord. The landlord could try and set your schedule, dictate your pricing, or overstep her boundaries in other ways to increase their bottom line.

In addition, it puts the landlord in a very questionable position. The IRS Cash Intensive Business Audit Guide contains six revenue rulings and court cases pertaining to salon classification suits. In all but one where the landlord claimed a percentage of gross sales as rent, the "independent contractors" were determined to be employees. One-in-six odds are crappy odds. So, I advise landlords to stick to fixed rent. If the landlord wants a percentage, tell her to hire employees and pay employment tax like every other business owner in the United States. They can't call you a renter and treat you like an employee. Stay away from landlords who push for this arrangement.

If you disregard this advice and continue on your merry way, understand this: any failures you experience are your own fault. I have spent a considerable amount of time putting this chapter together to help keep you from making the same stupid, costly mistakes countless booth renters make every year. When you're broke and crying, know that you brought your pain on yourself.

Mobile Salons

I have a confession to make. I think mobile salons, when executed properly, are the coolest. Right now, they're gaining in popularity because they're low-cost, quirky, and fun. Here's an overview of the pros and cons of mobile salon ownership.

Pros

No landlord. No leases to negotiate here! Purchase your mobile unit and enjoy your freedom!

Fixed investment. Similar to home salons, your investment in your mobile salon is fixed (aside from periodic maintenance and repairs).

Mobility. Unlike home salons, if you ever move, you can bring that investment with you.

Low overhead. If executed properly, your operating expenses will be very minimal. Utilizing solar panels for energy and the new, futuristic composting toilets will save you bundles on energy and water. Plus, you'll likely be plugged into whatever business you're visiting, so they'll be taking on that energy expense!

Very marketable. Mobile salons often enjoy oodles of publicity, particularly the themed units. Your options are limitless. You could create a cute seaside cottage pedicure salon in a tiny house unit and set up shop on the shore. You could buy a small vintage caravan and create a 50's-themed styling salon. Buy a retro Airstream and convert it into a swank barber shop. Unique theming draws attention! (Seriously, I have so many ideas for mobile salons, I can't even handle it. I love the concept.)

Cons

Not for hoarders or the claustrophobic. If you anticipate that you'll have difficulty keeping yourself organized and functioning in a tight space, mobile salon ownership probably isn't for you.

Initial setup requires diligence and connections. Successful mobile salons have standing relationships with local businesses and routinely visit those businesses to service their employees and customers. Many rely heavily on corporate parties or local events. Personally, I would have a regular fixed location where the salon would operate several days a week and have standing commitments with several local businesses also. Before you invest, do some networking, generate interest, and make arrangements with local business owners.

Conversion renovations. You're unlikely to find a mobile unit already outfitted to suit your purposes, which means you'll have to purchase one, gut it, and rebuild it. DIY-ers might consider this a massive pro, but those of you that aren't keen on the idea of taking on that project probably won't. You could always hire contractors to build out the interior of your mobile unit for you, but the cost may be considerable.

Tips

Plan in advance. Similar to home salons, mobile salons require a ton of foresight and planning to utilize that precious square footage. However, advance planning will be a regular part of your daily routine. Mobile units take time to cool and heat, so you might want to have some system in place for that. If you plug in somewhere, consider an automatic timer.

Get Insured. In addition to professional liability insurance specific to mobile establishments, you'll likely also require special vehicle insurance to cover incidents that may happen during transport.

Do it right. Don't half-ass this. If you're going to go mobile, do it properly. Nobody wants to get services in some dank, nasty, rusted-out RV.

Consider a tiny house. If you aren't yet aware of the "tiny house" movement, you need to educate yourself right now! They're extremely affordable, eco-friendly, and can be built to your specifications.

Home Salons

"If you're going to do it, do it right. Don't be taking clients in your kitchen like an amateur."

If you're considering establishing a microsalon in your home, this chapter will give you an overview of the pros and cons. I've also included some tips for those of you who choose to move forward.

Pros

Minimal Investment. Unless you want to end up homeless, you're destined to pay your mortgage every month. Depending on the type of mortgage you have, you should own the house completely in 15-30 years. However, a rented workspace will be an eternal expense, subject to increases and other fun surprises.

As mentioned earlier, most states require you to alter your home by erecting a permanent wall and installing a new door to separate the salon from the living quarters. The costs for these alterations are fixed and once they're paid for, that's it.

Because you will no longer have to travel to work, you will save money on gas and vehicle maintenance. Most people drive 10-20 miles to work. You'll commute 10-20 steps from your front door.

Last-minute cancellations suddenly become less obnoxious. Periodically, a client will experience some catastrophe (broken hip, sick kid, flat tire, or a standard lapse in judgment) and miss their appointment, leaving your schedule with a big, fugly gap. Instead of stewing for that hour, thinking about all of the things you have to do at home, you can actually do those things.

Cons

They'll know where you live. Some clients will abuse that knowledge. I'm not insinuating that your clients will rob, rape, or murder you (though that unlikely possibility also exists). What I mean is that some clients may not respect your time or space. (For example, home-based nail techs may have issues with clients "popping in for a quick repair" after work.)

You'll need to establish clear boundaries, set your working hours, and abide by them. Make it clear to the clients that under no circumstances are they to show up unannounced outside of business hours.

Even if you're not required to by your state to do so, you really should permanently separate your business space from your work space.

Stranger danger! Now I'm totally insinuating that clients will rob, rape, or murder you. This possibility exists in any salon ownership scenario, but the risks are much higher when operating independently out of your residence, especially if you're taking new clients. You have no way of knowing if your new pedicure "client" is a normal college girl seeking pampering or a thief's girlfriend who is there to case your property for a future burglary.

Consider this: you're working in your home salon as usual. A new client has booked a three-hour appointment at the end of the day for a cut, color, highlight, and conditioning treatment. Instead of the woman you spoke to on the phone, a man enters the salon with a gun. You live and work alone. It's mid-afternoon on a Tuesday and your nearest neighbors—the ones most likely to hear your cries for help—are at work. What are you going to do?

Don't discount this possibility. When designing your home salon, research the security options available to you. Magnetic or smartlock systems (like Okidokeys, www.okidokeys.com), switch-activated security systems, and video surveillance have become very affordable.

If you're not extremely disciplined, your quality of work and professional image will suffer. I have seen some talented, high-end hairdressers open home studios and absolutely fall apart professionally. Suddenly, it becomes acceptable to work in pajamas. One couldn't afford to install a proper shampoo bowl so she rinsed clients in her bathroom sink. This is unacceptable.

The only difference between your home salon and a traditional salon should be the location. Adhere to the same standards your clients have become accustomed to.

Cabin fever. If you have a problem with the fact that you will be in your home all day long and all night long, day in and day out—a home salon probably isn't for you.

Attracting new business might be difficult. If you're located deep in a residential neighborhood, forget walk-in business. You're not in a salon, so referrals may be hard to come by since you won't be working alongside other professionals. Some clients won't feel comfortable coming to a residence for their services. These are hurdles you'll have to overcome. That's why, in my opinion, it is better to establish your microsalon after your clientele is established. Without a clientele, you will be redirecting the rent money you're saving into your advertising budget for the first few years.

Tips

If you want to move forward, there are a few things that must be done before you can even start taking clients, and we're not talking about painting and decorating.

Know your restrictions. A lot of deed-restricted neighborhoods will not allow people to operate businesses from their residences. Make sure you don't require any clearance from your homeowner's association, city, or your county. You'll need to know how your property is zoned, whether or not a public hearing is required, if you're permitted to place signage, and more.

Know your state regulations. Some cosmetology boards absolutely forbid home salons. Those that do allow them often regulate them just as strictly as standard salons. Find out what your state requires for a home salon and abide by their guidelines.

Plan ahead to avoid making expensive mistakes. Plan before you apply for construction permits. Figure out your square footage, measure for furniture, and map your layout before you purchase anything or begin construction. Serious thought needs to be put into your workspace to maximize your square footage.

Save money for advertising. Unless your home is located in one of those quaint areas that are zoned for both commercial and residential with a bit of exposure, it's unlikely that someone is just going to walk up to your house off the street. Build a website and start researching your advertising options.

I've seen many gorgeous home salons and heard tremendous success stories. Although this option isn't one I would consider, I can certainly see the appeal of it. As long as you know your restrictions, commit to running your home business like an actual business, and establish clear boundaries, you should do very well in a home salon.

The Dollars and Sense of Microsalon Ownership

You should put the same amount of planning into your microsalon that you would a traditional salon. This requires a lot of research and math. Grab your calculator, fire up your laptop, and get a pen and paper ready.

Salary

How much money do you want to bring home annually? You can't pull some arbitrary desired annual salary out of your ass. Research your local economy and your demographic. These factors require consideration when figuring out your salary and your pricing.

Local Economy

Who lives in your town? Do the statistics indicate that your city is predominantly populated with families, retirees, or young singles and college kids? How much money does the average resident in your town earn annually? Your prices will have to be able to accommodate your local economy.

Demographics

Do you want to attract professionals, retirees, or teens? For example, my business was located in a podiatry practice and the majority of my clients were patients. My average client was age 50-70, retired, and on a fixed income. I enjoyed working with retirees because they're reliable, appreciative, loyal, and wonderful to spend time with. Most of my clients were diabetic and/or neuropathic and required monthly foot inspections and pedicures to maintain their health, so they set standing appointments.

Those were my preferred clients, so that was my demographic. Because I so thoroughly enjoy working with that clientele, it was critical that my prices be reasonable to keep within their budgets.

Taxes

You'll be self-employed, so account for your federal income tax responsibility (15.3% of your gross earnings). If you have state income tax on top of that, account for that also. You mustn't forget to deliver your pound of flesh to the tax man.

Billable Hours

How many hours will you be working annually? For the purposes of this example, we're assuming a forty hour workweek with one hour lunch breaks every day, totaling thirty-five billable working hours per week.

Sick days and vacation days are not billable time. There are roughly fifty-two weeks in the year. Subtract your vacation time and your sick days from those fifty-two weeks.

This can be calculated by weeks or days.

52 (weeks in a year) - [SICK WEEK(s) + VACATION WEEK(s)] = [ACTUAL WORK WEEKS]

365 (days in a year) - [SICK DAYS + VACATION DAYS] = [ACTUAL WORK DAYS]

For the purposes of this example, we'll assume two weeks for vacation and another week for illnesses. That leaves forty-nine working weeks per year. When multiplied by thirty-five billable hours per week, that comes to 1,715 billable hours per year.

This can also be calculated by weeks or days. Choose your preferred method.

[ACTUAL WORK WEEKS] x [WORK HOURS PER WEEK] = [TOTAL BILLABLE HOURS]

[ACTUAL WORK DAYS] x [WORK HOURS PER DAY] = [TOTAL BILLABLE HOURS]

Hourly Rate

[DESIRED ANNUAL SALARY] / [TOTAL WORK HOURS] = [HOURLY RATE]

For this example, these numbers would be $57,650 (desired salary)/1,715 (billable hours) = $33.61 (hourly rate).

Overhead

Welcome to the place where shit gets crazy. If you're compulsively organized like I am, you know exactly what your yearly overhead will be. Since I'm not psychic, I have no way of knowing what your expenses will be, but here's a rough way to calculate it.

[WEEKLY RENT] x 52 (weeks in a year) = [ANNUAL RENT EXPENSES]

[[WEB HOSTING] x 12 (months in a year)] + [DOMAIN NAME RENEWAL] = [ANNUAL WEBSITE EXPENSES]

[MONTHLY ONLINE BOOKING COST] x 12 (months in a year) = [ANNUAL ONLINE BOOKING EXPENSES]

[AVERAGE MONTHLY SUPPLY BILLS] x 12 (months in a year) = [PROJECTED SUPPLY EXPENDITURES]

[MISC. ANNUAL EXPENSE] + [MISC. ANNUAL EXPENSE] + [MISC. ANNUAL EXPENSE] = [MISC. ANNUAL EXPENSE TOTAL]

You get the idea. The formula is basically:

[MONTHLY EXPENSE] x 12 (months in a year) = [YEARLY EXPENSE TOTAL]

[WEEKLY EXPENSE] x 52 (weeks in a year) = [YEARLY EXPENSE TOTAL]

All annual expenses get totaled together separately.

For the sake of our example:
Rent: [$100/wk] x 52 = $5,200
Monthly Supply Bills: [$250/mo] x 12 = $3,000
Yearly License Renewal: $27.50
Yearly General/Professional Liability Insurance: $600
Yearly Advertising Budget ($200/mo): $2,400
Web Hosting: ([$0/mo] x 12) + 10.99 (domain renewal) = $10.99

ESTIMATED ANNUAL OVERHEAD EXPENSES: $11,238.49

(Don't forget your utilities or cleaning staff if you assume those costs.)

Break-even

Break-even is the point of zero loss/profit. This step will show you how much money you need to bring in per year to sustain your business and your salary.

[ESTIMATED ANNUAL OVERHEAD EXPENSES] + [DESIRED ANNUAL SALARY] = [ANNUAL BREAK-EVEN INCOME GOAL]

Our example looks like this:
$11,238.49 (annual overhead) + $57,650 (desired salary) = $68,888.49

Divide your break-even by the billable annual hours to figure out how much money you have to charge per hour to meet it.

[ANNUAL MINIMUM INCOME GOAL] / [BILLABLE ANNUAL HOURS] = [REQUIRED HOURLY INCOME]

In our example, this comes out to:
$66,286.49 / 1,715 = $40.16/hr

Pricing

Now you know how much money you have to make hourly, which makes setting your service prices as simple as calculating your service times and dividing or multiplying that time by that hourly rate. To get real specific, break your hourly rate down into minutes. Some beauty professionals swear by the $1/minute formula. The problem with that formula is that it doesn't take your demographic, overhead, or local economy into account. Not all areas or clients will be able to accommodate those rates and the rates may not sufficiently meet your needs, so it's preferable to use a system that factors those figures in.

Once you determine your service prices based on the hourly rate, they can be rounded up and adjusted where necessary. In many instances, the hourly rate won't match the service value. Specialty services will always require adjustment. I consider services like permanent makeup, sculpted nail enhancements, advanced nail art, and color correction to be "specialty." Any rare services that require a high degree of skill, a massive time (and/or financial) investment to master, or a significant equipment/product expense must be inflated to reflect the actual value.

Assess what you offer and the value of the service to the public to determine what adjustments to make.

For example, at $40.16 an hour ($0.66 a minute), rounded up to the nearest $5, my service menu looked like this:

Natural Care Manicure or Pedicure, 30 minutes, $25

($40.16 / 2 = $20.08. Round up to $25. Meets service value, no adjustment necessary.)

Signature Pedicure, 45 minutes, $35

($.66 x 45 = $29.70. Rounded up to $30. Adjusted to meet service value, $35.)

Toenail Prosthetic Application, 30 minutes, $65.

($.66 x 30 = $19.80. Rounded up to $20. Adjusted to meet service value, $65.)

[ADD ON] Polish Application, 15 minutes, $10.

($9.90. Rounded up to $10. No adjustment necessary.)

[ADD ON] LED Polish Application, 15 minutes, $15.

($9.90. Rounded up to $10. Adjusted to meet service value, $15.)

My Prosthetic Toenail Application serves as a great example of a procedure that warranted a price adjustment. The prosthetic toenails I applied look very natural. Nobody in the area offers that service. The prosthetics last eight weeks. The cost of the materials and the lamp required to cure the enhancement material are substantial. Learning to perform the service well required extensive training and practice. Therefore, the value of the service exceeded $20. To make the cost reflect the value of this particular service, the cost had to be increased to at least $50 ($6.25 per week the service lasts). I charged $65, which clients found to be more than reasonable.

Also factor in your worth when making adjustments. Your education and experience have value. My service prices for my area were beyond competitive, considering my professional value. I was highly experienced, exceptionally skilled, and had a massive collection of certifications that placed me well beyond my so-called "competition." I also came with enthusiastic podiatrist endorsements, sterilized my implements, and performed services with certified organic, homemade products.

My prices were not just "reasonable," they were obscenely low considering the value I delivered. Could I have charged more? You bet. I could have charged $70 an hour and clients in my area would still have considered those prices an accurate reflection of the service/experience value they received.

However, you have to keep your demographic at the forefront of your mind. To attract and retain my preferred clientele, I needed to accommodate their fixed incomes. For me, it was more important that those clients were cared for on a routine basis. Those are the people I wanted to serve. Although I easily could have, I had no desire to set my prices higher than what I had calculated, so I didn't.

Rounding up like this and making adjustments gives you a buffer against unexpected timesucks. Clients will cancel. Clients will drop off your book. A wedding party may book an entire day with you only to no-show. Then again, clients might upgrade their services during their appointments. Clients might come in and blow $1,000 on retail during a crazed shopping spree or give you a $500 check for Christmas. Gift cards will get purchased and go unredeemed.

In any case, it's better to be safe than struggling. Rounding up helps to accommodate for lost clients, missed appointments, and unforeseen emergency expenses. You never know what will happen from day to day. That is the nature of this industry and business in general. Accept it and learn to love it.

Competitors

The worst advice ever given regarding pricing (and it does get perpetuated throughout the professional beauty community to this very day), is, "price yourself in line with your competition." I don't even know where to start when trying to list all the reasons this advice blows.

First, most professionals have no clue how to evaluate their competition. Many have no idea who their competition actually is, nor do they have any information on how these competitors operate internally.

When considering competing businesses, find ones that most closely resemble your business in terms of the level of service, the amenities, and the quality of the services performed. Compare like with like when evaluating your business, not apples to masochists. No salons are created equal. Just because you offer the same services as Great Clips does not mean that those services are comparable.

For example, I'm a licensed cosmetologist that specializes in nail care exclusively. My local market is heavily saturated with discount salons: establishments that perform quick services with cheap product for very low prices. Sure, our businesses might be considered similar because we both offer nail care services, but in reality, our experience, professional philosophies, and services are worlds apart. Those differences separate me from the discount salons to such an extreme degree that we can't be compared in any aspect.

Even if your business seems similar to another on the surface, the operational differences (which you have no way of knowing) factor into their pricing. In our discount salon example, my internal operational factors differ from theirs considerably. Many of these salons make their money by outright violating tax and labor laws, utilizing high-pressure upselling techniques, and using garbage enhancement product. Most only take cash, don't have websites, and are located in high-traffic areas, negating the need for paid advertising. A good deal of them have developed a reputation for being filthy and I have been told by local inspectors that several in my city don't even have disinfectant or laundry detergent in their businesses (super gross).

In contrast, I pay taxes, carry insurance, don't upsell aggressively, use quality enhancement product, take credit and debit exclusively, launder my towels and linens (with detergent), and have an advertising budget. I also do not reuse abrasives or disposables like the vast majority of discount shops do. These are monetary and time expenses that I have to account for and charge for, which they do not.

So forget your competition. You don't know how they calculated their pricing and even if you did, it wouldn't matter because you're not them. Price what you're worth and adjust for your demographic and local economy.

When a client confronts you about your prices by comparing you to a competing business, instead of bashing that business, communicate the features that make your salon fantastic (like your commitment to exceeding your state's health and safety regulations).

Gratuities (Tips) and Retail

Neither can be counted on, so don't count on them.

On average, I would clear about $300 a week in retail sales. Eventually, I raised my prices and took on a "no tipping" policy, but before that, my clients tipped 20% per service on average. Your tips and retail income will pad your annual bottom line considerably, just don't bother trying to calculate it into your projections. It's not worth the aggravation and won't be accurate in the least. Consider that money a bonus. Set it aside for your retirement, a vacation, or blow it on hookers and booze. Your call. Either way, don't waste your time trying to count unhatched chickens.

Remember, these figures are estimates only. They are goals. Now that you know how much money you need to make; your job is to hit that figure consistently and hopefully exceed it.

Audit Avoidance Tactics

Cash-based businesses (like salons) are often targeted for random audits. Sometimes it happens through absolutely no fault of your own, but sometimes your return flags your business. The audit rate is roughly 1 in 100, but we're in a unique position that puts us at special risk. Salon owners and independent professionals who make $200,000 or higher have an audit rate of 3.26% (1/30). If you make more than $1 million, in addition to being the luckiest bastard alive, you have a 1 in 9 chance of being audited. The information in this chapter will help you avoid an audit.

Watch your deductions. Your deductions should be realistic and typical. Typical deductions include recurring business expenses, like your online booking service or your rent.

Don't claim questionable expenses. You can justify deducting a trip to a trade show. An extravagant European cruise? Not justifiable. Big deductions for meals, travel, and entertainment invite audit. To qualify for meal or entertainment deductions, keep detailed records that document the amount, the place, the people attending, the business purpose, and the nature of the meeting. No documentation? No deduction. If the deduction isn't verifiable, don't claim it. Get a receipt scanner and an expandable file. Scan your receipts and save them on Google Drive or Dropbox and back them up on a portable hard drive or USB drive. Keep the originals in the expandable file. Keep the storage device and the expandable file somewhere safe. (Fire-safe boxes are reasonably priced.) If you're ever audited, you can correspond your deduction with the original receipt. Some places give really crappy receipts, so if you need to notate what the expenses were, do so on the back of the slip.

A thorough consultation with a qualified tax professional will prepare you to properly categorize and claim your proper business deductions.

File online. Mistakes happen when IRS representatives manually enter handwritten return information. Numbers get omitted or added. Their mistakes could cause you to be audited. According to the IRS, the error rate for a paper return is 21%. The error rate for electronically filed returns is 0.5%. Eliminate the middle man entirely and e-file.

For the hardcore: eliminate the "cash" from "cash business." The IRS knows that those who receive primarily cash are less likely to accurately report all of their taxable income. So, eliminate it.

I don't like cash. It's nearly impossible to track and easy to lose. Counting it three times a day to balance the drawer was time-consuming and frustrating. I hated filling out deposit slips and making daily trips to the bank. So, I implemented a new policy and only took traceable forms of payment. This included checks, SpaWeek gift certificates, credit cards, and instant mobile transfers. Not only did this policy make me less likely to be audited (and robbed), it simplified my accounting, eliminated the bank runs, and gave me peace of mind. Most of my clients didn't pay with cash anyways, so I never heard a single complaint about it.

This was one of the best decisions I could have made for myself and my business, but it does have a downside. Payment settlement entities have been required since 2012 to report all credit card transactions to the IRS on Form 1099-K. This includes Visa, MasterCard, and American Express, as well as online merchant processors. The IRS compares your credit card and cash receipts with your industry average. The IRS may send you a letter asking you to re-examine your books to make sure you didn't omit any cash transactions if they feel your non-cash transactions make up too large a percentage of your annual revenue.

To protect yourself from this, make sure your no-cash policy is clearly stated on your website, your brochures, and posted in your business. Keep your appointment records and daily sales records. It shouldn't be difficult at all to compare each appointment from the book with the corresponding payment record, especially now that many merchant service companies provide and store digital signatures and digital receipts.

Hire a bookkeeper and accountant. Managing your own business finances puts you at risk. Turn that responsibility over to a professional. If you're going to be itemizing (which you most likely will be), hire a professional to keep you organized. Focus on making the money. Let someone else handle the paperwork.

Cross your T's and dot your I's. If you file yourself, make sure your social security number is correct. Don't round your numbers. Triple-check every figure. Leave nothing blank. If you aren't using software to file, get out of the stone age and start doing so now.

Incorporate if you're self-employed. Small businesses are a favorite target of the IRS—and for good reason. Self-employed people are most likely to under-report income and overstate deductions. The IRS makes no distinction between whether you're high-grossing or not. Corporations and LLCs are audited less frequently than other small businesses. Incorporating or forming an LLC also allows for more deductions.

Watch your charitable deductions. The IRS knows the average charitable donation at every income level. If you hold a charity event where services are rendered in exchange for donations to a particular charity, document everything. Always consult with a tax professional when claiming charitable deductions to ensure that you have all the documentation necessary to justify them.

If you hire support staff, classify them properly. The best way to put yourself at risk for an audit is to have employees classified as IC's. When it comes to payroll tax debt, the IRS has unyielding power and authority to collect. (They can lock your doors and shut you down without a court order.) You don't want any part of that.

Expect it. That's right. Expect to be audited and be prepared for it before it happens. Keep yourself organized and stay honest. Even the most minor illegal, fraudulent activities are indefensible in the eyes of the IRS. Run everything by your accountant/bookkeeper.

If what you're doing seems wrong, don't do it because it probably is wrong. Your best defense is excessive preparation and organization.

Resources for Microsalon Ownership

"Obligatory disclaimer: I don't get paid, compensated, or rewarded in any way for endorsing anything. Ever. It would be super cool if I did though, so if you're one of the manufacturers or companies I mention in this book—send me money. Make your checks payable to Tina Alberino. Thanks."

Dozens of tools are available to microsalon owners to help make running their small businesses simple and easy. The ones I've listed are those I have used and enjoyed myself.

1.) StyleSeat (www.styleseat.com)
Styleseat offers completely free salon scheduling and online booking. It boasts an easy to use interface and has a lot of great tools for evaluating and managing your business. They also have a free app so you can book on the go! For most microsalon owners, the free version will suffice, but if you would like access to more features (such as recurring appointments, automatic birthday cards, and more detailed reports), you can always upgrade to one of their premium packages (currently priced at $25 per month). I have been a member from the time they launched and I love it.

2.) Wix (www.wix.com) or Wordpress (www.wordpress.org)
Wix makes website creation as simple as point and click, drag and drop. Pick a template and edit it to suit your

preferences. To remove the ads and use your own URL (which I highly recommend), upgrade to premium.

I used Wix for years but because its hosting prices kept increasing (and its performance decreasing), I abandoned it in favor of a Wordpress site hosted at home. This allowed me to eliminate hosting fees entirely. However, I had to teach myself how to code and build my sites myself. If you have the patience or the technical skill to do so yourself, go for it. If not, Wix should suit you just fine.

3.) MailChimp (www.mailchimp.com)

MailChimp allows you to create and send beautiful email newsletters to your clients easily. Similar to Wix, MailChimp features a WYSIWYG (what you see is what you get) editor, so putting together your newsletters is simple. You can also create a registration form and link it on your website so your clients can sign up easily! Currently, MailChimp is free up to 200 subscribers.

4.) SpaWeek (www.spaweek.com)

SpaWeek allows people to purchase salon and spa gift certificates online, which can then be redeemed at any of the locations in its network that accept them. I joined because it costs nothing and I thought, "Well, it couldn't hurt." The gift cards are easily redeemed on its website and the money (minus a super small fee) gets directly deposited in your bank account at the end of the month. This brought me a lot of clients (who then became regulars). I cannot say enough good things about my experiences with SpaWeek or the clients who have discovered me through its service. I highly recommend joining.

5.) Square (www.squareup.com)

Square allows you to accept all credit cards (Visa, MC, AmEx, and Discover) through your smartphone or tablet. The apps have a clean, easy-to-use interface. They currently charge 2.75% per transaction—much cheaper than what you would be paying if you established a merchant services account. Square doesn't require you to sign a contract or pay out for expensive equipment like other merchant service companies do. (Seriously, who the hell wants to spend almost $300 on a receipt printer?) They make a ton of reports available online also, so you can track your microsalon's performance. You can also sell gift certificates or retail products through your own market, which Square offers for free. Funds get deposited into your bank account within two business days.

"Man Down! Call for Backup!"

Imagine this: you have come down with a sinus infection. It hurts. You thought you would be better this morning but when you awoke, you felt like someone had hit you in the face with a sledgehammer. Now, you have to scramble to cancel all of your appointments. Rescheduling them will be a nightmare since you're fully booked.

When you're ill, you belong at home. Too many professionals try to "tough it out" to avoid inconveniencing clients or losing income. However, because you're in close proximity with these clients each day, you run the risk of spreading whatever sickness you've contracted to the rest of them. I'm willing to bet that most of them would prefer to hold off on their haircut for a week or so if it means avoiding catching whatever funk you have.

"Lone wolf" microsalon owners won't have coworkers to rely on to pick up their slack when they can't carry it. Who will cover for you when you're sick, injured, have a family emergency, or are called to fulfill your civic duty as a juror? In these instances, it helps to have a substitute—a dedicated professional who conducts business similarly to you that you can rely on and refer to when disaster strikes.

Desirable Substitute Attributes

Integrity. Your backup must be trustworthy—someone who won't use your illness or injury to pull your clientele out from under you. Understand that some clients might prefer your substitute and leave you for her, but this should be the client's decision—not something they were coerced into by the substitute.

Similar Professional Values. This will be different for everyone since everyone has different professional values. I value promptness, quality, atmosphere, affordability, and experience. My substitute is prompt, does great work, has been in the industry fifteen years longer than I have, and charges the same rates that I do. The atmosphere at her salon differs greatly from mine, but the staff are welcoming, friendly, and accommodating and that's more than good enough for me.

Equals or Exceeds Your Technical Skill Level. Don't send your clients to a professional who does a shoddy job. Your clients deserve better and you don't want to have to fix whatever the substitute has done when you see that client next. Your substitute might do things differently, but she should deliver an end result consistent with what your clients expect from you. On the rare occasion that I've had to send my clients to my substitute, none have returned with any complaints—at least none that were reasonable. ("I liked her but she wasn't you," isn't a complaint you can realistically address.)

Tips

Keep your individual clients in mind. Consider each client's individual wants/needs before you refer them to your substitute. For example, I had several clients who required privacy during their appointments—either because their religious beliefs prohibit publicly exposing their feet or simply due to their personal insecurities—so these clients couldn't visit my backup tech since she was not equipped to accommodate those clients.

Take into account personality compatibilities also. My substitute was very animated and chatty. I am not. My reserved clients wouldn't have been comfortable with my bubbly, exuberant backup tech. If a few of your clients don't seem as if they'd be suited to your substitute, explain to them your hesitation and let them decide for themselves.

Having a suitable, trustworthy substitute will relieve that anxiety that comes with illness or last-minute emergencies. The process of finding a substitute also allows you to meet and network with other professionals in your area—professionals who can become an amazing support system. Get out there and start interviewing potentials!

Things Your School Should Have Taught You (But Probably Didn't)

Your Portfolio: Your Biggest Asset

Your portfolio doesn't have to be huge and aside from any prints you choose to have made, it shouldn't cost a dime. In this chapter, you'll learn how to create a portfolio, how to negotiate a creative collaborative project for the purpose of portfolio building, and what the most important components of an online portfolio are.

Getting Started

Build a network of other portfolio-builders to collaborate with. Join a networking site for other artists, like Model Mayhem (www.modelmayhem.com). Sites like MM allow photographers, models, stylists, nail technicians, makeup artists, wardrobe designers, and other creative professionals to post or participate in collaborative projects in their area. The last I checked, the vast majority of these sites offered free memberships, but also offered "Pro" accounts for a subscription fee.

You'll start by creating a profile—a pretty straightforward process. Keep it focused on your area of expertise and mention what you're hoping to get out of the site. Once you're done, view the profiles and portfolios of other professionals in your area. Reach out and make friends. Before you post a project, I recommend responding to project postings and working a few shoots first.

Search for and respond to "TF" (Time For) postings. Sometimes, these postings are listed as TFP (Time For Print) or TFCD (Time For CD). You may see different abbreviations, but they all mean the same thing: nobody gets paid. All professionals involved are participating in the project for the sake of portfolio building, so no currency changes hands. The experience and photographs you gain in return for your time will be far more valuable than money anyways.

You'll receive prints or (preferably) a disk of images from the shoot. Each photographer handles this exchange differently. Some give "raws" (unedited images), others only give fully-processed (retouched) images. Some watermark their images and some do not.

Research photographers before working with them. Stay away from those that have no reviews or have reviews that indicate that they don't honor their agreements. (You can discourage this by requiring the photographer to sign a TF Agreement, which I'll get into later.) When working with a photographer for the first time, I recommend only doing so under the condition that they physically hand over a disk of raws immediately after the shoot to hold as collateral until the finished images are delivered. Once you've established trust with the photographer, you can change your policy with them.

Staff a competent makeup artist (if you aren't one yourself). Some models are more than capable of making themselves picture perfect, but try not to ever go into a shoot without a MUA (makeup artist). Don't assume you can function as a MUA without proper training or product. Drugstore cosmetics will not withstand the power of professional lighting. If you've never participated in a shoot before, you probably don't realize this—but lighting eats makeup for breakfast. Trust me. Leave the makeup application to the professionals who have experience in photography.

Do not have the photos processed to death. Processing should be very minimal to keep from distracting from the work you have done.

Aside from a single line of credits—do not have text anywhere on the image. I advise staying away from photographers who insist stamping their name all over the photos you and several other professionals have worked so hard on. Just because they clicked the shutter doesn't mean they own the image or that they deserve the majority of the credit. Photographers that approach me for TF work and insist on watermarking the images are directed to my rates. I do not work TF for watermarked images and neither should you. Instead, I have a single line of text in a 10 point font that runs vertically along the left side of the image. The names of the photographer, the model, the MUA, the wardrobe stylist, the retoucher, and myself are all listed. Everyone gets credit, but nobody gets more than anyone else. That's how a collaboration works.

Do between five and ten of these TF shoots. You will likely end up with dozens of great images. The next part of this process will certainly break your heart.

Choose only 1-3 pictures from each shoot and put them into a black photo portfolio. Stay away from animal print, Hello Kitty, or any kind of glittery cutesy covers if you want to be taken seriously. Do not include photos you took on your cell phone or at your nail desk. Pick only the best 1-3 images from each shoot you've participated in.

Navigating TF Collaborations

When considering a TF project, multiple factors require evaluation, starting with the person who posted the project. In a true TF collaboration, there will be no "lead." Every participant will have their input considered respectfully by the other involved parties and together you'll agree on a direction and final outcome that suits all of you. The poster of the collaboration needs to be clear on what the word "collaboration" means. Just because they post the project doesn't mean they are the "boss" of the project.

Secondly, consider the talent of your co-collaborators. If their work doesn't meet your expectations or they don't have pictures of their work at all, either accept the risks that come with that or walk away. Remember, you're all amateurs, participating in the project to gain experience and build your portfolios. Don't expect perfection, but don't settle for garbage either.

Finally, draft a TF Agreement and have all involved parties sign it prior to working on anything. The TF Agreement will specifically outline your policies and will include: the photographer's name, shoot location, names of the models involved, and the services you'll be providing along with their respective monetary values. You will also list the trade items agreed upon. The TF Agreement should also clearly state that the photos shall not be watermarked and that the credits are to be listed in an inconspicuous place in a font not to exceed ten points. Include a release that clearly states you have the right to use and distribute the photos as you see fit and that nobody else can claim any profit from the photos—including yourself. Nobody can resell or relicense the pictures. Add model releases also. Take photos of their identification with your phone and attach them to the signed releases.

In bold, capital letters, write this statement:

"IF THE TRADE ITEMS PRODUCED FROM THIS SHOOT ARE NOT PROVIDED IN 30 DAYS, THE PHOTOGRAPHER IS RESPONSIBLE FOR PAYING THE FULL PRICE OF THE SERVICES PERFORMED"

...or something to that effect. Mine reads,

"The trade images can be delivered through email or on optical media delivered by mail. They may also be made available through a download link. Final images will be delivered by one month after the

date of the shoot. If the photographer fails to deliver the final images as promised, the photographer will be guilty of theft of services under false pretenses and will be held responsible for paying the full monetary value of the services rendered."

Include the estimated cost of your time, travel, and service values so the photographer understands what you're worth.

This TF Agreement serves as a covenant between you and the photographer. Have a signature line for yourself, the photographer, and the models to sign.

Like the parties that have signed the agreement, once you've agreed to work TF, you must follow through with that agreement. You aren't the only one committed to the shoot. Many professionals who regularly collaborate in freelance projects like this know one another. If you blow off a shoot or are difficult to work with, you will develop a reputation and will have a very hard time finding future opportunities.

Don't work with professionals who refuse to sign your agreement. You are not a charity worker and deserve to benefit from the shoot in some way. If the person that posted the project refuses to sign the agreement, direct them to your rates. This agreement protects you from fraudulent, opportunistic photographers and project coordinators.

Beware of "Commercial TF" Work

"Commercial TF" is when a commercial client seeks professional staff to create images for commercial advertisement use but only pays out in tearsheets or prints (usually with limited distribution rights). This isn't an appropriate use of TF because you're giving someone else the ability to profit from your work without receiving compensation in return.

If everyone starts working TF for commercial clients, our work no longer has value. If you're good enough to be printed in magazines, you're good enough to get compensated for your skills. Never work for someone else for free just so you can tell others that you did so. "Experience" and "exposure" are not good reasons to do commercial work TF.

Necessary Components of an Online Portfolio

Websites are not required of you or expected, but they do make you look extremely legitimate compared to other professionals. They show dedication and superior initiative. This also shows potential employers that you are proactive about attracting your own clients. Many online portfolios are a simple two or three page sites. I advise against adding music, ads, tacky widgets, or distracting animations. Keep it clean and simple.

In order to get the most out of your online portfolio, you'll need to ensure that it has eleven very important things:

Your name as the URL. Your portfolio URL needs to be easy to remember. Don't get cute here. "www.nailhottie.biz" and "www.hairrawkergurl.me" are not good professional portfolio URLs. If possible, use your first and last name and follow it with a .com. Other domain extensions are catching on slowly, but stick to what people know. ".com" is still everyone's default when they try to remember a URL. Finding you on the internet should be as simple as knowing your name. If your first and last name aren't available, include your middle name and make sure that middle name is on all of your business cards. Nicknames are acceptable only if your clients know you by that nickname.

Direct contact information. This can be your cell phone number, email address, mailing address, work information, or all of the above.

Professional images of your best work. You should have these in abundance by now! Continue to grow your collection by participating in shoots regularly and sharing your work on social media.

Your brief professional biography. Your professional biography should be 95% professional and 5% personal. Answer these questions: Where were you born and raised? How long have you been doing your profession? Where did you go to beauty school? What do you specialize in? Do you have anything to brag about? Why do you do what you do? What products do you use? What is your professional philosophy? Where do you currently work? When do you work? What are your hobbies?

If you follow that formula, your professional biography should read something like this:

"Hilda was born and raised in Nashville, Tennessee. She graduated from Prestige Beauty Academy in 1989. Since that day, Hilda has specialized in classic roller sets. She has won several speed perming and cap highlighting competitions. Hilda uses a variety of high-end salon products, like Majirel and Roux Fanci-Full. She is dedicated to keeping Nashville's seniors looking fantastic! Hilda understands that being restricted to an assisted living facility can be difficult for the lonely, aging residents of the facility, but she strongly believes that a human touch, some end papers, and a half can of Aqua Net can cure even the deepest depression! Hilda can be found in the salon at Rolling Hills Assisted Living Facility on Monday through Friday from 9am-4pm. When she isn't at the salon, Hilda can be found in the common room, watching reruns of Golden Girls and Murder She Wrote with her beloved clients."

...ok, I was screwing around with that, but you get the point. Writing the biography doesn't have to be complicated if you follow my super sophisticated Mad Libs method.

Online booking links. If the salon uses online booking, link directly to the service. If they don't, add a "Request an Appointment" button that brings up an email contact form. Give clients a way to get on your books with the click of a button. Put it in your header and footer, where it's visible on all pages.

Any social networking or blogging links. These also need to be in your header and footer. Use the icons and have them linked to the appropriate websites. Do not post the text links and call it a day. That's sloppy and unprofessional.

Mailing list subscription button. There are several free online services you can use to manage email newsletters (for example, MailChimp is free up to 200 subscribers). Since the clients sign up on their own, you're not violating any kind of non-solicitation contract you may have signed. They're coming to you, not the other way around. If you get fired, quit, or if the salon gets blown away in a hurricane (been there), you can easily update the clients without having call each and every one of them individually.

Your schedule. Put this in your "Contact" page right next to your email form.

Service descriptions and prices. The descriptions on my site are incredibly detailed and I list prices. Whether you choose to list your prices is entirely up to you. I chose to do so because I don't have time to answer a bunch of phone calls about pricing. I know of some professionals who prefer to have the clients call to inquire. They believe that clients are more likely to book when they've spoke with an actual person.

I believe the opposite. I think clients aren't likely to call at all if they don't see prices. Some would assume that the prices are out of their price range. Also, never underestimate the laziness of people.

A professional headshot. No duckface "selfies" and no group shots of you and your "gurls" partying at the bar (yeah, I've seen both of these on portfolios). If you're at a TF shoot, ask the photographer if they could take a quick shot of you looking like an approachable, classy professional in exchange for linking the picture to their website. Most photographers (if they're not jerks) will be happy to do this for you.

Client reviews. If you have any client reviews, add them. Word of mouth truly is the best advertisement. (Besides, reading them back to yourself at the end of a rough day can be a great motivator!)

"How am I supposed to do all this?! I'm a stylist, not a web designer!"

Chill out. With point-and-click web building sites like Wix (www.wix.com) you don't need to be a web designer to put a terrific site together yourself. Moonfruit (www.moonfruit.com) is another option, but I found it a bit more advanced and clumsy compared to Wix the last time I played with it. I'm certain more of these "drag and drop" web design services exist now.

If you're a quick learner and have superior technical skills, I consider Wordpress to be the absolute best builder out there. I spent some time learning how to use it and have since migrated all of my websites to it. For beginners, I strongly recommend Wix.

Lies, Bullshit, and Bad Advice

"Who makes this crap up? Why is the professional community still perpetuating this ineffective, useless, outdated advice? Is it working for any of you?"

Bad Advice

In schools, continuing education classes, business seminars, and professional forums, popular pieces of advice are hammered into the skulls of recent graduates. They're preached like gospel by professionals who swear by them. While these techniques may work, they certainly won't work for everyone and they definitely aren't the most efficient, effective, or productive strategies available.

"Be available." While building your book, you'll often hear this absurd piece of advice. "Be at the salon all day from open to close!" "Come in on your days off!" "Work late!" "Come in early!"

Instead, set a schedule and stick to it. Be available when you're scheduled to be available. Give the clients consistency. Do not be at their beck and call. In addition to risking burnout, you'll also send the message that your personal time can be infringed upon. We will talk more about establishing a work-life balance a little later, but for now set those boundaries and enforce them.

"Building a book is all about waiting. You have to do your time like everyone else." This terrible piece of advice usually gets thrown around to justify sitting in the salon for weeks or months, waiting until the clients somehow eventually decide to flock to you. Sitting on your ass, hoping for walk-ins will not pay off in a solid clientele at any point...well, it might pay off in several years, but unless you're a lotto winner or the spouse of an oil tycoon, I'm assuming you have bills to pay and actually want to make enough money to pay them.

"You should do heavily discounted or free services to get your name out there." You absolutely should not discount or give your services away—unless you're interested in attracting the wrong kind of clientele. Never devalue your work. You know who deserves discounts? The loyal clients who support your career, not some random person off the street looking for a handout.

You know how you get your name "out there?" Referrals, photo shoots, an online portfolio, social media participation, hitting the streets and handing out fliers, advertising in your area, making friends in your community, and above all—providing fantastic service. Word-of-mouth proves to be the most effective advertising. All of these solutions will cost you far less than a Groupon or huge discounts offered across the board and they'll attract the right clients—clients who appreciate great services at fair prices.

Repeat after me: "I am a licensed professional and this is my job, not a hobby. My work has real value. I will not work for free or for less than I'm worth. I'm not a volunteer or charity worker. I have bills to pay like everyone else. I will not feel guilty about charging my clients appropriately for the services they're certain to enjoy. I want to attract clients who appreciate my effort, education, and attention to detail, not clients who can't recognize the value of my talents. I want to attract clients who are serious about their personal care and are sure to become regulars, not coupon clippers that only obtain services when the price is right or when they receive a gift certificate. I will be successful and I will do it without compromising my pricing."

Woo-saaah. Deep breaths. Calming waters. Chirping birds.

Got those crazy discount thoughts out of your system? Good. Let's move on.

"Price your services to match or beat competing businesses." You never, ever price match or engage in a price war with a competitor. Not even once.

"Fake it 'till you make it." This has to be the most horrifying, damaging piece of advice I've ever heard. What are you going to do? Fake your way through a service, botch the job, and lose the client—or worse, injure them?

When people do services they're not licensed to perform and when licensed professionals perform services they're not confident in performing (or those outside of their scope of practice), the clients are the ones who suffer. Those clients are happy to pass their suffering on to the person responsible in multiple ways. At best, they will tell everyone they know about their terrible experience. At worst, they'll report you to the necessary authorities and press charges in civil court.

Your reputation is your currency in this industry. Don't risk your business by performing services you are not proficient in or can't guarantee. Be honest and set realistic expectations. Never compromise.

Bullshit

"The customer is always right." Except that they aren't. Clients are almost never right. If the clients were so damn smart, why are they soliciting the services of licensed professionals? As a licensed professional, you know what will suit a client and what will not. If you don't think moving forward with a service is a good idea, explain why and offer an alternative. Clients don't understand the ramifications of some of the truly crazy crap they ask for. (The first time you hear a client say, "I want my hair cut into three layers," you'll understand.) It's your responsibility to inform them.

A perfect example of this would be the mother that comes into the nail salon with her eleven-year-old daughter. "She wants super long nails," she tells you. What do you say?

You explain to her that it's unsafe to give a girl so young enhancements to begin with, let alone super long enhancements. You offer gel polish instead and list off the benefits of gel polish.

Oh, but the little brat throws a tantrum and her mother insists you do the job. Do you perform the service even though you know it's a big mistake? Is the customer "right" in this situation?

Hell no. Refuse to compromise your professional integrity and refer them to another salon. Let another technician be responsible for that inevitable disaster.

"I have my license. I've learned all there is to learn." Some graduates come out of school thinking they know everything. You went to school for anywhere from four months to two years (depending on your license and your state's requirements) and suddenly you're a master of the profession? I don't think so.

No matter how great your school, you've only learned the bare minimum. You are far from done with your education. Successful professionals never stop learning. It doesn't matter whether you've been in for four months or forty years, you always have room for growth and improvement. Be humble and keep your mind, ears, and eyes open throughout your career. The second you think you've learned it all, shred your license and walk away for good because you either weren't cut out for this industry or your time in it is up.

"Personality is critical to your success. If you can't form connections or build personal relationships with your clients, you'll never build a book." Are people skills important in a customer service industry? Of course. Does you success as a professional depend entirely on your ability to make your clients like you? Absolutely not.

If you're skilled, polite, conduct yourself professionally, and provide fantastic services, the clients will return. Courtesy and professionalism are sufficient—you don't have to make every client your BFF.

Lies

"You have to market yourself." Do you have to market yourself? No. Should you? Sure! However, as an employee, you aren't responsible for bringing clients to the business. Doing so will certainly benefit you, but you shouldn't feel obligated to. Remember, the owner's job is to get clients into the salon—it is your job to make them happy and retain them. If you wanted to be responsible for "marketing," you could have gone into business for yourself.

I firmly believe that employers are responsible for their staff's welfare and the success of their own business. They're responsible for making sure you receive a livable income. If they didn't have the clients to accomplish that, they shouldn't have hired you to begin with. An owner cannot point the finger at her staff and blame them for the salon's piss-poor performance by demanding they "market" themselves. They are the captain of the ship and their leadership determines whether or not the salon succeeds. Every salon has a few staff members that under-perform due to their own professional inabilities, but if every single one of the employees are floundering, the owner has failed as a leader. Don't ever allow them to push their responsibilities as an owner onto you.

"You have to apprentice for a few years or you won't be successful." You don't have to apprentice. If you can afford to, definitely do. However, not all of us have the means to work for minimum wage (or free) in exchange for experience and training. Don't get discouraged about your future if you can't afford to work through an apprenticeship. Failure to complete an apprenticeship won't guarantee failure any more than it can guarantee success.

As an alternative to apprenticeship, invest in some training materials as you can afford them and practice during your downtime. Nail techs, buy some cheap acrylic and a practice hand. Stylists, get yourself a mannequin or find some people willing to serve as hair models. Watch videos, read books, attend classes, practice always, and be responsible for your own advanced education, but don't let anyone tell you that you can't succeed without an apprenticeship.

"You're fresh out of school. You don't deserve 50% commission until you've gained more experience." Experience does not equate to expertise. I have hired girls right out of school that were naturally gifted (or worked damn hard while in school to become fantastic). These recent graduates put out better work than licensed pros that have twenty or more years of experience.

Just because you're fresh out of school does not mean that you deserve to be compensated less. Your services should be priced according to your skill level regardless of how much experience you have and commission rates need to be set according to overall job performance. How does it make any sense for an owner to take a bigger cut of your percentage if they're charging the same price for your services as they are the "experienced" professionals working next to you? (That's a trick question. It doesn't make sense.)

Unless the owner stands at your side, working with you on a daily basis, there's no reason for them to take a bigger cut. If your technical skills aren't quite where they need to be for you to play ball with the big girls, then you need to be started as a Level 1 and have your service prices set accordingly. It isn't fair for the client to be paying the same rate for an inexperienced professional as they would be an experienced one. This is one of those "only benefits the owner" situations.

"You have to pay your dues." You'll hear this from senior coworkers and sometimes owners who think treating a new staff member or recent graduate like a servant is acceptable. We're adults working in professional salons, not sorority girls hazing pledges. You do not have dues to pay. Paying your tuition, graduating, and becoming licensed was sufficient. You're nobody's shampoo girl, personal assistant, or laundry wench. Don't accept that immature behavior.

"Owning a salon is easy." You'll always hear this from people who don't own a salon and have never previously owned a salon—people who have absolutely no idea what they're talking about. Salon ownership is extremely difficult. Your salon owner probably wishes periodically that she had picked an easier business to operate, like a retail store or a dog food manufacturing plant.

Here's some insight into what salon ownership entails: the services provided combine artistic skill, technical skill, and people skills. If the business doesn't perform well in all three areas, it fails overall. Finding good staff can be a maddening process. "Creative types" (I'm looking at you, stylists) often have a hard time working together under the same roof. It becomes the owner's responsibility to keep the peace between the stylists, ensure the clients are happy and the business profits. On top of that, she has to order product, manage payroll, advertise, provide continuing education (if she chooses to), keep on top of new products and new trends, keep the building in good repair, and make sure the salon is in compliance with all board of cosmetology regulations.

Salon ownership is a bitch. Give your boss some credit. If your salon is successful and the owner makes it look easy, it isn't because her job is simple, it's because she's good at what she does. Don't assume you can do it better just because it "seems" like a no-brainer.

It isn't as easy as it looks. If it were, all those dumbass coworkers of yours would be doing it too.

Build and Maintain Your Clientele

"Until you learn how to retain what you obtain, you will struggle to build."

Many professionals consider the process of building and maintaining a clientele to be a nearly impossible, monstrous task. Don't allow that kind of absurd, negative thinking to hold you back or get you down. Nothing about the process of building a book is complicated.

In a perfect world, microsalon owners wouldn't open up shop without first having secured their clientele and salon owners would accept responsibility for keeping their employees busy. However, our work situations are rarely perfect (or even well-managed). You might find yourself in a position where you have no choice but to build your own clientele from scratch, or maybe you're just an ambitious professional and you feel you could benefit from more exposure. This chapter will provide many techniques for client acquisition and retention. I have tested and tried every one of these over the course of my career and can vouch for their effectiveness (or else I wouldn't be sharing them).

Retain What You Obtain

Rebook. Never, ever forget to rebook a client's next appointment before they walk out the door unless they're one of those toxic clients we discussed. (Some clients you're better off without.)

Build Trust. Let clients know they're in good hands. You may think this means acting like you know it all, but the best way to build trust requires having the ability to be honest with clients, admit your limitations, and seek outside help when necessary. Some professionals worry that this will make them look like an amateur and will shake the client's confidence in their ability, when actually the opposite holds true. Being honest about your skill level and potentially disastrous service outcomes communicates to your client that you're honest, trustworthy, and have professional integrity. It tells them you care about the quality of service they receive. Never be afraid to take a step back and say, "Let me bring in another professional for a second opinion on this. I just want to make sure we're doing what's right for you before we move forward."

Focus and Listen. In our consulting chapter, we will discuss listening at length, but for now we need to address focus. Many veteran professionals will work multiple clients simultaneously. While this practice will get you closer to that six-figure salary you dream of, it won't win you any points with clients. In my experience, clients prefer to have your undivided attention. In my opinion, they deserve it.

I don't recommend double or triple-booking. In addition to being a stressful way to work, it makes you more prone to mistakes and oversights. You cannot deliver great customer service if you're running back and forth between multiple clients. In the end, you'll be run down, stressed out, and left with two or more dissatisfied clients. Double-booking staff members often struggle with client retention. Don't be one of them.

Protect Your Reputation. Never let your pride or greed jeopardize your reputation. If a requested service has the potential to end unfavorably, educate the client about why moving forward is a bad idea and offer an alternative. Refuse to perform services that will end poorly. The Compulsive Drugstore Colorist serves as a great example. She's dyed her hair all fifty-five shades of Natural Instincts over the last two months and now she wants to go blond. Do you want to be responsible for turning that kitchen beautician's hair into overcooked spaghetti?

Remember, word of mouth is a double-edged sword. Unhappy clients will tell nine people on average about a poor experience, but a client with jacked-up hair will tell everyone they know. A client with jacked-up hair and the ability to use Yelp can harm your reputation significantly and indefinitely, especially if they include pictures. You don't want your name attached to that.

It's always preferable to have a client complain that you refused to perform a service you couldn't guarantee the quality of than to have them complain that you executed a service that ended in disaster. However, the vast majority of clients will appreciate this honesty and will thank you for it.

Deliver Consistency. Before you clock in to work on Day 1, have your service protocols memorized. Consistently great service delivery keeps clients loyal. You can't do a kickass job on the first appointment and then slack off on subsequent appointments. Every service has to be as good as the first. Any idiot can do a pedicure, but the tech that works efficiently on the nail care portion of the service to ensure she has fifteen minutes at the end of every service for a full massage is the one that will fill her book.

Be Reliable. Consistency doesn't just apply to your service protocols, it also applies to your scheduling. Set your hours and be there whether you're booked or not. If you're an employee and your boss sets the hours, make sure she puts you on a regular schedule. This makes it easier for clients to remember your availability and will enable them to book standings since that schedule doesn't change every week.

Be Prompt. Never, ever leave clients waiting on you. One of the fastest ways to lose clients is to disrespect their time by running behind. Live by the ten-minute window.

Professionals who live by the ten-minute window are dedicated to having their services completed ten minutes prior to their next appointment. This allows them time to break down, clean up, and prep for the next client. Failure to schedule this ten minute buffer will set you back massively as the day progresses. Sometimes, complications will arise and you will run behind, but this should never become a routine occurrence. Schedule your time appropriately so you can have your last client out the door, your station cleaned up, and be at the front desk with a smile when the next client walks in for her appointment.

Also, don't be tempted to "squeeze in" an upgrade service if you know it will set you behind. Your clients deserve better than that treatment.

Be Special. Learn new techniques, try new products, and design new services. Come up with ways to keep clients interested in you. If all the competing salons in your area are going left (Brazilian blowouts and crackle polish), veer right (hair extensions and rockstar gel services). Set yourself far apart and make sure your clients know that you're always one step ahead. Commit to being "special."

This tip in particular sets apart the stellar from the mundane in this industry. Either take what everyone else does and do it much better, or do something none of them do better than any of them ever could.

However, there are plenty of wrong ways to distinguish yourself from your competition, like performing services in lingerie, serving alcohol, or conducting weird services like fish pedicures or foreskin facials. These techniques are desperate, gimmicky, inappropriate, and unnecessary. Once the novelty wears off, clients will abandon you.

Keep other professionals scrambling to catch up with your education and what you offer. You want their clients to say, "Well, I heard a stylist in the next town over is offering a revolutionary new color technique," not "Have you heard about the crazy nail technician who is doing *pig placenta pedicures?* Gross!" Get clients talking because you're an educated, experienced trend-setter, not because you're a freakshow.

Keep Them Informed. If the client chooses upgrades during her service, always make her aware of the additional charge and how that will impact her total. Some clients don't give this enough consideration, so to keep someone from freaking out at the register, keep them informed. For example: "The deep conditioning treatment will cost an additional $15 and will take another twenty minutes. That will bring your total to $120. Is that alright?"

Be Better. Attitude truly is everything. Believe it or not, the customer service experience you deliver will often trump the beauty services you perform. You can be a mediocre professional (most of us are starting out), but you can still build a loyal clientele simply by having a better attitude than your competitors. Lately, it seems like every business is staffed with incompetent, inconsiderate, disrespectful, rude, lazy people who don't care about customer service or satisfaction. Customers have become accustomed to being treated as if they're an inconvenience. This is unacceptable in every business, especially ours. Stand apart by being welcoming and pleasant.

Exceed Expectations. Under-promise and over-deliver. Don't oversell yourself and your services. Keep your clients' expectations reasonable and consistently exceed them. Show them what you can do; don't just tell them.

Follow Up. I often enjoyed using my staff as guinea pigs and performing experiments in the salon. For three months, I implemented a policy requiring the staff with the lowest retention rates to make follow-up calls within ten days of each appointment. They followed a similar script. "Hi [Client]! This is [Professional]! I just wanted to call and see how you like your [cut, color, nail enhancements] and make sure everything is going well. What kind of feedback have you received? Are you having any issues I can help with? Do you have any questions I can answer for you today?"

The staff that made follow-up calls saw a massive retention rate increase. Nearly all of the clients who received follow-up calls rebooked. Now, in addition to making random follow-up calls myself for quality assurance purposes, I require staff to do the same.

Socialize for Professional Gain

One of the fastest ways to build a book requires being visible and meeting people in your community. However, I don't encourage attending local "networking events." They're full of people who are focused on selling to you. Not many of them give a crap about what you do. In my experience, they yield nothing but irritation. Go ahead and give it a shot, but don't set your expectations too high. Hopefully, your experiences will be better than mine.

Utilize these tips to maximize your networking time and eliminate the frustration that accompanies social interaction in environments that are crafted solely for the purpose of self-promotion.

Get to Church. If you're religious (or a shameless heathen looking for a fast way to make a bunch of contacts), find a popular place of worship to attend regularly. I can't walk into churches or I'll burn alive, but I have hired new graduates who were fully booked their first day on the floor thanks to the support of their church family. The people they attended church with were very loyal and sent tons of referrals.

Hit the Bars. Like churches, bars are a great place to meet lots of new people. (Also, you're unlikely to run into your new church friends there.) As a manager, I organized weekly cocktail evenings at a lounge a few doors down from our salon. In addition to giving the staff the ability to blow off steam and strengthen their relationships, the events also netted new clients. Our standing booth reservation paid for itself ten times over in growth.

Recreational Classes and Clubs. When considering activities that will maximize your networking efforts, chose those with a high degree of interaction and group participation. Good options also include one-day workshops (for instance, those held at craft stores). One-day workshops will expose you to new classmates each time you attend, so you'll meet more people than you would in a standing, multi-week class.

Charity Work. The only people who deserve free services from you are those who truly need them. Spend one day a month at your local domestic violence shelter or home for displaced mothers. These activities, in addition to being emotionally gratifying, will often draw local media attention and the attention of socially conscious clients who appreciate your efforts. Your fellow charity workers may also become clients of yours.

Volunteering. The best places to volunteer are those that expose you to a wide range of potential clients—so, don't expect that your hours of pouring soup at the soup kitchen or scooping poop at the animal shelter will pay off in new clientele. Great options include your local library, hospitals, and Habitat for Humanity.

Referral Programs: Get Others to Spread the Word

Client Rewards. Establishing incentives for referrals will motivate existing clients to build your book for you. (Remember, only loyal clients deserve discounts!) There are many ways to implement a reward program. Most salon software tracks referrals. You (or your employer) can set a target number. Once the client refers that number of clients, they can be rewarded with a salon gift card.

Cross-Promote. Make contacts with other professionals and businesses that you can cross-promote with. As you're building your portfolio, you'll meet tons of photographers, makeup artists, fashion designers, and other stylists who can send business your way. Wedding planners are also a great source of referrals.

Book Building During Downtime

Did a client cancel her two-hour appointment, leaving you with a big fugly gap of open space this afternoon? Instead of busting out your cell phone to play a rousing game of Angry Birds, spend some time on self-promotion. The tips that follow can be done in and near the salon, for free.

Meet the Neighbors. If your salon has neighboring businesses, take a walk down there with some cards and introduce yourself. Encourage the staff at the neighboring businesses to visit you for services and refer you to their customers. Neighboring businesses are excellent referral sources.

Connect. Update Facebook, Twitter, Pinterest, and Instagram. You don't have to post anything new, just reach out and remind people that you exist. You can share information on new techniques or new products, post one of your portfolio images, or update everyone with some positive salon news. Be visible and be sure to tag and hashtag!

Write. Put together an original article or newsletter about your profession. The most effective ones address the big issues: dirty implements, unsanitary environments, and unlicensed professionals. This content attracts consumer attention more effectively than generic information about products or services. Write about the perils in our industry and highlight what makes you and your salon different. Be certain to include the salon's name, location, and contact information.

Don't be tempted to plagiarize content. Your article must be an original creation. Don't copy and paste the work of others. If you want to quote someone's content or use an excerpt, contact that person and ask for permission. Most of us are more than happy to grant it.

When you're finished, post it on your networks and print it out. These articles can be posted on bulletin boards found in community centers, apartment complex lobbies, college campuses, laundromats, and public libraries. You can also ask for permission to leave them in the waiting rooms in physician's offices.

There are tons of creative ways to build a book. These are just some ideas to get you started. Keep your eyes open for what other professionals are doing!

Consult With Confidence

"If you're doing more talking than listening during the consultation, you're very likely doing it wrong."

The most important part of every service is the consultation. During this time, you'll need to learn what your client expects and what their tastes are. During their first appointment, the consultation give you the opportunity to gain the client's trust in your professional abilities. This chapter will help you learn how to communicate clearly and effectively and gain a lifetime client.

I struggled with consultations for the first five years of my career. The textbooks, lectures, and hundreds of articles I read on the subject yielded nothing useful. Other professionals may have benefited from their information, but as I gained experience, I realized that the techniques they shared just weren't effective and a few of them are really inadvisable. In this chapter, I'll share with you my consultation techniques that I know to be effective and explain to you why I consider the popular techniques to be flawed.

Five-Step Consultation Process

Consultations can be broken down into five parts.

1.) The Q&A: Sit across from the client and ask effective questions. Effective questions require more than a "yes" or "no" answer. The first portion of the consultation should happen with both of you seated face to face. Ask open-ended questions and listen to the client's answers.

Many professionals spend their consultations behind the chair, touching the client's hair and analyzing while questioning them through the mirror. Don't create this distance between yourself and your client and don't attempt to multitask during consultations. The client deserves your full attention. You can't listen and analyze thoroughly at the same time and you shouldn't even attempt to. The only acceptable way to multitask during a consultation is to take notes during the process. This shows the client you care about what they want and the notes will help you repeat back to them what your interpretations are. Notes will also make cross-questioning easier. (During cross-questioning, you'll address any areas you need clarification on by asking the same question a few different ways.)

Before moving on to the analysis, repeat what your interpretation of the client's expectations and desires back to her. For example, *"So, to be sure I'm hearing you correctly, you're unhappy with your texture and are interested in straightening options?"*

2.) The Analysis: Analyze the client's hair, skin, or nails. Ask questions that relate to the area being serviced. Once you have a good idea what the client's looking for, you can begin the analysis. During this portion of the consultation, you evaluate the hair, skin, or nails and ask questions relating to the area you're servicing.

When you ask these questions, don't do it with your head down and your attention focused on their scalp, hands, or feet. Make eye contact and open your ears. This is the only point speaking to the client through a mirror is acceptable.

Continuing with our example, let's assume our texture client has relatively healthy hair. It has been colored darker than her natural tone with professional product. She has expressed to you that she doesn't want to commit to styling every day.

3.) Recommendation and Education: Make your professional recommendations and explain your reasoning. When you make recommendations, do so face-to-face. Get out from behind that chair, lift your head from your nail desk, and communicate like a professional. This portion of the consultation is your opportunity to let the client see that you're thorough, educated, and competent. It's her turn to ask questions, so invite her to do so.

Educate her. Utilize visual aids like pictures and color swatches. If you think she'll benefit from a particular service or product, make that recommendation and explain why. Likewise, if you think her requests or expectations are inadvisable, unobtainable, or unsuitable for her lifestyle, communicate why and offer an alternative. (Some professionals will end the consultation here if the client's requests don't conform to their policies.)

Make sure the client understands the aftercare and maintenance commitments required before continuing. If you're doing a chemical service, I strongly recommend performing a 24-hour swatch test. (Seriously, neglect swatch tests at your own peril. The first time you have a client return with her eyelids swollen shut due to a lash adhesive allergy or a blistered scalp due to a chemical allergy, you'll realize how critically important this process is.)

Using our straightening client as an example, you decide to suggest chemical straightening. You would say, *"Because you don't want to spend time styling your hair every day, I recommend a chemical straightening procedure. However, this procedure will likely pull out some of your color, so you may require another color service. Chemical straightening may cause a small degree of breakage, so I also recommend that you purchase [products] for home care. I think you'll also benefit from regular deep conditioning treatments every [X] weeks. Chemical straightening does require regular maintenance. Your roots will have to be straightened every [X] weeks, which will cost [$X]. The service cannot be reversed, so if you decide to return to your natural texture, you will have to wait for the straightened hair to grow out. During that time, you might have to commit to straightening your roots with a flat iron. This is a chemical procedure, so our policy is to perform an allergy test in advance for your safety."*

To illustrate how you would tactfully decline to perform an inadvisable service, let's pretend the client's hair is in rough shape and you refuse to move forward since you know the straightening treatment will do more harm than good. *"Due to* the condition of your hair, I can't guarantee a favorable outcome with a chemical straightening service. Instead, I can make a few recommendations on how we should proceed. We can find a cut and style that works with your existing texture while we improve the health of your hair, I can teach you how to straighten your hair in a way that requires a minimal time investment, or you can come in twice weekly and have me straighten it for you. If you're willing, we can design a plan together that will allow you to enjoy your desired result while getting your hair into optimal condition for a more permanent solution. However, at this time, I don't recommend a chemical straightening service and can't proceed with it."

4.) The Plan: Agree on how to move forward. At this point, you and your client should come to an agreement about how to execute the service. Communicate the price right now so there are no surprises during checkout.

Clients have been known to sue salon professionals for "emotional distress" when services don't meet their expectations, so for chemical clients, I recommend signed consultation agreements to ensure you're both on the same page and to protect yourself from frivolous litigation.

For example, "Alright! So, you want to go ahead with the chemical straightening. That service starts at $70, but because of the length and density of your hair, the final price will be $100. The cut and style are included, but the conditioning treatment is an extra $20. Your services, when totaled with the home care products you're purchasing will bring your bill to $160. If that's alright with you, I'll have the receptionist put your products together and I'll make sure that an aftercare sheet is put in the bag in case you need to reference it at home, then we can get started."

5.) Confirmation: Ensure the client understands the service outcome before proceeding. Recap what you're doing and what the outcome will be. Ask again if the client has any questions.

Keep the education and feedback going throughout the service; explain what you're doing, the products you're using, and how each procedure and product benefits the client.

"Before we continue with the chemical straightening service, do you have any questions for me at all?"

"First, I'm going to apply this barrier cream to protect your scalp from the product."

"Because your hair is colored and you don't have coarse hair, I've chosen a mild formula, which will minimize the damage to your hair while still achieving the desired result."

"How are you feeling? This product is known to be very mild, but if you experience any irritation or itching, please let me know. No portion of this service should be uncomfortable for you."

Craptastic Consulting Advice

This consulting advice can be found everywhere. Remember, the opinions below are my own based on my experience. If you want to test your luck with them, go for it—but first, consider the drawbacks to these strategies.

Flattery. *"Start the consultation by complimenting one of the client's features."* Most people likes to hear nice things and if you genuinely want to compliment the client, by all means, do so. However, flattery for the sake of "scoring points" with the client isn't advisable and can come across as forced or fake. Instead of trying to court favor through flattery, gain trust by projecting professional competence.

Covert Psychology. Many resources will encourage you to "mimic" or "mirror" the client and to keep your chair lower than eye-level to keep the client from feeling intimidated. These tactics are premised on the assumption that by utilizing submissive positioning and mimicking the client's body language, rate of speech, and facial expressions, you can gain their trust on a subconscious level. As cool as these subtle brainwashing techniques sound, I urge you not to do this. Mimicking and mirroring often happens naturally without us putting conscious effort into it anyways. Observant clients might be creeped out by it.

The best way to gain a client's trust isn't to assume their body posture and hand gestures. Be genuine and listen attentively. Instead of focusing on mimicking the client (and running the risk of weirding them out), focus your attention on their responses to the questions you ask and concentrate on delivering educated answers to theirs.

Observational Assumption. This popular piece of advice requires you to make assumptions about the client's tastes based on your observations. *"From the first time you set eyes your client, observe her body language and mood. Is she talkative and animated, or quiet and timid? Are her clothes flashy and trendy, professional, or casual? What about her hair and makeup? Does she look like she spent a good amount of time grooming before her appointment? These observations will give you insight into what kind of person she is and what kind of service she expects."*

To some degree, observations can be helpful, but you shouldn't base your judgment regarding a client's lifestyle or preferences on the clothes she happens to be wearing that day. Your first impression of a client will rarely be accurate.

Discriminatory Observational Assumptions. *"Younger clients will want more fashionable styles. Older clients will want more conservative styles."* Do not ever make observational assumptions like this, especially ones that are discriminatory. I'm not sure why this is considered acceptable or advisable. It's just as inappropriate to make discriminatory assumptions based on age as it is to make assumptions based on race. Seeing this advice being perpetuated makes me angry and it's a surefire way to piss off a client. You know how to determine what a client wants? Ask questions.

Constant Contact. *"Touching your client helps them feel at ease and gives you the ability to analyze their hair or nails while you consult."* Touching your clients constantly also weirds them out. Only touch your clients when necessary—during the analysis portion of the consultation.

Personal Questions. *"Getting to know what your client wants requires getting to know them personally. Ask questions about their hobbies, interests, career, and home life."* These questions aren't relevant and are a waste of precious consulting time. If you aren't directing the conversation, the client can get carried away talking about themselves.

Remember, you have to maintain professional distance, so keep the conversation pertinent to the service. Clients may find personal questions to be inappropriate and some employers won't permit that kind of discussion in the salon. In addition, clients may feel entitled to (or obligated to) reciprocate by expressing interest in your personal life. Don't open that door.

Give Them What They Need, Not What They Want. By far, the worst advice I've ever heard. A lot of consulting advice will encourage you to manipulate the client into accepting something other than what they're asking for.

In some cases, suggesting alternatives will be necessary. (For instance, *"If we cut your hair short on the sides but leave the length, the outcome will be what we refer to as a 'mullet.' This isn't an outcome that I think will suit you, but here are some alternatives for you to consider..."*) However, aside from refusing to perform services that will end poorly and hurt your reputation, there's no excuse to manipulate or coerce a client like this or worse—deliver a different service "for the client's own good."

Either give the client what they request or refuse them service. Never take it upon yourself to give them a look they didn't ask for.

A great consultation will secure rebookings, ensure favorable service outcomes, and will show the client that you can be trusted to deliver fantastic results. Your recommendations and referrals will skyrocket. Never begin a service without a thorough consultation.

Rebooking, Retailing, and Upselling

"Not all professionals will agree with my professional philosophies—but this is my book, not theirs, so they can bite me."

Rebooking, retailing, and upselling are skills every salon professional must have because they are critical to your bottom line—and unfortunately, they are skills that are not taught in many schools. This chapter contains my personal beliefs and strategies that have worked for me. There are tons of other techniques out there. You should learn and test each of them to determine which works best for you. I will also address other popular techniques that I don't particularly agree with (along with my reasoning for why I don't agree with them). Just understand that my way isn't necessarily the right way and it definitely isn't the only way. Experiment and utilize the methods that are effective for you.

Rebooking Techniques

Technique 1: "Do you want to schedule your next appointment before you leave?"
This passive technique has the massive drawback of giving the client a wide window to decline. In addition, the professional doesn't sell their availability to their full potential.

That being said, it can be effective if the client really enjoyed her service and prefers to make appointments in advance.

Technique 2: "You will be due for your next appointment on [DATE]. Currently, I only have [TIME] or [TIME] available. Which works for you?"

With Technique 2, you close that "declination window" and communicate to the client that your time is at a premium without rubbing their face in it. She gets the underlying message loud and clear: you are an in-demand professional and the possibility exists that she might not be able to secure an appointment with you when she's due to come in if she doesn't do so before she walks out that door. For clients who seem hesitant, I let them know that my clients book in advance and my availability can't be guaranteed. I then offer to book the appointment "just in case" and inform them that they'll be getting a confirmation 48 hours in advance. If they need to cancel or reschedule, we can just book them in the next available slot that works for with their availability, put them on my cancellation list, or fit them in with whoever has availability.

In my experience, it is extremely rare that a client doesn't rebook when Technique 2 is used. It is incredibly rare that they cancel or no-show that appointment. (Although, my cancellation and no-show policies combined with the 48 hour reminder calls also help deter that.) Let clients know that rebooking is standard procedure for all of the clients you service, so those slots fill quickly. This technique also makes it very easy to transition a client to a standing appointment schedule.

Technique 3: "We'll see you for your next appointment on [DATE] at [TIME]!"

I hate this technique. It's too presumptuous and could offend your client, who may not appreciate that you didn't bother to ask if she wanted another appointment or take her availability into consideration. It's a step too far. Auto-rebooking might boost your repeat percentage, but that inflation will be artificial and you'll likely be looking at a considerable amount of cancellations and no-shows.

Retailing Techniques

Technique 1: "We sell things for this." "We're running a special on this."

Unless they have prior experience in sales, a lot of new salon professionals are very passive retailers. Technique 1 isn't so much a "technique" as an ineffective, half-assed way of suggesting products. The professional doesn't provide reasoning behind the recommendation other than the fact that the salon carries a product or has a current promotion. They are not demonstrating their education, their competence, or their professional expertise.

Technique 2: "I have taken your lifestyle and personal needs into consideration and really think you could benefit from [PRODUCT]. It contains [MAGIC INGREDIENTS] that will [PERFORM SOME KIND OF MIRACLE FOR YOU OR MAKE YOUR LIFE MORE AWESOME IN SOME WAY]. To use it, simply [SMEAR IT ON YOUR FACE/SPRAY IT ON YOUR HEAD/SLATHER IT ON YOUR HANDS OR FEET]. I'll use some of it on you today to give you an idea of how it works so you can see the results for yourself. We sell it here and a bottle costs [TEN BAGILLION DOLLARS]. If you like it and decide to purchase it, let me know and I'll have them reserve a bottle for you."

Technique 2 practically guarantees a sale. If it doesn't guarantee a sale, it impresses the hell out of your client and builds trust. The client will be more likely to ask for your professional opinion on products in the future—and that's fantastic.

The professional displays confidence, concern, and shows off their professional expertise. The recommendation gets made and the sales pitch stops. From there, the client can ask questions if she likes. Spark her interest and let it go where it goes. Don't sell—educate and recommend. Then, get back to doing your job. You aren't a sales person; you're a service provider. Selling isn't everything.

Only recommend products or services you truly believe will benefit your client in some way. Don't be pushy or aggressive. Educate your client about the product: explain how it's used, her how it will benefit her if she were to use it regularly, and let her make the decision to purchase (or not) for herself. Your client's comfort and trust take precedent over a product commission. Clients who believe you have their best interests in mind are more inclined to purchase products or services you recommend than clients who perceive you as being hungry for retail income.

Technique 3: "You need this product. Seriously. I mean it. You need it. It does [EVERYTHING AND MORE]. [INSIST.] [PUSH.] [KEEP PUSHING.] I'll go put it up front for you."

You'll see these aggressive sales techniques in salons that impose retail quotas on their staff. I don't advise or agree with the retail quota practice at all—particularly when the owner hinges the staff's continued employment on whether or not they can meet those quotas. Goals should be set and those that reach those goals deserve rewards—but setting mandatory sales objectives and intimidating your staff to meet them creates a stressful work atmosphere and forces salon staff to resort to desperate tactics (like forcing the product onto the client), which turn clients off to the staff member and the salon.

This pushy technique might close a few sales, but clients tend not to appreciate it and are unlikely to return to a salon where retail products are practically shoved down their throats at every appointment. Don't lower yourself like this and don't work somewhere that makes your employment conditional on your ability to meet their quotas. Remember, you're a service provider, not a salesman. If you wanted to work in beauty retail, you could have spared yourself the expense of beauty school and pursued a career at Sephora or Ulta.

Upselling Techniques

Service sales are the easiest to close, in my experience—especially if the client has processing time to kill. Find a way to make their downtime profitable for the salon and enjoyable for your client. Here are some techniques for service upselling.

Technique 1: "Would you like a quick manicure while you wait?"

Don't be passive. The professional leaves that declination window wide open again! She's not informing or educating! She doesn't seem enthusiastic about maximizing the client's time in the salon! If you want to guarantee an instant income boost, move on to Technique 2.

Technique 2: "Your hair has to process for thirty minutes, but I noticed that your polish is chipping off. I would love the opportunity to give you a polish change with our new spring collection of gel polishes that just came in. We guarantee that you color will remain chip-free for fourteen days. If you'd prefer, I could remove the polish and give you a natural nail manicure with a hydrating, relaxing warm paraffin treatment, a treatment I firmly believe every woman should experience at least once in

their lives. Since you would be having the service in conjunction with a color, cut, and style, I would happily give you a 10% discount on whatever manicure you choose. It would sure beat sitting here flipping through magazines!"

With Technique 2, you achieve several things. First, the client learns about your new gel polishes; if she doesn't decide to get the service that day, she might decide to one day in the future. Secondly, she learns that your gel polish services include a quality guarantee, which communicates that your salon believes in that particular product and service so much that they're willing to promise quality results. She also might not be familiar with gel polish or its benefits. A fourteen day manicure might just blow her mind and open an entirely new dialog—giving you yet more opportunity to show your expertise and share your salon's offerings. Next, you're making that paraffin treatment sound damn good! This also opens up a window for dialog and introduces the client to a service she may not have heard of before! You're communicating to her that you personally love the service, which gives that recommendation weight. Finally, the discount sweetens the offer and reminding her of her alternative makes the services even more appealing.

Does this work? Damn near every time. I rarely advise discounting services, but this instance serves as the exception to that. Even at 20% off, you're making additional money you would normally not be making.

Before I move on to Technique 3, do you notice something about the services recommended? They are fast, low-overhead services that encourage frequent repeat appointments. If you're going to recommend a "filler" service upgrade, make it low-cost and make it something that demands frequent upkeep. Turn those 4-6 week color clients into two week manicure or waxing clients.

I know I said before that my methods may not be the right way—I lied. This technique is totally the right way to upsell services.

Technique 3: "Your bill is [X] because I did [THIS] and [THIS] without your permission."

Oh, silly discount salons. We have all had this happen to us at one point or another—usually at salons that advertise rock-bottom pricing and rely on speed and nickel-and-diming their customers to turn a profit. "You want gel topcoat? $5 extra." "You want your nails cut down? $5 extra." "You want callus removal? $5 extra." This practice can be irritating, even when the extra costs are disclosed during the service, but nothing will infuriate a client more than a higher-than-expected bill at the end of an appointment because the service provider took it upon herself to provide unsolicited upgrades. Don't ever take away your client's freedom to choose.

Deep Discount Dumbassery

"People that pay for things never complain. It's the guy you give something to that you can't please."
-Will Rogers

Most salon owners have wised up by now and are staying far, far away from Groupon and similar discount deals. Hopefully, you're too smart to require this chapter, but at some point in your career, your employer or one of your microsalon owning friends may experience a lapse in sanity and give serious consideration to a group discount scam. This chapter will help you talk them down off that ledge.

Group coupon deal sites are vampires. They feed off their own customer base, bleeding their merchants dry. If you're not familiar with how these deals work for merchants, here's an overview of how Groupon works, as an example.

Groupon requires their merchants to discount their products or services by at least 50%. Groupon runs the deal and collects 30-60% of the voucher's sale price. You read correctly. First you discount your services by 50%...and then Groupon takes 30-60% of your remaining 50%. The discount equates to at least a full 75% off (the average Groupon deal leaves merchants with $0.23 on the dollar). How can any business afford to give away 75% of their income for a promotion? How do salon owners fall for such an obvious hit-and-run marketing scam?

In addition to utilizing high-pressure sales tactics, Groupon reps runs "projections" for merchants to sell their product, but these reps don't understand that merchant's individual business or how that merchant's staff are compensated. They also don't know their overhead, service times, demographic, or any of the other factors that go into salon marketing and management. Unfortunately, salon owners fall for this pitch often because they also don't understand their financials, marketing, or overhead. Cost analysis is the most important factor in any marketing decision and it's one only the salon owner can do with any accuracy.

Groupon also doesn't cap sales. Why would they? They're making 50% on the voucher cost and don't have to deal with the consequences that the salon owner will face as a result of those unlimited voucher sales. Owners hear Groupon's promises of cash windfalls, but don't consider the cost of redemption (product, staff, scheduling, and utilities) or how a flood of business will affect their client experience.

Group coupon sales reps also like to promise, "You'll never have to advertise again after running a Groupon." Owners want to believe this so badly because advertising is an ongoing expense all of us wish we could do without. Unfortunately, we don't live in Groupon's fantasy land where all Groupon clients upgrade their services, purchase tons of products, and book standing appointments before they leave. We live in reality—and in reality, salons can never stop advertising, Groupon clients don't spend money in excess of the voucher, and the vast majority will never return.

To add insult to injury, most of these discount clients don't tip. The few that do tip will tip on the voucher cost, not the service value. Legitimate marketing tools net long-term results and lifetime premium clients, not one-time results and unprofitable customers.

The ideal group coupon business has fixed costs, high profit margins, and the ability to offer small-value coupons. We're not a fixed-cost industry. Our operating expenses are high and fluctuate with product usage. To contrast, theaters are great group coupon businesses. It costs a theater the same amount of money to run a show with an audience of five as it does for them to run a show with a full house. These businesses benefit from high traffic and aren't dependent on loyalty, but in our industry, traffic alone doesn't equate to profitability.

For salons and spas to succeed, we focus on acquisition and retention. Loyalty is our bread and butter. The demand generated by oversold vouchers often exceeds the salon's ability to redeem them. Staff get booked out months in advance with a flood of group coupon clients, making it impossible for their loyal, full-priced clients to get an appointment. This causes both the displaced loyal clients and the demanding group coupon clients to leave nasty reviews—destroying a salon's online reputation.

These group discount deals are nothing more than a way to sell services at a massive loss, and smart salon owners won't sell at a loss—especially in quantity—because smart salon owners aren't in business to give things away.

Owners devalue their business and the services of their staff when they offer anything for free. A smart salon owner builds a strong client base by offering excellent services for a fair price. They invest in their current clients and won't betray their loyal client base or devalue their loyalty by forwarding deep discounts to new prospects in a desperate effort to capture these coupon-snatchers. Smart salon owners know that strategy just isn't realistic or sustainable.

Do you see the importance of clarifying how you'll be compensated for deep discounted services in the initial interview and getting that policy on paper in your employment contract? Neglect this important discussion at your peril. These deep discounts will kill your commission and often force owners to violate the FLSA because many will not meet their minimum wage obligation. These deals hurt salons and the staff they employ.

I gathered emails from my readers regarding their experiences with Groupon and similar deals and here's what they had to say.

The Sales Pitch

"They made me feel like I would be an idiot for not using them."

"They spouted these numbers about how much money I would make. They didn't mention how much I would be losing."

"My rep made promises about how the Groupon clients would be customers for life. How stupid I was for believing that."

Massive Losses

"The decision to run this group deal nearly destroyed my salon. Our saving grace was that expiration date."

"Running a Groupon was the biggest mistake I've ever made as a salon owner and the most expensive lesson I've ever learned. I lost money, loyal clients, and employees."

"They talked me into offering one-hour facials (normally valued at $50) for $20—60% off. They took 50% of each voucher sold, leaving me with barely $10 per voucher. At 50% commission, the esthetician stood to make $5/hr. I had to make up the difference to meet my state's minimum wage of $9 an hour. So, I lost $30 per service right off the bat just to run the damn deal, gave $10 to Groupon, netted barely $10 per service, and paid $9 of that every hour to my esthetician. This left me with $1 per service to cover product and overhead. I can't express how many ways this scam hurt my salon."

"So far about half of the vouchers have been redeemed. If the other half are redeemed, my salon will definitely go out of business."

Bad Reviews

"Groupon clients feel entitled to everything. They want a $100 service for $10, and somehow feel justified in posting cruel, slanderous reviews on Yelp when the service they receive doesn't meet their absurd expectations."

"Would I do it again? Not a chance in hell! Why? Because group coupon clients have been rude and nasty to deal with and the reviews they left for the services they paid practically nothing for have ruined my salon's Yelp rating."

"These demanding, bottom-feeding discount hunters were a nightmare! They would throw a fit when we tried to enforce the fine print. Then, they left bad reviews because we wouldn't cater to their unreasonable demands. It will take me years to repair the damage they've done to my rankings on Superpages and Facebook!"

"Groupon people have got to be the biggest cheapskates I have ever met and therefore some of the biggest complainers. They complain because they didn't read the coupon's terms and somehow their inability to read was my fault. They cannot seem to wait to publicly crucify our salon."

Poor Customer Quality

"These clients told my staff that they would never be willing to pay full price for beauty services under normal circumstances. We didn't attract loyal clients, we attracted opportunistic spa tourists. We attracted vultures."

"Groupon clients are some of the worst individuals I have ever met. They wanted all that we had and more. They wanted it all and they wanted it for nothing."

"The group coupon clients were cheap, rude, unappreciative, and low-class. They made my employees miserable and killed morale in the spa. They were not the type of clients we would want to have return. I will never do another similar deal again."

"I cannot believe what negative, mean, rude, hurtful people this 'deal' sent to our salon."

"Groupon clients book, cancel, and rebook repeatedly. They arrive late for appointments or won't show up at all…but still insist they should be able to redeem their coupon at a later date. My salon is better off without that type of client."

Don't become a victim of these "group deals." The horror stories still vastly outnumber the success stories.

Salon Policies: Lay Down The Law, Sheriff

"Your professional reputation is your most valuable asset as a beauty industry professional. Protect it by establishing policies."

Policies are rules that you set and boundaries you define as it applies to the services you provide. For example, "We do not apply drugstore haircolor." That policy communicates to clients that they can't show up with a box of Natural Instincts, slap a $20 on the counter, and expect you to apply it for them. Salon policies are important because they allow you to protect your professional reputation and can deter toxic clients.

Where policies are concerned, there are three types of professionals.

1.) "I'll do/allow anything as long as I'm getting paid." These professionals don't have any policies. The client wants Cruella deVille's dye job with Miley's unfortunate Beiber haircut? No problem. That'll be $110. Show me the money. You want to bring all five of your children and let them tear the salon apart while you text your boyfriend? Okay! You're the boss!

These professionals often feel that clients should be given whatever they request, regardless of the consequences. Some of them simply love money and others are so eager to please clients that they're scared to refuse them anything.

2.) "I won't do/allow X...unless Y or Z. Then, I guess it's okay." These professionals have a rule or two, but they're relatively flexible. For example, "I won't do nail enhancements on teenagers...unless they're a 'mature' teenager and/or their mom gives permission."

3.) "I won't do/allow it. Period. If you don't like it, there's the door." These professional know how they like to do business and they're very specific about it. Their policies are non-negotiable. Professionals with rigid policies like this value their reputations highly. They would rather risk angering a client by refusing them than compromise their professional integrity.

Everyone works differently and we all hold different professional philosophies. For the majority of us, those values evolve over time and our policies change to accommodate that. I could say I don't advocate any position over the other, but I'd be lying. I believe policies are necessary and to operate without them would be foolish. Whether or not you choose to implement policies is entirely up to you, but for your consideration, here are some of the pros and cons.

Pros

Quality Control. When you set clear rules and boundaries, you retain complete control over your output and environment. By refusing to allow certain behaviors in the salon, you can guarantee a pleasurable experience for all of the guests. By refusing to perform services with questionable or unfavorable outcomes, you can protect your reputation and ensure client satisfaction.

Mutual Benefit. Many policies benefit the clients and the professionals—even policies that seem crappy. For example, a lot of spas have policies that state, "If you are delayed in your arrival, please remember that your service will end at its original time." While this policy benefits you by deterring late arrivals, it also benefits the clients because it doesn't allow latecomers to inconvenience the clients who arrive promptly.

Toxic Client Deterrent. A confident, passionate professional attracts quality clients. That same confidence will absolutely repel toxic clients. For example, some clients might look at your late arrival policy and say, "Screw that place! What a ripoff! If I'm paying for the service, I should get the full service regardless of how late I am." Good clients will consider that policy reasonable and appreciate that you value promptness.

Cons

Toxic Client Deterrent. The clients you lose tend to be the ones you probably didn't want to attract to begin with. Nonetheless, if you are a "show me the money" professional, policies may compromise your traffic and pose a problem.

Negative Client Perception. Some clients disdain professionals who know their worth. Again, the people who hold these opinions often belong to that class of undesirable clients. Some professionals hold themselves to a higher standard. We've worked hard to be good at what we do. We shouldn't be ashamed of that and we shouldn't be humble about it. Do we refuse to do cheap, crappy work? Hell yes. Why? Because we actually give a shit. Do we charge no-shows for disrespecting our time? You bet. Why? Because this is our career, not a hobby. This a "con" that I wouldn't take seriously for a single second, but some professionals really care about what other people think of them. Obviously, I'm not one of them.

Client Opposition. Clients who are disdainful of policies tend to be those that violate them. These clients tend to be those treat service workers like slaves while shouting, "The customer is always right!" Reasonable clients won't oppose reasonable policies.

Choosing Policies

When you think about forming policies, a few things should come to mind immediately. Make a list of them and prioritize it by severity. Things you absolutely will not allow go at the top of the list and things you might be flexible on go at the bottom.

To serve as an example, my list looks like this:
1.) Non-Negotiable Policy: "No children in the spa."

2.) Non-Negotiable Policy: "We do not fill or repair enhancements we didn't apply."

3.) Non-Negotiable Policy: "No shows and late cancellations will be charged 100% and will be required to prepay all future appointments at booking."

4.) Conditional Policy: "No food or drinks in the spa treatment areas."

Wording, Placement, Enforcement, and Justification

After you've made your list, you'll know where you draw your line and how firmly you press your pen down when you draw it. With this knowledge, you can move on to wording, placement, and enforcement.

Wording. On policies you feel strongly about, be clear. Use firm wording and keep sentences concise. "Please," "kindly," or "we ask" should not anywhere in those non-negotiable policies. Those words are soft and make the policies seem optional. Phrases like, "do not," "will not," "not permitted," and "no exceptions" are strong and form an immediate impression. They make it clear the policies are mandatory.

Placement. Don't slap the guests in the face with a rulebook. Think about where you can place these policies so the clients will see them only when necessary. Important rules will go in multiple places. More specific ones will go where they're relevant.

Enforcement. Have a plan for enforcing your policies.

Justification. If you're ever questioned by a client, having logical reasoning behind your policies can be helpful, but you're not required to justify them to anyone. For example, I don't do facials on men anymore. My reason? When I was eighteen, a male client propositioned me for sex during his facial in an aggressive, threatening way. Is it likely to happen again? Probably not. Does that mean I'm going to start taking male facial clients again? Nope.

Also, don't apologize for your policies. Any apology you provide will be disingenuous anyways, since if you were truly "sorry for the inconvenience" you wouldn't have implemented the policy to begin with.

Now you can start constructing your policies. To illustrate, we'll work from the list above.

1.) "Children are not permitted in the spa for any reason."

Wording: Notice the firm, rigid wording. "...not permitted." "...for any reason."

Placement: This goes on the spa website, brochure, and a plaque in the waiting room. It also appears during online booking and in the appointment reminder emails.

Enforcement: This policy pervades the business materials and can be found on a plaque in the waiting room. Unless blind, clients can't claim they didn't see it. Clients who violate this policy are sent home.

Justification: We use a lot of dangerous chemicals and sharp implements. We also have expensive equipment. We cannot be held responsible for a child's safety while we're working. It also interferes with the relaxation of the other clients and can be distracting for the staff. Children do not fit in the atmosphere the spa creates.

2.) "We do not fill nail enhancements that we did not apply. No exceptions."

Wording: Again, strong wording communicates that we're serious about this policy. "...do not..." "No Exceptions."

Placement: This goes on the spa website and brochures, but only where the nail enhancement prices are listed.

Enforcement: When new clients attempt to book a Fill & Rebalance service, they're told they must book an Enhancement Removal & Full Set. If they refuse, they're denied the appointment.

Justification: We don't know how well the natural nails were prepped prior to application. If an infection manifests due to another technician's negligence, we don't want our name attached to it. If the enhancements pop off due to bad prep or crumble due to garbage product, we're not fixing it or assuming blame for it. If clients want to walk around telling people they're wearing our nails, they need to be wearing our product, sculpted and finished our way.

3.) "No shows and late cancellations will be charged 100% and will be required to prepay all future appointments at booking."

Wording: The wording explains, in no uncertain terms, how we handle no-shows and last-minute cancellations.

Placement: This goes out with the reminder emails, pops up during online booking, and is posted on the reception desk where people sign their credit card receipts. It's also on brochures and the website.

Enforcement: The policy itself clearly communicates how we plan to enforce it.

Justification: We're running a business. Staff get paid for the time clients reserve whether or not they decide to show up for the service. We're not going to take a loss because a client "forgot" or blew us off for another activity. Clients that don't respect our time or skills are not welcome.

We use sharp tools and e-files. To reduce the risk of injury, we require their full attention.

4.) "No food or drinks are permitted in the spa treatment areas. Thank you!"

Wording: The first part of the policy comes across strong, but the "Thank you!" softens it.

Placement: This can be found on a sign on the door that leads to the treatment rooms. They can enjoy a snack or beverage in reception or the transition room, but not in the treatment areas.

Enforcement: Unless the client's food or drink interferes with the execution of the service, this policy won't be enforced. If a client wants to ingest their own toenail dust, we won't stop them.

Justification: Clients enjoying hand services need to have their hands free throughout the appointment to keep the professional on schedule. Clients getting foot services shouldn't be eating in the treatment room because it's just gross.

Comprehensive policies that are worded appropriately and placed strategically will communicate your guidelines, boundaries, and expectations for you. Most successful salons have policies in place and most professionals have at least a few of their own, so ask your peers to gain insight into what others are doing and why. Finding out what works for them and what doesn't will help you form your own policies. You can also search online and view the policies of other salons, but remember, your wording must be your own. Be original. Don't plagiarize the work of others.

Relocating: How to Inform Your Clients

"You're not just informing them that you're moving—you're thanking them for their business and showing your gratitude for their continued support. Don't think of it as a notice; think of it as a love letter that comes with a gift of appreciation in the form of a discount on their first service at your new place of employment."

Have you decided to make a change and find employment at another salon? **Assuming you have the legal right to solicit your clients,** this chapter will tell you how to notify your loyal clients of your move from one business to another tactfully and professionally.

Call the clients who have appointments scheduled during the next two weeks. Those clients need to know immediately, so make your calls. Leave voicemails for those that don't answer and be sure to follow up again within a few hours or the following day.

Update your portfolio and websites to reflect the changes. Anyone who searches for you should see your new place of employment. Even if you perform the following steps, a few clients may fall through the cracks, so make it easy for them to find you online.

Invest in stamps and nice stationary. Don't just send an email. Emails are informal and many of the clients may not even read it. You might not even have all of their email addresses and half of the ones you have may not be current. So, type up a nice letter and have it printed at a local copy shop or office supply store on heavy paper.

Write a letter. Tell them about the great new place you've moved to. Let them know about what the new place will offer them (a full coffee bar, a more serene atmosphere, or a higher quality product line). Not all clients will be willing to follow you, so be sure to include a recommendation for them should they chose to remain at the salon. Sign each one by hand. If that means signing your name 300 times, then that's what it means.

For your top ten clients (you know who they are), go a step further and send them a nice card with a handwritten message. You can get a pack of ten with matching envelopes for as little as $1 at Target, Walmart, and sometimes even Office Depot.

Offer incentives. This may not be necessary, depending on how far you're moving and the disposition of your clientele. Whether or not you offer incentives is really up to you, but if you're going to do so, offer a deal on a service your clients haven't tried before instead of offering a dollar or percentage off. (For example, 15% off a revolutionary new conditioning treatment.) Another good choice would be to combine a value-added service with a full-price service (like a free brow wax with a haircut or a free paraffin treatment with a manicure). These services are low-overhead, low-cost, and high-maintenance. Putting a time restriction on your incentive is advisable because it encourages your clients to take advantage of the offer sooner rather than later, making it less likely that you'll lose them.

Send an email 3-5 days after you mail the letters. Give the clients time to receive the letters by mail and then send an email. Tell them that if they haven't already received one, a letter has been sent. Tell them that things are going great at the new location and you look forward to seeing all of them there. BE SURE TO USE THE BCC LINE. If you put everyone's email addresses into the "To" line, you will have disclosed those email addresses to everyone on that list and you will thoroughly piss off your clients. So, BCC ONLY!

Don't stalk the clients. Make the calls, update your sites, send the letters, and send the emails. Then, drop it. Not all of your clients will follow you. Don't be obnoxious. I have heard of professionals who tracked down their clients on social media, showed up at their offices, and called them relentlessly. Have some dignity.

Sample Letter

In your letter and your communications, don't mention or discuss why you left the old salon. If clients ask, tell them that you desired a change. Don't bitch about your old boss, the salon's policies, or any injustices you may have suffered. It's unprofessional and you don't want word getting back to your old salon.

Dear Valued Client,

It has been a pleasure doing your hair at [PREVIOUS SALON], but sometimes a change of scenery is needed! Effective [RELOCATION DATE], I will be located at [NEW SALON]. I would love to have you join me! I'm happy to offer you [INCENTIVE] at your first appointment with me at [NEW SALON]!

[NEW SALON] offers many exciting new features and services! Including:

[LIST FEATURES, PRODUCTS, AND SERVICES].

It is located at [ADDRESS], approximately [DISTANCE] miles away from [PREVIOUS SALON].

Should this change not suit you, the stylists at [PREVIOUS SALON] will be honored to serve you with the professionalism and style you have enjoyed in the past. If you choose to remain at [PREVIOUS SALON], I personally recommend my good friend [PREVIOUS COWORKER] and know she will provide you with the same level of service you have come to expect from me.

If you'd like to book your next appointment with me at [NEW SALON], please call our reception desk at [NEW SALON PHONE NUMBER].

Again, it has been my absolute pleasure to be your stylist and I look forward to seeing you soon!

Best regards,
[SIGN YOUR NAME]
[TYPE YOUR NAME]

Sample Email

Dear Valued Client,

If you haven't yet received the letter I sent, I have recently moved from [PREVIOUS SALON] to [NEW SALON]. I would love to have you join me there! I'm happy to offer you [INCENTIVE] at your first appointment with me at [NEW SALON]!

[NEW SALON] offers many exciting new features and services! Including:

[LIST FEATURES, PRODUCTS, AND SERVICES].

It is located at [ADDRESS], approximately [DISTANCE] miles away from [PREVIOUS SALON].

The move has gone smoothly and everything is great at my new professional home away from home!

Should this change not suit you, the stylists at [PREVIOUS SALON] will be honored to serve you with the professionalism and style you have enjoyed in the past. If you choose to remain at [PREVIOUS SALON], I personally recommend my good friend [PREVIOUS COWORKER] and know she will provide you with the same level of service you have come to expect from me.

If you'd like to book your next appointment with me at [NEW SALON], please call our reception desk at [NEW SALON PHONE NUMBER].

Again, it has been my absolute pleasure to be your stylist and I look forward to seeing you soon!

Best regards,
[TYPE YOUR NAME HERE]

Preserving Your Health

"Your body breaks down little by little every day without you even realizing it. Do your part to slow down the breakage by taking preventive measures."

The beauty industry will be hard on your body. Damn near all of us have joint issues. Hip and knee replacements are common. Many of us have required carpal tunnel surgery on at least one wrist. Some of us have lost time at work to recover from rotator cuff tendonitis, a condition that requires ongoing physical therapy and eventually surgical correction. A large number of professionals have serious issues with their necks and spines from hunching over every day. We may develop product allergies from overexposure, asthma and other breathing issues from dust and chemical inhalation. We're exposed to viruses from being in close proximity to a wide variety of people every day. This chapter will tell you how to protect your health and slow the gradual deterioration so many of us experience.

Stay Healthy. Get healthy and stay healthy—starting today. Eat better and sleep better. We get plenty of exercise at work, but a short walk several times a week won't kill you (unless you step in front of a bus or something).

You must stay hydrated! Simple hydration contributes to your health in such a significant way and helps prevent the majority of issues we suffer from. Take your body weight and divide it in half—you should be drinking that many ounces of water each day.

Muscle, Back, & Shoulder Problems. If the salon doesn't provide padded anti-fatigue mats, purchase one. Standing on hard floors all day will strain your feet, knees, neck, and lower back. Wear sensible shoes with arch support and do your best to pay attention to your posture—if you're bending over, lifting your arms higher than your chest line, or leaning at weird angles, you're doing it wrong.

To prevent back, neck, and joint strain, consider a hydraulic cutting stool. Saddle seat stools provide the best support. These stools are adjustable and allow you to work at the correct height. I strongly recommend that every stylist invest in one. Trust me, you'll be so very glad you did.

You may run into a veteran stylist or two that wears stabilizing belts. Some of us can't be trusted to maintain good posture and will wear rigid braces with contoured lumbar inserts periodically to re-train ourselves to stand and sit properly. If you start noticing that you're violating ideal body mechanics, consider utilizing one a few days a week.

Venous Disorders. Invest in a pair of compression stockings and commit to wearing them at least half the week. Compression stockings prevent and guard against extremely common venous disorders that plague our profession by delivering a distributed amount of compression at the ankle and up the leg, which aids in circulating blood and lymph fluid and improves lactic acid removal. They also improve the efficiency of your muscles by stabilizing them. Because they encourage healthy circulation and decrease swelling, you'll also notice that your legs, ankles, and feet ache less at the end of the day. Added bonus—you're less likely to develop blood clots and nasty, distended, permanent varicose veins or spider veins

Carpal Tunnels. Our jobs require a lot of repetitive hand and wrist movements, often in combination with vibrating equipment like e-files and blow driers, putting us at a significant risk of developing carpal tunnel syndrome. Don't trust yourself to abide by perfect ergonomic guidelines or body mechanics. You won't. Unless you're a ten-foot-tall stylist or working exclusively on children or very short adults, you'll never be able to keep your hands and wrists in line with your forearms while working. You'll seldom notice how tightly you're gripping your tools. You won't have time to take stretching breaks (those are fantasies they sell you in school).

Don't wait until you start experiencing cramping or tightness. Take preventive measures now. Get wrist splints and wear them a few nights a week. Wrists splints stabilize your wrists during sleep, reducing pressure on the median nerve and giving the joint a period of rest. Stretch your wrists every morning to keep them flexible.

Get Insured. You need insurance—no excuses. It isn't optional and you can't shrug it off, cross your fingers, and hope you won't suffer a car accident or end up with a debilitating illness.

Not only does insurance protect you against extremely expensive sudden injuries or illnesses, you are far more likely to get routine preventive care, which will decrease the likelihood of you getting seriously ill or injured to begin with. Without it, you're likely to skip physicals and put off important annual checks like mammograms. Do you realize what's at stake here?

I do. I was diagnosed with stage two cervical cancer at the age of 22. It had already started spreading into my uterus when they found it. Because I experienced no symptoms, I skipped my annual appointments for five years. If I were screened yearly, it would have been detected so far in advance that it likely wouldn't have progressed at all.

I didn't have insurance and had to pay for all of my treatment, drugs, and surgeries out of pocket. I spent two and a half months unable to work because the side effects made me incredibly ill. This drained my savings, causing me to live off credit (which I maxed out). My lack of income made it impossible for me to pay my bills and almost caused me to file bankruptcy. I am still recovering from the damage cancer did to my credit rating.

Prior to the Affordable Care Act, insurance companies could refuse coverage to people with pre-existing conditions, so no insurance company would take me on after I received my diagnosis. Now, insurers can't refuse you and they have to cover annual checkups and preventive care without co-pays. They also must provide essential health benefits in ten categories (preventive, wellness, ambulatory, emergency, hospitalization, maternity/newborn, pediatric, mental health/substance use, prescriptions, and rehabilitative/habilitative services). Plus, you're now eligible for tax credits and subsidies to offset the cost of premiums and expenses.

You have no excuse to be uninsured, you lucky bastards.

Now, my family and I have the best, most inclusive health care plan available. My lesson was an expensive, terrifying one to learn but I will never let the coverage lapse like that again. Now, if I get sick or something seems "off," I'm at the doctor's office within days. Do not let what happened to me happen to you. I used to say, "Everything will be fine. I'll just be careful." At 22, I thought I was invincible. Now, I know better.

Don't be an idiot. You can't predict the future, Ms. Cleo.

Preserving Your Wealth

"Don't allow poor financial planning to put you in a position where you're forced to work through your golden years, living paycheck to paycheck. The only sixty-year-olds that should be working behind the chair are those that genuinely want to be there."

You must achieve and maintain your own financial security. Quit spending, pay your debts, and commit to saving. This chapter will tell you how.

Budgeting

Many people falsely believe that budgeting is difficult, stressful, and restrictive. In reality, the opposite is true. Budgeting tools are widely available and make the process effortless. Knowing your budget and living within your means relieves stress and gives you incredible freedom. You know what's stressful? The consequences of living without a budget—drained accounts and shockingly high credit balances combined with massive interest rates.

Budgets give you a clear picture of your finances. They show you how much you can afford to spend on essentials and recreation and keep you motivated to contribute to your financial goals and priorities. A well-balanced budget also ensures that you'll always have enough money in savings.

Plenty of budgeting tools are available on the internet through financial management services like Mint.com (a free service offered by Intuit) and Simple (www.simple.com, a completely free online bank with great tools for saving). However, your budget will be highly individualized to your needs and will change over time. Do some research on budgeting and structure one to suit you. Dave Ramsey (www.daveramsey.com), has fantastic budgeting and financial management advice and resources available online for free.

Spending Habits

Mint.com and Simple allow you to categorize and monitor your spending habits and provide you with comprehensible charts and reports to keep you on top of your finances. These tools make it easy to see your spending habits and determine how to adjust your spending to stay within your budget.

Here are my quick tips for curbing impulse spending:
Know Your Weaknesses—And Avoid Them. We all have weaknesses. Mine are designer eyeglass frames and handbags. To curb my designer purse addiction, I no longer allow myself to walk into purse areas at the mall. I can't be

trusted. Unfortunately, I can't avoid the optometrist's office. The glasses I wear? $340 Coach frames. My backup pair? $270 DKNY frames. My insurance covers over 50% of my frame cost and 100% of my lenses, but there's no insurance plan in the world that provides designer purses (unfortunately for us all). So, I budget for my frames and allow myself this luxury once every two years. If you know what you're most likely to splurge on, stay away.

Shop Without Money. Go to a store without cash or credit. Walk around and browse. Take note of the things you'd like to buy and their prices, then set aside the money you need to purchase it. If you still really want it by the time you've accumulated the money to purchase it, buy it. (Chances are, you won't.)

Keep Transactions Tangible. Credit is dangerous, so avoid using it except in emergencies (and no, that $800 leather jacket does not qualify as an emergency expense). The reason credit can be so easily abused has to do with the how credit transactions are conducted and how that transaction registers in your mind.

With cash, you hand over an amount and receive less back. You have physically given something away in exchange for something else and you have a hard limit on what you can give away. With credit, you hand over the card and the card gets returned to you immediately. There's no perception of loss or limit. You can easily forget that anything was spent at all since there's no tangible sense of sacrifice. That's how credit cards get maxed.

Everyone falls victim to this manipulation of perception, so avoid using cards altogether whenever possible. When you are spending tangible currency, you are far less likely to overspend. You are more conscientious about what you do spend and you're more selective about the items you purchase.

Calculate Time Sacrifice. That pair of designer shoes you're salivating over cost $388. Sure, it's easy to cackle maniacally and loudly proclaim, "My credit limit is $2,000! The shoes are mine!" But instead, ask, "How long would it take me to make $388 and are these shoes really worth that sacrificed time?" Let's pretend you're a nail technician. Your most popular service is a $40 pedicure that takes you an hour to complete. You make 50% commission, which ends up being less than $20 after taxes. Those shoes would take you twenty or so pedicures to pay for.

Twenty hours of your time.

For a pair of shoes.

Assess Value. Coach just launched their fall collection and you want one of their new handbags so bad that it keeps you up at night. The problem? It costs $795. You've calculated how much time you'll be sacrificing to purchase it, and even though the time sacrifice is considerable, you're still determined to have it dangling from your arm, holding your pack of gum, cell phone, lip gloss, and wadded up receipts in style. But how much value can that product really deliver for the cost?

If you wear the purse for a year, that averages out to $66 a month (over $2 a day)! At two years, it's $33 a month! Can you justify that expense? If you were to wear the purse diligently, how long before it would break down? Coach bags are spectacular quality, but leather is leather and purses get abused even with the most careful treatment. Maybe you'd be better off with a reasonably-priced bag (something that won't send you spiraling into a deep depression if it gets stained, scuffed, or ripped).

Use Giftcards. Small expenses compound fast. Instead of allowing these small costs to accumulate, buy a gift card and load it on the first of every month with your budgeted amount. When the card runs dry, you're done.

$20 Happy Fund. Some financial advisers would prefer you identify the emotions that trigger you to spend and be aware of your vulnerability during those times, but I don't. Instead, I suggest a $20 Happy Fund—because sometimes people feel the need to spend due to achieve some mood boost. Restricting yourself could lead to what I call an "entitlement splurge." (If you've ever said, "Consequences be damned, I fucking deserve to blow $2,000 on things I really don't need," you've experienced it too.) Instead, make a list of things you love that you can purchase for $20 or less. (My short list includes Kindle books, Starbucks coffee, and vanilla soft serve.) Keep a $20 somewhere "in case of emergency." Break it out when you feel the urge to splurge.

Debt

If you're in debt, your top priority needs to be paying it down as soon as possible. Commission industries and the American economy overall can be extremely unstable. The beauty industry in particular gives the term "feast or famine" a terrifying new meaning—particularly in more touristy areas. Consider this an investment in your future; the money you save in interest fees, late fees, and penalties can be diverted into other areas of your budget...like costly designer eyewear (or less cool things, like your retirement fund).

There are a few different strategies people use to pay off debt fast. The two most common are debt stacking and debt snowball.

The traditional method, debt stacking, requires you to make list your debts by interest rate in descending order. You hit them from highest to lowest—making large payments on the cards with the highest rate and paying the minimums on the lowest rates. You repeat this process until you clear the list. Debt stacking saves you the most money in interest, but since some of your cards with higher balances might take a while to pay off, you'll have to wait for that feeling of gratification that comes with crossing debt off your list.

The debt snowball method requires you to list your debts in ascending order by balance, not interest rate—making large payments on the cards with the lowest balance and paying minimums on the others. Again, repeat the process until the list is cleared. This method reverses the pros and cons found in the debt stacking method; the interest costs more, but the psychological payoff is higher.

When paying off my considerable debt caused by my uninsured cancer disaster, I utilized the debt stacking method because I hate interest. (You might as well light your money on fire.) However, you may need the morale boost that comes with crossing a card off your list for good to keep you motivated to clear those debts. Whatever method you choose is the right one if the end goal—a life free of credit card debt—gets achieved.

When it comes to making large purchases, never finance unless you absolutely have to. Few people can afford to save up the money to purchase a home or vehicle outright, but you can save as much as possible to keep your debt low. I suggest making larger payments to pay down the principle faster also.

Emergency Savings

An emergency fund is a safety net you only touch when you have no choice, like when you get laid off, or when your refrigerator breaks down, or when your transmission blows. Once you put money into emergency savings, that's where it needs to stay. Forget it exists until your rainy day morphs into a devastating flash flood. You can't afford not to have an Emergency Fund. If you're living paycheck to paycheck (which is what you're doing if you don't have savings built), you're one unforeseen, emergency expense away from financial ruin.

You know where emergency savings belong? Savings accounts or safe investment accounts. Not stocks or mutual funds. A 2% interest rate might sound measly, but it will offset inflation. Contribute regularly and save enough to cover six months or a year of necessary expenses (mortgage, health insurance, car payments, groceries, utilities, etc.) to protect yourself from disaster. At bare minimum, have three months of necessary expenses saved. Our income can be unstable and uncertain, especially for those of us who are self-employed, so our emergency funds should hold larger balances.

I recommend keeping your emergency fund at in its own account at a separate bank to make it harder for you to pull money from. Cut up the bank card, shred the checks, and establish recurring direct deposits scheduled at regular intervals to keep on track. When you pay off each credit card in your debt list, consider diverting the money you would have spent each month on that payment into your savings until you meet your goal.

Investments

"Invest in yourself. Your career is the engine of your wealth."
-Paul Clitheroe

Before you consider investing money into anything, do considerable research. Savings accounts are sure bets, but the gains are minimal. In the same way that your savings doesn't belong in investments, money you want to see a significant return on doesn't belong in savings. However, investing comes with considerable financial risk that most industry professionals can't afford, so I don't advise it unless you have the disposable income available and really know what you're doing.

I advise investing in your most important assets—yourself and your career. Advance your education, learn new skills, attend trade shows, and buy books that will help you develop into a better, more profitable professional. These are things you're certain to see a return on.

Retirement

Retirement planning is not something to push off until "someday." Start planning now, not later. Few salons offer retirement savings options, leaving it up to you to plan for your future. Save early and save as much as possible. No amount is too small.

Again, we return to the employment classification discussion. Misclassification and tax evasion doesn't just hurt you in the short-term; it destroys your future. Social Security, your financial safety net, is based on what you pay into it. Your earnings help you accumulate credits. As of the writing of this book, you get one credit for every $1,200 you earn, and can only earn four credits maximum per year. Each year, the dollar amount you need to earn to be granted a credit increases with average earning levels.

You cannot claim retirement benefits until you have earned forty credits. If you are misclassified and do not pay your self-employment taxes, you are not contributing to Social Security and only prolonging the time it will take for you to collect it.

Before you say, "I'll never see a penny from Social Security anyways," (as some of you young kids like to do) do some research. Even if the SS Trust Fund were to empty entirely, you would still get your benefits because the fund itself is just a supplemental source of Social Security funding; the majority of the benefits being paid out are refunded from taxes collected from current taxpayers. The Trust Fund held excess taxes (overpayments) up until 2010, when the taxes collected weren't enough to fund the benefit payments and money had to be pulled from the Trust Fund, but even then, the Trust Fund's interest earnings are more than enough to cover the losses—at least until 2033, when the Trust Fund is projected to run dry, requiring Congress to agree on a plan to close that gap or reduce the benefits so that the our taxes can cover the benefits. In that worst-case projection, retirees would still be seeing 77% of their benefits, not zero. So, as long as Americans are paying FICA, benefits will be available. However, you shouldn't be relying on Social Security to carry you through retirement. Social Security should supplement your retirement fund.

If you want to be rich in retirement, start contributing early. If you begin in your twenties, you can invest smaller amounts over the course of your career and end up with a larger fund by retirement. Failure to save early will require you to make larger contributions over a shorter period of time.

If your salon offers a 401(k) plan, get enrolled (and play the lottery, you're clearly the luckiest SOB alive if you've been able to find a salon that offers retirement options). In most plans, employers match up to 3% of your salary. Another bonus? The money you put into the fund doesn't get taxed.

Unfortunately, not many salons offer retirement plans, so you may have to establish a Roth IRA. The money you contribute will be taxed, but withdraws won't be. If you're able to contribute $4,000 a year into your IRA for forty years at 8% annual interest—you'll be a millionaire at retirement.

There are tons of retirement investments you can make, from stocks to bonds to mutual funds. (Playing the lottery is not a retirement plan.) Personally, I don't gamble. I'd rather contribute to a sure thing than take any kind of financial risk.

Do some research, read some books, and talk to a financial adviser to determine what options will suit your situation best.

Assess Yourself Before You Wreck Yourself

"'Good enough' isn't good enough anymore. You need to consistently deliver above and beyond your competition and strive for excellence."

Perform self-evaluations periodically to identify your strengths and weaknesses. This will help you monitor where you are in relation to where you want to be and whether you're doing everything necessary to get there or if you need to make adjustments and correct your course.

Where are you in relation to where you want to be? Look at where you are right now in your career. Are you in an environment that encourages growth and continuing education? Are you satisfied with where you are or are you feeling like you want more? What do you expect out of your career? Do you have a goal? If not, make one and set attainable, realistic mini-goals to help you get there. Write them down. Put this list in a place where you can see it every day. Keep one at home and one at work. Set deadlines for these goals and put them on your calendar. Taking steps towards (and accomplishing) career goals will greatly increase your job satisfaction.

Are you still excited about work, or has it become "just a job?" Periodically, every professional goes into a creative slump. Working on clients becomes a chore instead of an adventure. Want to break out of it? Attend a class or push yourself to do something daring and creative. Look through some fashion magazines and let the images you see inspire you to create. Buy a piece of clothing, design an entire look around it, and schedule a shoot. Bringing a concept to reality can get your creative juices flowing. Plus, the images are a nice bonus! Reading fashion or beauty industry blogs can also help keep you interested and motivated.

Are you maintaining your professional standards? How are you dressed and groomed? How do you behave in the salon? Are you setting a good example for your coworkers? Is your attitude likely to attract potential clients?

Are you following the state sanitation laws and regulations? Inspect your workspace and analyze your disinfection protocols. Clients today are very aware of sanitation laws. Don't get a reputation for being unclean.

Is your portfolio updated? How long has it been since you've added new pictures to your portfolio? How about the content on your website? Is everything accurate?

What's the status of your online reputation? Have you been adhering to responsible internet etiquette? Are you on top of those online reviews? Are you engaging your clients and continually generating interest?

If you're a microsalon owner, are you marketing yourself to the best of your abilities? Are you preparing new incentive, referral, and loyalty programs to reward your clients and gain new ones? Are you developing new services to keep your menu interesting and fun?

It can be very easy to slip into bad habits. Assess yourself at least once every six months to keep your career on track. The competitive nature of this industry requires this careful attention and your continued success depends on it. Push yourself to continually improve.

Achieve a Work-Life Balance

Do you suffer from workaholism? A workaholic's mind revolves entirely around work-related issues and responsibilities. They never "clock out" and are compulsively at the expense of career pursuits. For some of us, work can become an addiction. With a job as badass and satisfying as ours, it certainly isn't hard to fall into a workaholic lifestyle, but failure to separate yourself from work and enjoy outside activities can hurt your personal and family relationships. Chronic workaholics will eventually experience burnout.

Burnout is a state of exhaustion and depression that follows a long period of job stress. You won't find work satisfying anymore and you'll feel disillusioned about your career. You may lack the desire to work entirely and even experience physical symptoms like chronic headaches and fatigue.

Before learning about burnout, I referred to these periods as "Craptastic Career Crises." These periods would manifest once every year or two and would last roughly a week, during which I spent my days anxious, aggravated, short-tempered, and second-guessing my career choice. The lifestyle of a compulsive workaholic is unsustainable, so you need to find a middle ground and maintain a healthy work-life balance.

A work-life balance means different things to different people. To me, someone with a healthy work-life balance knows how to prioritize their time between work and stuff that has nothing to do with work. They set firm boundaries and have the discipline to enforce them. They also have the ability to keep things in perspective. In this day and age, many people consider the concept of the work-life balance to be a myth. Fortunately, our industry allows us the freedom to achieve it.

Unlike other professions, nothing is so critically important in the beauty industry that it can't wait until business hours. It's extremely unlikely that you will ever be required to answer emails, make phone calls, or do paperwork off the clock. However, for pushovers, doormats, and those prone to workaholism out there, here are some tips for keeping work where it belongs.

Create a schedule and stick to it. "Oh, I'm sorry, I forgot you leave at 6pm...I booked you a color retouch and a cut."

Talented professionals often have their schedules violated both intentionally and "on accident" by salon owners and receptionists. Often, when schedule violations occur in our industry, they aren't simple little tasks that set you back ten minutes—they're thirty-minute haircuts, one-hour color retouches, or two-hour highlight, cut, and style appointments.

Your employer won't like what I have to say about this: make them cancel those appointments immediately. When you are off, you are OFF. If you allow a trespass like this once, they'll never respect your personal time and these violations will become a routine occurrence.

Make it known up-front in your interview that you write your schedule in stone. You don't stop taking appointments when your book closes out, you walk out the damn door when your book closes out. If you're scheduled to leave at 6pm, your last appointment needs to be scheduled to end at 6pm—not scheduled to begin at 5:45 or 6pm. Failure to draw this line will cause your 9am-6pm shift to become a 9am-9pm (or longer) shift. You'll soon resent your employer and the clients for being so inconsiderate of your time and eventually you'll burn out altogether. Intelligent owners understand the importance of giving their staff personal time.

You deserve to have a life outside of the salon. Don't feel obligated to take late appointments, come in early, or work an extra day to accommodate excess clientele. If you need the money and really want to work a little overtime here and there, that needs to be your decision, not one an employer or client imposes on you. We've all had to work an extra shift to cover a sick coworker now and again, but outside of those emergencies, it's not your job to sacrifice your free time to the business. Learn to say no without guilt or remorse. You don't owe anyone your time off.

If you're consistently being asked to work extra, the salon may be outgrowing the staff's ability to accommodate them. At this point, the owner should a.) jump for joy and b.) start interviewing new employees.

Have a separate work number. Some bosses don't understand what a "weekend" is. Clients might call or text you at extremely inappropriate times. To keep work from encroaching on your personal life, get a separate phone number that forwards to your cell phone and turn off forwarding after business hours. I have a Google Voice number that my readers, work colleagues, and consulting clients can call any time. However, that number won't forward calls to my phone until 9am on weekdays. At 5pm, forwarding automatically disables for the evening.

Leave it at the salon. When you clock out, forget work exists. Take time to appreciate your family and cultivate the relationships you have with the people in your life. Don't let the day's events bleed into your personal time. Difficult clients will break you down, coworkers will aggravate you from time to time, and your boss might decide to take her bad day out on you. When the shift ends, let it end. Don't dwell on it or bring it home. These things happen and they pass.

Keep failures in perspective. The easiest way salon professionals let their work impact their personal time is by dwelling on professional failures.

We work in a creative industry. Like all creative industries, the desirability of our output is subjective. When a client dislikes the outcome of a service it can be devastating, particularly if you're new to the industry. Incidents like that can kill your confidence and the fallout could impact your personal and professional life for a considerable length of time.

When I was a cosmetology student, a friend coerced me into attempting an extremely difficult graduated, asymmetrical bob. When I finished, it looked beautiful—but then she asked me to go shorter. I cut another inch off and discovered that her roots were curling as they dried. Her hair was chemically straightened. Before, the length and density of her hair hid the roots, but without the weight of the length to pull the curl out—the outcome was disastrous, let's just end it right there.

It plagued me for nearly two months. I cried over it. I had nightmares about it. It scarred me. From Halloween until Christmas, there wasn't a single day I didn't think of it and berate myself.

My friend (who is probably the most laid-back person alive) didn't even care that the haircut was so horrible. She shrugged and said, "My bad. Let's just relax my roots and reshape it." I did and it came out great, but knowing the cut was fixed didn't make it any easier for me to move on from the botched cut. It took longer for me to forgive myself than it did for her hair to grow out. I let that bad cut own my life.

In retrospect, I realize that the experience made me a better professional. I learned several valuable lessons. 1.) Consult thoroughly. 2.) Never perform a service if you're unsure of the outcome. 3.) Don't let a mistake define you.

Don't torture yourself like I did. It took me several years to learn this lesson. Not every service will go as planned and even if the service gets properly executed, not every client will love the results. It comes with this job. Accept it and don't let it consume you. Do your best to learn whatever lesson you can from the experience and move forward.

The Interwebs

Protect Your Rep

"Don't be stupid. Was it really necessary to upload those pictures of your drunken table dancing episode? No. All of these things that seem so cool in your early twenties are going to look really inappropriate and immature when viewed by prospective employers or clients. You have a reputation to protect now. Keep both your public and private posts squeaky clean."

Now that you're entering the workforce, the time has come for you to completely wipe everything questionable that's related to you from the internet and build an impressive professional presence. Business owners know how to Google potential job applicants—and many do. What are they going to find when they search for you?

PHASE 1: Out With The Bad—Evaluate, Scrub, and Revoke Permissions

Sign out of Google and all other social networking sites. Google personalizes your search results, so make sure you're signed out before you search for yourself. You want to see what everyone else sees, not what Google thinks you want to see. Google does have a system for removing pages from its search results, so read their Removal Policies.

Check each search result that leads to you. Anything questionable must come down—preferably months in advance of your job search since it takes time for things to be cleared. If you're a member of online communities you'd rather not be associated with professionally, either close your account or alter identifying information.

Analyze your various online profiles carefully. Remember to ensure you're signed out of each social network you belong to. Search for yourself and view your public profiles. Title a blank document with the network's name and take notes on unflattering posts, photos, and videos that need to be removed. Make sure to notate the dates of the posts. This makes it easier to find them when you scrub the profile.

Scrub-a-dub. Sign in, refer to your list, and remove the offending public posts on all sites.

Check the associations you've made. You don't want a potential employer to see that you "Like" "having sex in public" or are a "Fan" of "kicking puppies." Those page owners can change the names of their pages at their discretion.

Sign out again and double-check to make sure the profiles look great.

Deep cleaning. These steps are optional, but recommended.

I work for myself and answer to nobody. As a blogger, writer, and lecturer, I'm expected to be authentic. That authenticity draws people to my blog and sells copies of my books. My "realness" fills my classes and my honesty secures consulting clients. I have a great deal of freedom when it comes to what I say and do because of the nature of my job. You are extremely unlikely to have the same amount of freedom since your career success depends on your ability to attract a diverse range of clients and requires you to represent the salon you work at in the best way possible. So I recommend taking your profile scrubbing a step further than just cleaning up public content.

Comb through every single post you've ever made (both public and private) and delete controversial, offensive, and inappropriate posts. You can carefully manipulate your privacy settings, but I don't recommend that route. First, even if you only share something with a specific group of people, one of them could screenshot the post and circulate it. Secondly, if you read through the Terms of Service of every "free" service you utilize, you'll notice that many of them retain the right to alter their privacy practices at any time at their discretion. While some of these services do provide advance notice of Terms of Service changes, many don't notify you of upcoming changes or require your acceptance of those terms. Your continued use constitutes your acceptance of their TOS. If one of these sites decides to change their policies, your "private" content could suddenly become very public. Technical complications and user errors have been known to cause "protected" content and images to become publicly available without the owner's knowledge. These policies and errors have destroyed marriages and cost people their jobs.

Revoke all tagging and wall posting permissions on social networking sites. In addition to scrubbing your profiles, you also need to protect your profiles from inappropriate posts made by others.

Disable auto-sync and auto-post. Some social networking apps, like Google+, will automatically upload and post your images and videos. If you insist on allowing the app to auto-upload, make sure that everything being uploaded goes into a protected album so you can control the distribution of that content.

PHASE 2: In With The Good—Craft An Impressive Presence

Now that you've polished your existing online reputation, you can work on enhancing and expanding it. If you can, do this well in advance of your job search efforts. Since you will be creating new profiles and websites, you want to allow ample time for them to appear in search results.

Type up a biography/about me. Your bio/about me can be as professional or casual as you want, but you should read it through several times with fresh eyes; once with those of a potential employer and again with those of a potential client.

As an example, mine reads:

"*A licensed cosmetologist and beauty industry advocate, Tina Alberino is a trusted resource, providing a wealth of information and personalized advice. Her areas of expertise include employment law, tax law, ethical salon management practices, and professional development. She is an educator, management consultant, blogger, and freelance columnist whose work can be found on her blog, This Ugly Beauty Business and in The Stylist each month.*"

You'll find this bio for me pretty much everywhere. We'll discuss how to craft yours in detail in the section, "Your Portfolio."

Strike a pose. Professional headshots aren't necessarily required, but will make you look very professional. Utilizing the same image across all platforms will eliminate confusion as well—a must if you have a common name like Jane Smith.

Create public albums of your work. This allows potential clients and employers to see what you can do. Update these albums regularly as your skills evolve and make sure those images are watermarked!

Link every site to your portfolio and vice versa.

Keep it consistent. Aside from your email and other contact info, keeping your profile image and bio consistent is up to you. Personally, I chose to keep everything the same. I know what each site says, where each site points, and what profile images are up, but those preferences are my own. As long as your phone number, email address, portfolio URL, and mailing address are the same on all sites, you're fine.

Only be where you need to be. Social media participation can be a time-consuming pain in the ass. Create a system for monitoring the multiple platforms you're on.

For example, every Monday, my calendar reminds me to check my networks. The calendar event lists these networks in the notes—LinkedIn, Facebook, Twitter, Tumblr, and Pinterest. Each are bookmarked in a "Social" folder on my browser's bookmark bar so I can easily click through each and check any messages or notifications. I recommend setting up a similar system to make monitoring and participating in social media as quick, easy, and painless as possible.

Make Google do your bidding. Search "Google Webmaster Tools Submit URL." Put your URLs into the box and submit them. This prompts Google to send its army of "spiders" to crawl your sites and index them appropriately.

The internet has incredible power, but like Stan Lee says, "With great power comes great responsibility." Harness it to work in your favor.

Get Social

"Post with caution. The immediacy of the internet makes it very easy to destroy yourself in a very fast, very public way."

In addition to having online portfolios, many salon professionals now have profiles on various social and professional networking sites, such as Facebook and LinkedIn. Like most of us, you probably enjoy adding people to your vast list of friends and colleagues. These sites make keeping in touch so much more efficient, after all. But what do you do when your clients want to befriend you online?

In this chapter, you'll learn how to utilize these sites to boost your visibility and increase client retention rates, without damaging your professional image.

What Social Networking Can Do For You

Social networking sites are great business tools when used properly. Status updates and photos keep you and your work at the forefront of your clients' minds and help you get noticed by their friends. Posting special offers generates interest and attracts new clients. Blogging gives you the ability to keep your clients updated on salon news and other important consumer information. Facebook allows you to organize salon events and fundraisers that clients can RSVP to with the click of a button. You can even take advantage of YouTube and upload advertisements for your business if you please. If managed well, the internet can be a priceless asset.

The Issues

The same things that make social networking a great asset also make it a potential liability. You don't want clients to be able to see inappropriate images your best friend posted of that crazy night out a few weekends ago. (You know, the pictures of you taking body shots off a male stripper's washboard abs? Mhm. Good times.) You definitely don't want your clients reading inappropriate posts made by careless friends and family members. If you integrate social media apps with your smartphone, remember that uploads and status updates are instantaneous. Once they're out there, they can (and will) be viewed.

By carefully manipulating the privacy settings, you can potentially limit your clients' exposure to your personal life, but as I said before, the best way to manage social networking is to refrain from posting anything inappropriate to begin with.

This is a great time for you to start changing the way you behave in public as well. Remember: others have cameras and the ability to upload content. Do you want your potential employers (or worse, clients) to stumble on inappropriate content that you have no control over? You can't control others or keep them from recording you, but you do have control over yourself. If you're not acting like a moron, you won't have anything to worry about.

Dos and Don'ts

DON'T lie or compromise. You can't hide on the internet. If you use your real name, real workplace, real hometown, add your relatives and friends and post to their walls, your clients will find you. Don't tell them you don't have an account just because you don't want to "friend" them. If you want to keep your personal and your professional lives separate be honest about it. Start a blog or a Facebook fan page as an alternative to adding clients to your personal profile.

DON'T get hijacked. Protect your account. Change passwords frequently and make certain to log out after each session, especially when using a shared or public computer. If your account links to your smartphone, make sure that the phone itself is locked with a passcode. Never loan your phone out without first logging off your networks. You don't want someone posting things on your profile without your knowledge.

DON'T be an asshat. Never post anything controversial (specifically political opinions or commentary on volatile subjects). I'm not sure when the internet community started thinking that those topics were acceptable, but they aren't. You never know what values your friends, clients, or potential employers hold dear. Your conspiracy theories, anti-vaccine rants, and extremist political views will cost you clients, jobs, and the respect of your peers.

DO stick to universal truths. If you post anything unrelated to work, stick to universal truths: puppies are cute, babies are adorable, coffee is delicious, the world is a beautiful place. Stay positive. Everybody loves that fluffy crap.

DO post images of your work regularly. Posting images of your work will gain you a considerable deal of exposure. Watermark them so others can't rip them off and use them as their own.

DO tag like a boss. Tags allow you to link a profile to a status update. On most networks, to tag someone, you preface their name or username with an @ symbol. Hashtags are labels that allow people to sort posts by category. Preface hashtags with a # symbol.

When you update any of your networks with anything work-related, tag and hashtag appropriately. Example: "@SalonFusion in #Cincinnati now offers #microbond #hair #extensions from @CinderellaHair! Make an appointment with #hairstylist @MindySamson to get your #longhair today!"

Anyone who follows any of those hashtags (Cincinnati, microbond, hair, extensions, hairstylist, longhair) will have your post appear in their feed. They'll also be able to contact the salon, the extension company, and the stylist directly by clicking their linked profiles. On some networks, the post will even appear on the tagged members' profiles (if their permissions allow it), which means people who follow @SalonFusion, @CinderellaHair, or @MindySamson will see the post also.

I don't think I need to explain why this process is incredibly useful.

We're beauty industry workers, not doctors or lawyers. You can post personal photos, status updates, and videos; just don't post anything trashy, inappropriate, controversial, or negative. Participation in social media outlets has become expected. Use it wisely, think before you post, manage your profiles carefully, and represent yourself professionally and it will serve you well.

Respond to Reviews

"Negative online reviewers give you a great gift by venting their grievances publicly; they give you time to craft a deliberate, appropriate response. Unlike a complaint made in person, everyone that sees their negative review will also see how you address it. That negative review and your response to it may net you more clients than all of the positive reviews combined."

So, you've finally gotten your first (and hopefully last) negative review online. Many sites like Yelp allow you to respond to them. You have two choices here: you can attempt to rectify the situation and save face for others that may see the review and your response, or you can flip a bitch and make yourself look like a complete idiot.

Regardless of the situation, you need to show others that you care and are willing to do anything necessary (within reason) to make this client happy. This chapter will give you the tools you need to respond with dignity and grace.

Form Your Response

Apologize. Don't hesitate. Apologize in the first sentence.

"I am so sincerely sorry that you had such a negative experience with me and I would love the opportunity to make it up to you."

Show gratitude. Let the client know that you appreciate that they took the time to write the review (even though you very likely don't appreciate it at all).

"I am truly apologetic that I did not meet your expectations during this visit, but I appreciate that you took the time to write a review. These reviews are incredibly helpful to me, so thank you for communicating to me where I am falling short so that I can rectify the problem immediately!"

Make an offer. Offer the client something for her inconvenience. She may not take up the offer, but at least make an effort.

"If you would be willing to give me another chance, I would love for you to enjoy [SERVICE] for [PERCENTAGE/DOLLARS OFF]!"

Let it be known that you take her complaint seriously and will improve in the future. Make it clear that you have taken action to correct the problem.

"I have addressed the problems you have communicated in your review."

If the problem was caused by a communication issue, say that you are now going to be more conscientious in your communications with others. If it had to do with a bad service, inform the reviewer that you are having your skills reassessed to see if there's room for improvement.

Promise it will NEVER happen again—and mean it. Take the feedback you were given and learn from it. Adapt your business to ensure that nobody ever has a reason to leave a similar negative review in the future.

"I am taking proactive steps to ensure that this issue doesn't arise in the future. I am doing this by ___. I promise you that nobody will ever experience this problem again."

Apologize again. Yeah, really.

"I want you to know how sorry I am about your experience. I do appreciate your feedback and hope that you'll give me another chance to earn back your business."

Don't get confrontational. I have seen responses to reviews that were downright nasty and unprofessional.

"This woman is obnoxious and rude. We're all glad that you're leaving the salon, you miserable cow. We pity the next hairdresser whose chair you sit in."

"This client fails to mention in her review that she ALWAYS tries to haggle the staff for lower prices when she comes, even though the price is clearly communicated to her prior to the start of her service."

"This review is completely bogus. This never happened. This person is a liar."

Don't attempt to explain your side of the story or discredit the reviewer. Even if you know the review is unfounded, unjustified, or made up entirely.

Common Complaints

Pricing. If a client complains about your pricing, showcase the benefits that set your business apart. (I'm assuming the prices are higher because the services/products justify them.) If you offer monthly specials, mention that. Some people just can't afford to (or don't want to) pay higher prices. You shouldn't renegotiate your prices unless they negatively affect your business on a massive scale. If one or two clients complain about the price every so often, fine. What you really need to look out for are people who complain about the services they receive.

Rude staff. Tell the reviewer you have reprimanded the person responsible. In booth rental situations, this can be difficult to deal with since your "coworkers" can't be held accountable for their behavior, but do what you can to ensure that the client will not have the same experience again should they return.

Bad services. Make a commitment to continuously improve. Continuing education doesn't have to cost tons of money. Find a mentor or partner with another professional for practice sessions.

Dirty salon. In a booth rental arrangement, this could become a serious problem. I have left salons because they failed to commit to keeping the place clean. If you're renting with a group of slobs, consider finding a new location where the renters are more considerate and respectful of their workplace.

Miscommunication. Clarify the miscommunication in the review. Sometimes, they are honest mistakes. If you said something in error, apologize and explain the reason why you may have been confused. Never blame the reviewer.

Your response should be classy, upbeat, apologetic, and humble. Others should read the response and think, "What a great way for them to handle that situation!" Don't let potential clients see you rage out on a customer online. Keep it together and not only will you salvage the relationship with the reviewer, but you might actually gain the respect and admiration of potential clients who read the response.

Consider Your Source

"There are a considerable number of vultures, parasites, and con artists in our industry—particularly in education, consulting, and business services—who make their livings off the naivety, gullibility, and passion of salon professionals."

The technological revolution brought us awesome things; among them, 24/7 access to both formal and informal career education, uploaded regularly by people from around the globe. Take your pick—there are blogs, videos, forums, webinars, and picture tutorials. From Youtube to Pinterest to eHow, at any given moment you can find ten thousand (plus) solutions to whatever problem you're experiencing, but can these resources be trusted in an environment where anyone can publish anything whenever they please? Who is on the other side of the monitor? How can you separate valid information from garbage? The internet can be a treacherous place full of liars, amateurs, charlatans, and snake oil merchants. You need to know how to critically analyze information from all sources so you can avoid falling victim to bad information.

When dealing with online information and when considering continuing education or coaching opportunities, consider the source. Who is giving the information? Can you find any evidence that this person has some authority or expertise? What specific qualifications make the information valid?

Too often, these "authorities" are not licensed or experienced at all. In many cases, there is no way to identify a particular author or check credentials. For all you know, the person doling out career advice on the other side of the monitor could be someone with absolutely no industry experience. Unlicensed "DIY-ers" frequently share technique tutorials—if you saw the DIY-er showcasing how to "safely" remove acrylic nail enhancements by prying them off with dental floss, you know exactly how dangerous the perpetuation of some of these amateur tutorials have the potential to be. (If you haven't seen it, Google it if you dare.)

That being said, some of these tutorials (particularly those regarding nail art and makeup application techniques) can be incredibly helpful to both established professionals and newly licensed professionals. Be sure to remember your own state's laws and regulations regarding your scope of practice when it comes to more questionable, advanced professional techniques—like ingrown toenail filing, eyelash perming, or certain chemical services. Services or procedures that are legal to perform in another state or country may not be permissible in yours. Unfortunately, the people creating this content are often unaware that regulations even exist, let alone what your particular regulations are—so verify that a particular practice is legal before integrating it into your service menu.

When evaluating information that pertains to tax or employment law, check the post date to verify that its current. If reference links are provided, check them. Find out where the writer pulled their information from. The information cited must be verifiable through legitimate sources.

A lot of my subscribers consider me to be legitimate source, but I disagree. (I'm not being humble here, just honest.) Sure, I'm informed and I have a reputation for providing accurate, trustworthy information, but I'm not a lawyer, accountant, or government representative.

I consider the links I provide that lead directly to federal statutes to be the most legitimate sources available. Their authenticity can't be argued with. They are regularly updated and even minor changes are usually publicized in popular news outlets.

Unfortunately, unlike the federal websites, many state statute websites are not updated regularly so for the really important local stuff you need to make a call to the correct state agency for a definitive, current answer. Statutes change a lot, so even if you are reading information recently authored by a trustworthy professional, always ensure to check the statutes since ultimately, you are the one responsible for ensuring your own compliance.

Regarding non-technical education, specifically business advice or coaching, consider the source's motivation. What does the source of the information have to gain by your acceptance of their information? Who do they affiliate with and why? A source's affiliations often lend clues to their bias. For example, an educator that works for or is sponsored by a major product company has an interest in promoting that company. That interest might conflict with their ability to provide you with honest, accurate information.

Evaluation of business advice requires some critical thinking—particularly if the source has a system or service to sell you. If the source can't demonstrate the legitimacy of their opinions and strategies with logic, rational explanation, or case studies, the odds are pretty good that they're selling you empty fluff. Move on to someone with a better reputation.

Be vigilant, cautious, and selective about whose information you trust. The internet can be a great resource when you know how to critically analyze the information you're presented with!

Keep Smiling

This bonus section has been written to motivate you. When you feel discouraged, angry, or upset, please refer to it.

Empowerment and Entitlement: Know the Difference

"If all salon owners are such greedy, incompetent morons, why are you still working for anyone at all? You might be the best stylist on Earth but you certainly aren't winning any awards for intellectual prowess if you've been in this industry long enough to convince yourself that the generalized assumptions you make about salon owners are true but still have yet to actually do something about it."

What is your relationship with the business you work with? How do you treat the entity that ensures your continued welfare? Is it a child you nourish, support, and provide guidance to or is it that annoying guy who you've friend-zoned but is always there for you to use at your convenience? Most salon professionals are dedicated to their salons. They go out of their way to build it up, maintain it, keep it clean, and keep it functioning. Some of them even do these things at great personal sacrifice (commendable, but not something I recommend).

However, some professionals view the salon they work at as a tool they use to satisfy their needs. Their motives are entirely selfish. The salon's problems aren't their problems; they're the salon owner's problems. That's why she's the owner, right? They believe all they have to do is show up and do their clients, and they'll be damned if they'll do it for anything less than 50% because they have *pride*.

To a degree, these assertions are right. Salon staff work because they need to make an income. The salon isn't their business and managing it isn't their job. The owner really should be bearing the bulk of the responsibility—but it takes an entire staff to effectively run a salon and keep it successful. Those "proud" professionals are going about getting what they want in the least productive way possible.

You will encounter entitled professionals with superiority complexes who mistakingly believe that every owner who has ever had the supreme privilege of employing them should just throw money at them while simultaneously kissing the ground they tread on. Do not turn into one of them.

Often, these professionals are not as hot as they think they are. They might be great at what they do, but if they come into the salon with the incorrect assumption that they are somehow better than everyone in it, they have failed as an employee, as a professional, and as a human being. It doesn't matter how big of a book that professional brings or how many years of experience she has, with an attitude like that she is a vicious cancer that will eat away at whatever establishment she works in. People like this kill morale and suck the life from the business. They see the salon as an ATM. They don't give a shit if the salon struggles, as long as the owner pays them whatever insane commission they've demanded.

A lot of these professionals consider themselves to be "empowered" professionals who "know their worth." They aren't. They're tyrants—entitled, parasitic idiots with no clue how this industry works.

To be fair, their development into this deplorable breed of asshole probably wasn't entirely their fault. One day long, long ago, all of them were fresh, starry-eyed professionals with crisp new licenses and rose-colored dreams of how fantastic their careers would be—just like you. Their dreams were chipped away, a little at a time, by a long line of really crappy, exploitative owners until the day what remained of their dreams shattered right in front of them. That day was the day they said, "I've had enough."

But they went about ten steps too far and became the monsters that created them.

I'm a huge champion of professional pride. I'll be the first person to preach the importance of knowing your worth and standing up for yourself when someone else tries to trample on you or push you down—but it is one thing to carry yourself professionally with dignity and self-respect; it's another to forcibly demand respect by abusing others or holding them hostage. The former makes you a queen, the latter makes you a terrorist. What these monsters call "pride" isn't pride. It's superiority. It's arrogance and conceit, selfishness and misplaced contempt. Ultimately, it's poor character and a complete lack of integrity.

Their income may be considerable and their following may be great, but because of that lack of character, they're not valuable employees. All of the professional accomplishments they're so eager to spout off to anyone that will listen are worthless because their respect and consideration are conditional on everyone else's unconditional compliance with their demands.

When you're an employee, you don't work "at" a salon, you work "for" a salon. Should you be managing it or performing charity work for the owner without guaranteed hourly pay out of the goodness of your heart? Hell no. In America, nobody works for free. However, you should never operate under the delusional belief that you deserve more money than the business you work for, because you don't. You're at the salon to earn money doing what you love and to ensure that the salon's doors remain open for as long as possible so that you and your coworkers can continue to make a living there. If you're only there to bleed the salon dry, you're a detestable piece of human garbage that has no place in this industry.

I've noticed a common trait with these elitist professionals over the course of my career—none of them have ever owned a salon. They have no idea what the actual costs of doing business are. They believe that every owner is some overlord whose only interest is working them and their coworkers like slaves, while they swim in a sea of gold coins in the back room like Scrooge McDuck in DuckTails. I've seen those owners first-hand. They do exist. However, many owners want the salon and the employees in it to thrive. An owner shouldn't be begrudged for wanting to succeed if they're earning that success ethically.

Admittedly, I hold owners to high standards and I'm brutal on them when they fall short. As I said on the back cover, this book is a collection of harsh lessons—many of which I learned through experience. I've been misclassified, manipulated, lied to, and stolen from. I've been treated like a slave and disrespected by employers who weren't worthy of my time or skills. Now that I work in consulting and career coaching, I'm more exposed to employment abuses than ever. If anyone has a right to be jaded, it's me; but I'm not. Great salon owners exist and more are coming into the industry every day. This industry has been changing for the better and I'm happy to be a part of that change. I urge you not to let your bad experiences break you.

Never allow yourself to become that miserable, selfish, entitled bitch. You're better than that.

Facts

"A good deal of the injustices salon professionals fall victim to could be prevented with a little education and self-esteem."

These aren't affirmations. They're facts. I'm not going to give you some false mantra to repeat to yourself every day in the hopes that it will someday magically come true. Read these statements until you get it.

You're a professional, not a charity worker. Your time, experience, and talent are valuable. You deserve to be appropriately compensated. Nobody works for free.

What you do matters more than you realize. You are more than the service you provide. You're more than your education, the color you apply, and the products you recommend. On the surface, your profession might seem superficial, but you make people feel better about themselves every single day. You give the gift of self-esteem. It matters.

You're more intelligent and capable than you give yourself credit for. Never allow yourself to feel helpless, useless, or worthless. You're a competent adult. You are not a pawn. You are not powerless. You are capable of enacting change—in your personal life, in your professional life, at your work, and in your community. You can make a difference.

Asking for help does not make you a bad professional. Never be afraid to ask for help or to seek out a mentor or coach to pull you through hard times.

You deserve to be treated with respect. You're too smart and too valuable to allow yourself to be victimized by an opportunistic salon owner or made to suffer a hostile work environment.

You're not a slave or a servant. Clients and employers who treat you as such do not deserve you. Dismiss them.

You chose to serve others out of love and compassion. You could have taken any job in the world, but you chose one that allows you to make others feel better about themselves. This is admirable and should be commended.

What you do is a career, not a hobby. Never allow others to belittle your chosen profession. It's your source of income and deserves to be taken seriously.

You are not perfect and nobody should expect you to be. All you can ever do is your best. You can (and should) strive for perfection but do so with the knowledge that you will never achieve it. Perfection is unattainable. Don't be discouraged by this. You're human. Admit your shortcomings and accept your personal limitations. Do your best every day and be satisfied with your achievements. Don't dwell on your failures. Keep your expectations of yourself reasonable. You can't be everything to everyone.

Your Happiness Equation

"Your Happiness Equation" began as a singular, motivational blog post but evolved into a series. The response I received from the subscribers was tremendous. These posts quickly became the most widely distributed and most frequently hit on This Ugly Beauty Business. I have cleaned them up considerably and expanded upon them for the readers of this book. I sincerely hope you find this chapter as helpful as my subscribers have.

Are You "That Girl?"

"Aren't we playing for the same team?"

We've all worked with "That Girl"—the one that shows up early, works late, and has energy and enthusiasm in excess. She's the one with all the bright ideas for salon events, new services, and strategies to streamline the salon's operations. She dresses spectacularly and is always the picture of professionalism. She's motivated and takes initiative. Love her or hate her—she's going places.

A lot of owners see That Girl as a threat to their leadership. They interpret her enthusiastic suggestions as backhanded criticisms of their management style. Many owners eventually see That Girl as some breed of mutineer in the making. These owners often butt heads with That Girl and fire her before she can become a competitor. I've seen it happen over and over again. I've even been ordered to fire That Girl by insecure salon owners more than once and have argued against it every time.

You want to know the reasons these owners had for ordering me to terminate That Girl?

"If we don't get rid of her, she'll end up being our competitor." Insecurity.

"I'm the owner, not her." Intimidation.

"She isn't as great as she thinks she is." Jealousy.

Salon owners fail to realize that firing That Girl will not stop her from reaching for the stars. They'll never kill that spark. They'll never break her because she's bulletproof and she's in this industry to stay.

That Girl is a natural-born leader, and those professionals are to be coveted, not discarded like trash or excommunicated like traitors. Instead of letting their ambition, motivation, or ability to take initiative intimidate them, salon owners should be helping That Girl develop them. By firing That Girl, they ship a massive asset directly into a competing salon owner's hands. That new salon owner might actually utilize That Girl's talents properly.

That Girl is the definition of management material. She needs challenges and thrives from seeing the business grow. To her, failures are valuable lessons that motivate her to work harder. Successes are incredible victories that encourage her to bring the business to the next level.

Are you That Girl in your salon?

My first employer recruited me into this industry when I was fifteen years old because I was That Girl. She utilized my talents, helped me grow professionally, and made me the professional I am today. She taught me everything I know about salon management and how to treat people.

Three years later, when Hurricane Charley destroyed our salon and my mentor lost her battle with cancer, I ventured out alone in search of a new job with obscene naivety. Everything was sunshine and rainbows! I had a great career in a wonderful industry where my hard work was appreciated and well-rewarded! My job was the best! Surely my professional life would be eternally wonderful! Right?

Wrong. The next two years were torture. I learned first-hand how new professionals without mentors experience this industry. Nothing about it was pleasant.

My subsequent employers weren't like my first. They didn't appreciate my input or my hard work. I was accustomed to working without direction or instruction. If something needed to be done, I just did it. My first boss always said my ability to take initiative was an admirable quality.

Under new ownership, I found myself getting yelled at for dusting shelves, arranging retail displays, and refilling backbar without "asking for permission." I thought, Since when do I have to ask permission to do my job?

"If I wanted to have the salon's work featured on models on runways at Sarasota Fashion Week, I would handle it. I don't need you trying to run this business for me." My friend is a coordinator for the show. She asked if I'd relay the offer...

"What is this IRS shit about employment classification? Don't you think I know how to run my business?" If you did, you wouldn't have everyone in here misclassified. You'd know that if you looked at the packet of paperwork I provided you with. Sorry for trying to keep you from being audited.

I spent that small portion of my early career being treated like an enemy, eyed with suspicion, and getting "put into my place" for being competent, motivated, and self-directed. I was even accused of corporate espionage once (yes, really). I spent nearly every day defending myself, not just against the owner, but against the attacks of my disdainful coworkers also.

"You're stupid if you think doing all that extra work is going to get you a raise or something."

"I hope you know that you're never going to get promoted, no matter how hard you work here. Why do you bother?"

"I remember when I was new, young, and naive as a freshly fallen leaf. You're so green, girl. This industry will eat you alive."

I could do no right. On the rare occasions my hard work was acknowledged by whatever asshole owner I was working for, the backlash from my coworkers was brutal.

"What are you trying to prove? You're making all of us look bad."

"You're an asskisser."

"Aren't you a loyal little pet?"

I made the mistake of desperately trying to befriend my coworkers. I swept their hair, shampooed their clients, worked late for them, took their reception shifts and their Sunday shifts. Nothing worked. Instead of gratitude, they gifted me with more hostility.

"My client booked with you! That's the real reason you're helping us! You're poaching clients!" (I wasn't.)

"Get Tina off the front desk; she's stealing walk-ins." (I was nearly fired because of that accusation. Thankfully, I was able to prove that I hadn't taken a new client—walk-in or otherwise—in three weeks, which pissed them off more because not only did I not get fired, they discovered that I had established a following of regulars.)

"You're just trying to win points with the boss. You're transparent." (I was trying to win points with them at that point. I had long since learned the owners were a lost cause.)

I was depressed and fed up. What the hell was I doing wrong? I was loyal, reliable, and hard-working. I just wanted to help make the salon owner's life easier and keep the salon running smoothly for everyone. Weren't we all on the same team? Why the hell was I being treated like a criminal?

One day, it hit me. The owners and the staff felt threatened. I never earned a client complaint. My retention and referral rates were the highest in the salon. I consistently exceeded performance goals, and all of them hated me for it.

Weak, insecure salon owners don't recognize how big of an asset That Girl is. Professionals who have worked under that kind of incompetent management don't thrive. They become just as miserable as the owners who shoot them down every day. These owners need their staff to be incompetent. It's how they exert their dominance and stroke their ego. These damaged coworkers and owners look at That Girl and see the various places they're falling short. Instead of becoming motivated to improve themselves, they do whatever they can to drag That Girl down into the miserable pit they're all wallowing in.

Don't become a victim like I did.

I learned a lot during that experience and I came through it greatly improved. My next job interview went down very differently. I was upfront in my resume about my dedication and my work ethic. I interviewed the owner intensely. I explained to her that I had experience in management and was not interested in working somewhere that wouldn't utilize my strengths. I was young but I was trained by the best and damn good at my job. I had no problem proving so, but I wasn't about to allow myself to be taken for granted and disrespected again.

She hired me and I enjoyed another three and a half years of bliss before I moved to Tampa. Since I asserted myself in that interview, I have not been mistreated. A few owners tried and failed, but because I knew my worth, I knew better than to tolerate it.

If you're That Girl, you need to start commanding respect also. Starting now.

And if you're one of those asshole coworkers, start treating That Girl better. She may end up being your boss one day.

Eliminate The People You Could Do Without

"Miserable people will consume you. If they don't bring value to your life, they don't deserve to be a part of it. We deserve better than 'mediocre.' So, surround yourself with people who love and accept you—the people who bring out the best parts of you and make you a better version of yourself."

I'm a very different person than I was ten years ago. You start to figure out who you are in your late-twenties. Your vision of how you want your life to be begins to fully materialize and you're finally at an age where you can take progressive steps to make that vision a reality.

Unfortunately, not everyone matures at the same rate. Some people don't seem to mature at all. In itself, this can be mildly irritating if you're somehow forced to be exposed to them regularly. It can be infuriating if "those people" feel the need to sabotage your life to pull you down with them.

I've always been a forthright, honest person—and not necessarily by choice. It's my nature. I've had people question whether or not my blunt honesty were a psychological disability or social functioning impairment, but I'm pretty sure it's the result of several biological factors combined with the way I chose to interpret and respond to my experiences over the course of my lifetime.

I'm different, not broken. That makes me special, not socially handicapped.

As I've said, I have high expectations of myself and hold others to high expectations as well, but I wasn't always this way. I spent a vast portion of my late childhood and eight years of my early adulthood compromising those expectations for others. They were the worst years of my life.

Throughout the experience, I thought I was doing the right thing. I told myself that my integrity and loyalty were admirable qualities and although I was miserable and could feel myself slowly growing colder, more reserved, caustically cynical, resentful, and bitter—I took comfort in the fact that I was making sacrifices that would surely be recognized and appreciated at some point in the future.

They weren't.

Each transgression against me cut two ways—I hated the transgressor for doing it and I hated myself for allowing it. Eventually, my skin thickened into dense scar tissue and the transgressions no longer hurt. I quit caring. I retreated further into myself, deeper than ever before and I stayed there.

I learned a lot about myself and a lot about sacrifice and loyalty—specifically, how freely granting unearned loyalty and making repeated sacrifices for someone who didn't deserve or appreciate them can destroy you a little bit at a time. I also learned a lot about happiness and how selfishness can be an extremely positive quality. I learned never to gamble my happiness on a potential payout that may never come.

I was young and stupid with a distorted view of what the word "loyalty" really meant. At that time, loyalty was defined as: "*n. To constantly strive and sacrifice to secure another person's happiness and approval without expectation of gratitude or reciprocation and to take abuse indefinitely without complaint."*

I'm a better person now—a harder person, but definitely a better one. The only regret I have is that it took me so long to learn these lessons.

Aside from those two isolated incidents, I have never had problems eliminating people entirely from my life, permanently. I don't form sentimental attachments to anything and that includes people. One of my shortcomings (according to others) is that it doesn't take much at all for me to write someone off for good. Personally, I don't see this as a shortcoming. Adults cannot be genuinely sorry for a trespass committed knowingly against another person. If you did something with the knowledge that what you were doing was going to hurt someone else, you can't claim to be "sorry" for it after the fact.

Genuine remorse cannot follow premeditation. At some point, the asshole weighed the risks against the benefits and chose to move forward. If they didn't weigh the consequences against the benefits, they're either too inconsiderate or too stupid for you to have associated with in the first place. False apologies are an insult to your intelligence. They aren't sorry they did what they did—they're sorry they have to suffer some sort of consequence for it.

I see everything in formulas. That's how my brain has always worked. It doesn't take a lot for me to calculate that some people don't fit into the equation that determines overall positive, meaningful contribution to my life. If their variable in that equation results in a negative, neutral, or negligible result—they go. Forever. Bye bye. No great loss. Sorry, not sorry.

I feel no remorse. I have no regrets. Neither should you.

You don't owe anyone your forgiveness. You don't owe them your time or energy. You aren't required to participate in their mind games or allow them to attempt to manipulate you. You can and should just walk away. Close that door and forget they existed, because from this point forward, they don't exist and you're better for it.

Until someone proves to me otherwise, I operate under the assumption that this life is the only one we have. As far as I know, when it is over it is over forever. Those with religious inclinations disagree, and that's fine, but there's no reason why you should allow others to attempt to sabotage your happiness for any period of time, whether you believe that death is the permanent end or a second beginning (or third, fourth, or fifth beginning—for those that believe in reincarnation). My theistic friends have often asked, "What if you're wrong?" I ask, "What if I'm right? Do you want to spend any portion of the life you know you have as a victim of others who have no respect for your happiness? I don't."

Your religion shouldn't factor in to your Happiness Equation when evaluating whether or not someone fits into your current existence. So ask yourself: "If this life is the only one I will ever have and each second is ticking closer to the hour of my permanent death, do I really want to spend any portion of my precious time dealing with this person in any capacity?" The answer will always be no, because if the person were truly contributing to your life in a meaningful way, you wouldn't feel the need to ask this question in the first place.

In the Happiness Equation, negative variables tend to come with exponents. You might be able to see that this person is a problem, but you're unlikely to be seeing the various ways they're negatively impacting your life until that person has been removed from it entirely. With each subtraction I have made, my overall satisfaction with my life has increased exponentially. If your life isn't continually trending upward, you need to be making changes.

Memorize these sentences and speak them when necessary. Being genuine requires speaking your mind earnestly without reservation. Be direct. Never cushion your words or lower yourself to sugar-coating.

"I will not be baited into your drama."

"I will not subject myself to your manipulation."

"I refuse to be taken advantage of."

"I am not a fool and I won't be treated like one."

"I am better than this and I deserve better than you."

"I am not a tool to be used at your convenience."

"This friendship/relationship/job is no longer serving my best interests."

"I am done."

Never compromise your expectations for anyone. Write them in stone and don't deviate. Have the confidence to defend yourself and shape your own happiness. Look at your Happiness Equation and figure out who/what is dragging you down and drop it. Your life is the single most precious thing you have and you alone have the power to make beneficial changes to it whenever you want. Be selfish and don't apologize.

Letting anyone compromise your level of satisfaction (or worse, allowing them to attempt to sabotage it) is committing a crime against yourself. Hold people responsible for their actions, then let them go for good. You are nobody's bitch and martyrdom has been out of style for centuries.

What Are You Compensating For and Why?

I have some social functioning difficulties. Specifically, I have issues recognizing social cues, evaluating facial expressions, interpreting vocal tones, and deciphering body language. I am tactless and my direct, blunt honesty takes some getting used to. I have social anxiety I refuse to treat with medication.

Please don't offer me solutions. I don't require them. My one experience with SSRIs wasn't a good one. It did its job—it altered my personality. Here's the problem: I like my personality. My flaws make me who I am. I'm imperfect but that's what makes me unique. I'm cool with that.

However, for a long time I wasn't.

My years in school were difficult at best (as they are for most socially crippled bookworms who would rather play Dungeons & Dragons than sneak out and get wasted at the beach). When I started high school, I decided that I wanted my last four years to be better than the prior eight years. I dumbed down my language ("I'm impartial" became "whatever"), dressed differently, feigned interest in shit I found truly trivial ("Shoes! Boys! TV! Squeeee!"), and tried to emulate others so I could "fit in." I spent far too long trying to integrate with the average.

Despite repeated failures, I didn't cease this idiotic practice until recently.

Even after high school, I saw my personality quirks as weaknesses that I desperately needed to compensate for somehow. I compensated by erring on the side of caution. Silence when in doubt. Excessive politeness as a default position. Apologizing when uncertain.

I wasn't walking on eggshells, I was tiptoeing through a minefield.

Trying to "blend" proved to be more stressful than it was worth. Not only was it getting me nowhere, it made me unhappy. I felt fake and even more isolated than normal. I wasn't Tina, I was some meat-puppet version of myself that I carefully directed every second of every interaction. It was exhausting.

It doesn't matter how hard you try to keep from giving people a reason to judge you—some people will always find something. Ask yourself: Would you rather be hated for who you are or accepted for someone you're not? For me, the answer was clear. Compensating didn't suit me.

So, what are you compensating for and why are you doing it? Is it really in your best interest to go out of your way to accommodate others to make up for your perceived shortcomings?

We're not talking about basic consideration here. Consideration is important in both your personal and business relationships. We're talking about crossing the line that separates consideration from concession.

Instead of trying to counterbalance your faults, be honest about them and accept them. Nobody is perfect—not you and not the people whose judgment you fear. It is unfair of them to expect anything from you that they're unable or unwilling to give themselves. This doesn't just apply to perfection; it applies to honesty, courtesy, respect, and appreciation. Reciprocity isn't a one-way street.

Our strengths and weaknesses are what make us different and allows us to compliment each other. Admitting where you fall short shows strength of character. It is very liberating to be able to look at yourself objectively. If your faults are holding you back, make the choice to improve upon them—but unless you're making that decision yourself to serve your best interests, the gesture is empty.

The Power, Strength, and Freedom Behind "I Don't Know"

"I'm a human, not Google."

If you try to fail and succeed, which have you done?

What color will a Smurf turn when strangulated?

If the professor on Gilligan's Island can make a radio out of coconuts, why can't he fix a hole in a boat?

Don't fool yourself into thinking you have the answer to these questions. They're ridiculous and unanswerable. The only correct answer is, "I don't know."

For some reason, many people have a serious problem with speaking those words. It can be almost painful. Somehow, a lot of us have been programmed by our teachers, our employers, and our peers to believe that admitting ignorance is a display of weakness, stupidity, or incompetence. It's a personal failure and failure is unacceptable.

Whenever you're tempted to fake your way through a question, remember that if the person asking the question knew the answer to begin with, it's highly unlikely that they would be asking you for it. So, don't be afraid to say, "I don't know." You aren't admitting failure. You won't be letting anyone down.

Nobody has all the answers and for someone else to expect you to have all of the answers is unfair, unrealistic, and unreasonable—so release yourself from that burden and enjoy the bliss of ignorance when necessary. Embrace it.

Uncertainty is full of mystery and possibility. Creating theories and exploring possibilities opens up the room for productive discussion. At the same time, it communicates to others in your company that it is okay to not know. If you're a salon owner or manager, this is an important lesson for your staff to learn and it's critical that you be the one to demonstrate it. You need to show them that you're willing and able to admit your limitations so that they can feel more comfortable doing the same when necessary. Uncertainty stimulates growth and jump starts creativity. By removing that burden of expectation from yourself and your staff, you are cultivating an environment that encourages confidence and inspires others to learn.

Don't fake your way. It is far better to risk looking incompetent periodically than to be exposed as a fool regularly. Saving face just isn't that important and allowing others to burden you with their high expectations is a happiness killer. It causes stress and uncertainty—both of which you don't need in your life.

Eliminate that pressure. You don't need it. It's weighing down the result of your Happiness Equation.

How to be Unhappy

"In order to be happy, you have to be unhappy (at least a little bit)."

Now that I've addressed the variety of ways you can negate your unhappiness and maximize your overall satisfaction, we'll discuss how unhappiness is actually an important variable in your Happiness Equation that fuels your happiness directly. (It's going to make sense, I promise. Stick with me here.)

I thought happiness was an unattainable thing. It was something to aspire to but impossible to achieve—one of those "shoot for the moon, land somewhere in the universe in the general vicinity of the moon," kind of things.

I was both wrong and right. You can achieve happiness, but you should never achieve complete satisfaction. To be truly satisfied with everything is an end to upward mobility. A large portion of your happiness stems from the improvement or correction of the imperfect.

Simply put: happiness can be boring.

Making things better makes us feel good.

When everything is perfect—what do you do? You stagnate, professionally and personally. This is why continuing education classes are loaded in every trade show. None of us want to stagnate. We thirst for knowledge, for change, for improvement.

Unhappiness is the strongest motivator out there. Unhappiness inspires you to aspire to perfection, solve problems, and to make things better. It drives your creativity every day of your career, whether you realize it or not.

Don't believe me? Consider this: if people were happy living in the dark and using fire for winter heating, would electricity have been invented? If people were cool with sending letters or telegrams, would we have phones or the internet today? If we were truly satisfied with the speed and convenience of using horses for travel, would we have planes, trains, or cars? If we were fine with polish that chipped off after three days, would we have gel polish?!

No. We only have these awesome things because someone said, "This sucks. I'll bet I can make this better somehow." Someone was unhappy with the method of doing things and that unhappiness inspired them to come up with more convenient solutions. A lot of innovations ultimately stem from some degree of dissatisfaction.

Every client who sits in your chair is dissatisfied when they arrive. They desire improvement and you deliver it. I'm willing to bet that "fixing" whatever your client considers imperfect contributes significantly to your own job satisfaction.

It's not enough to just be dissatisfied with everything all the time. In order to take full advantage of your dissatisfaction and transform it into happiness, you have to take steps to improve whatever causes the dissatisfaction and reap the feel-good benefits of knowing that you did something awesome—no matter how small that "something" is.

Identify the things in your life that could use improvement and systematically address each one of them.

Develop a strategy and tackle the items on the list with righteous fury.

When you accomplish your goals, celebrate them. No task is meaningless or without merit. For example, today I made three meals for my family, did two loads of dishes and a load of laundry, cleaned up some of my lecture content for my trade show classes next year, wrote 2,000 words for this book, edited my third draft for my column in *The Stylist*, and wrote a blog post. I have been productive and that feels awesome! +20 to my Happiness Equation today.

Even simple improvements like replacing those old, outdated window treatments you hate or developing a more efficient system for tracking gift card sales will contribute to your happiness and personal sense of accomplishment—and the satisfaction gained from a job well done can't be understated.

So, get critical. Focus your hatred...then get productive. Never settle for "good enough." There's always room for improvement or advancement. Be the one that makes it happen and be sure to congratulate yourself afterwards—right before you move on to the next thing.

Dissatisfied people change the world; be one of them.

Maintain Forward Momentum

"Negative experiences aren't meaningless if you learn something from them."

As much as I hate to see bad things happen to people in this industry, I also hate seeing professionals dwell in their own misery and refuse to take responsibility for their portion of (or learn from) whatever nightmare they endured. This chapter was written to help you move on from a negative professional experience.

Stop Crying. The severity of what happened is irrelevant. Wasting time feeling sorry for yourself accomplishes nothing. Don't waste a single second placing blame on others or playing the victim. Those behaviors are unproductive and self-destructive. Make a decision to end this useless behavior immediately and instead use that time to start taking steps to rectify your situation.

Take Responsibility. You played a part, whether you know it or not. Think hard about how your choices may have contributed to this. It's possible someone chose to make you a victim and there was nothing you could have done to foresee or prevent it—it happens. However, if you can identify where you went wrong, you need to acknowledge that and make a promise to yourself never to allow it to happen again. Blaming others might make you feel better for a little while, but ultimately, shirking responsibility like that implies that you have no control over anything, and that's a really inaccurate, depressing assumption to live by.

Learn. Instead of letting this experience make you miserable, squeeze a lesson from it. See this experience not as a loss, but as an investment in your professional education. Consider yourself a better person from this point on for having endured it.

Gain Perspective. This singular event doesn't define you. You aren't a bad person or a stupid person—even if you played a substantial role in the event. Maybe you made a mistake (or a series of them). So what? Mistakes are how we learn, grow, and improve moving forward. Don't brand yourself with titles like, "idiot," "naive," or "bitter unlikable loner whose passing shall not be mourned." The pity party has ended, remember? Be nice to yourself. See the bright side: you've learned where you went wrong and you know how to prevent it from happening again! Your user/abuser gave you the gift of knowledge and increased awesomeness—that silly fool.

Take Control. Bad things are going to happen to you—that's just how life works. Assholes exist. Accept it. You can't control the actions of others any more than you can control the weather, but you can control your own actions. Continue your forward momentum by proactively changing your own life and directing your future. You control your destiny! Go forth, make a plan, and make that destiny legendary.

Embrace Freedom. You're an adult! You can eat ice cream for breakfast! You can get in your car and drive to Vegas on a whim! Nobody owns you, you rockstar son of a bitch! Bad things happen sometimes, but it's cool. You know why? Because you have the freedom to flip that jerk the double-bird and blow $50 on gourmet chocolates, that's why. If you continue to let the negative experience occupy space in your mind or affect your life, you are giving the Bad Guys what they want. Letting them win is unacceptable. Don't give them that kind of power over you.

If you fail to learn from your experiences and refuse to turn your misery into proactivity, you're only hurting yourself—and you deserve better than that.

Before You Throw in the Towel...

"We all have those days where we sit down, wonder why we're still in this industry, and struggle to come up with reasons. Anyone who says they haven't is a damn liar."

This industry can be rough, especially when you're a fresh new graduate. A lot of owners take advantage of employees, clients can get vicious and cut you down, your coworkers might be catty and cruel. Even veterans have a hard time staying positive during the dark times. All of us have considered giving up for good at least once.

For now, get your license away from the paper shredder. Make yourself a cup of coffee, sit down in a quiet room, take a deep breath, and read this chapter. I'm not going to downplay your struggles and disappointments or make you feel silly by "putting things in perspective." (We all know that crap doesn't work anyways.) Hopefully, by the time you're done reading this chapter you will feel empowered and at ease and better equipped to make that major decision. Sometimes it helps to have someone tell you that you aren't alone, you aren't crazy, and you are capable of taking charge of your career.

You are your own boss, regardless of your employment situation. A lot of owners feel like their business owns them (I know that I do sometimes). Employees feel like they're at the mercy of their salon owner. Don't fall into this false belief. You alone control your destiny. You are the boss of you. If the salon you own or work at no longer serves your needs or makes you happy, you have the power to leave—and if you're miserable, you absolutely should.

You owe nothing. I don't care what contracts you signed or how close you are with your boss, your clients, or your staff. You don't owe anybody anything—not your time, not your energy, and certainly not your unconditional loyalty. You're a free human. Don't let others guilt trip you into giving more of yourself than you're willing or able to give. You are nobody's hostage.

Standing up for yourself does not make you selfish. You are your own advocate. If something doesn't feel right or affects you negatively, you should absolutely stand up for yourself. You have the right to be happy in your career and in your life overall. Don't let others take that from you and don't feel bad about defending that right. Fight for yourself and don't apologize for it.

Stop making yourself miserable. Life can be stressful enough. Don't dwell on mistakes or regrets. Learn from them and move on.

Put your pride aside. You can admit when you're wrong. Apologizing for making a mistake is an admirable trait and one that nobody can fault you for. Don't let pride hold you back from releasing negativity and anxiety. That behavior is counterproductive at best and self-destructive at worst.

Remember why you chose this industry. Really think about your reason for pursuing this career. Ask yourself if that reason still holds true and if it's enough to motivate you to continue on. (Hint: if your answer is "the money," odds are that you got into this industry for the wrong reason and are learning a harsh lesson.) Most of us went into this industry so we could work with people, helping them feel better about themselves. We care about our clients. That compassion drives us. Some of us are in it for the liberation that we get from being able to create all day long. That freedom of expression drives us. Whatever your reasons were, remember them now.

Identify what threatens your happiness. What instigated this career crisis and can it be corrected? If you have a bad boss, find a new job. If the salon you own has been staffed with toxic people, fire them and re-staff. If you have a few evil coworkers that seem hell-bent on ruining your work life, either get it handled, handle it yourself, or go in search of greener pastures. Identify what threatens your happiness and correct or eliminate it.

Absence makes the heart grow fonder. Don't be ashamed to take a break. Sometimes, a few days or weeks away from the job might help you remember what you love about it. The absence might make you realize that you're better off pursuing something else entirely. You owe it to yourself to find your own happiness, wherever that is. People who don't understand that or don't support that don't matter.

Education stimulates motivation. If you're suffering from a lack of excitement and motivation, sometimes a new product, new class, or trade show trip can correct it. These things all have a magical quality that has the power to infuse excitement into your job. If basic boredom is your malady, education is your remedy.

You know best. You worked hard for that license you're thinking about abandoning, but the choice is yours entirely.

I've been there. Renewal time has arrived. The checkbook sits in front of me right next to my renewal forms. A $75 fee and a fifty cent stamp are the only things standing between me and another two years of licensure. Am I sure I want to do this for another two years? If I let the license lapse, I won't have a choice in the matter anymore.

Even in my lowest career crisis moments, I always cut the check, paste the stamp, and send the form in...because you never know.

Do you know? Maybe you do. Maybe it's time to cut ties completely and walk away forever—then again, maybe it isn't. Maybe a career in this industry is worth fighting for.

Why You Should Quit

I have included several motivational chapters that are beloved by my readers. "Know your worth!" I say. "Take control of your career!" I proclaim.

This chapter is the polar opposite of those chapters. This chapter is about knowing when to quit and why you should embrace it and not let it shame you.

There is a concept in economics called "the sunk cost fallacy." The basic premise of this theory is that the more you invest into something, the more difficult it is to abandon it. You let your investments justify your continued investment—despite the fact that the route you're taking has been unsuccessful.

People are programmed to avoid waste; we call this "loss aversion." Whether it's concerning a monetary investment or a time investment, we can't stand the thought of wasting anything. For example, let's say that you have purchased a ticket to a play. The ticket is non-refundable and non-transferable, but you have since decided (for whatever reason) that you no longer want to attend. Many people would feel obligated to see the play because doing otherwise would be a "waste" of the ticket price.

People also do not like to quit or break commitments—probably because we've been trained to believe that quitting is shameful or an admission of failure. By purchasing the ticket, the person in this scenario has made a monetary commitment to see the play and may choose to see it—even though they really don't want to—based on that monetary commitment. This is what we call "throwing good money after bad." In this case, your "good money" is the time you could be spending doing something more enjoyable.

Basically, you have fooled yourself into believing you are doing the logical thing when you are doing the exact opposite.

The psychological theory of "cognitive dissonance" states that humans strive for internal consistency. If you've acted a certain way, over time you will overly justify your behavior. If we struggle or suffer for something—whether it's a career or a relationship—we will convince ourselves that we love it to justify our actions. Cognitive dissonance halts personal evolution.

Over time, we gain new information that shapes our opinions and may change our course of action. You shouldn't feel obligated to continue investing your time or effort into anything if you have gained new information that has lead you to the conclusion of, "Hey, maybe this wasn't the right decision for me after all..."

Let's assume you've been working in this industry for ten years. When your license renewal comes up biannually, you sit down and evaluate your career. You teeter on the fence. "Well, this isn't making me happy and I'd rather be a skydiving instructor. I'm not completely miserable, but I've already invested ten years into this career. I know how to do my job well and I make alright money. It isn't my passion but I'm getting by. It would be stupid to quit now that I've invested $20,000 into my education and thousands into my equipment and untold amounts into continuing education certifications. I'd hate to just walk away after spending all that money. My parents always said this was a stupid career move and that I should have been a lawyer. If I quit now, they'll think I'm a fool. My clients will never forgive me if I quit. I think I'll go ahead and renew it and maybe things will improve."

And thus your cycle of mediocrity continues for another ten years.

When you're evaluating your career, forget what you've invested. That money and that time is long gone. You will never get it back. Do not let your aversion to loss factor into your Happiness Equation. Ignore your past investments when making decisions about your future. Make a decision that promises a better future outcome, not one that attempts to justify the feeling of loss in your past, to satisfy your pride, or avoid criticism from others. In the scenario above, the decision should have been made and that renewal form should have been shredded immediately before the first "but."

The reason for this is a microeconomic concept called "opportunity cost." Opportunity cost is defined as, "the loss of potential gain from other alternatives when one alternative is chosen." For example, the opportunity cost of going to college is the amount of money you would have made if you had chosen to enter the workforce immediately after high school instead. It is the loss of "what might have been." It is the cost of the opportunity you're not taking advantage of by continuing to pursue your sunk cost endeavor.

When you allow yourself to fall prey to the sunk cost fallacy, you're not taking into account the opportunity cost. You are wasting your time doing something you don't like doing when you could be investing your time in a new project that could potentially offer you greater satisfaction—like becoming a skydiving instructor, for instance.

You should be leading a life that satisfies you. If this career no longer does so—do yourself a favor and walk away.

"But what will they think?!"

Who cares what they think? Who determined that quitting is shameful and why are you going to allow that fear of shame to dictate your happiness?

As I said before, we learn over time. Maybe when you entered beauty school you entered with false assumptions about the industry. Now you've realized that you were wrong—or maybe your assumptions about the industry were right, but your lifestyle or personal aspirations have shifted with your experiences. You have evolved and so have your needs. This doesn't make you a failure, this makes you a learning, thinking human being. Continuing as you have despite this new knowledge is illogical and irrational.

Tell me—what's admirable about that?

Nothing.

Who are you serving by continuing to walk a path that makes you miserable?

Not yourself—and you are the only person that matters when you're working on your Happiness Equation since the equation is designed to maximize your benefit.

As I said before, I have been that person, sitting at my desk, staring at my license renewal papers and wondering if I should continue. I've always enjoyed my career, but for a long time I struggled with what I should be doing. I've been criticized by family, friends, and college professors for not "taking full advantage of my intellectual and academic potential."

My intelligence level ranks among the top 2% of smart people in the world. Let me make this clear—being smart is not an accomplishment. It is not something I worked hard to achieve. I was born with a superior intellect. It was bestowed upon me through a series of random genetic pairings. I had absolutely nothing to do with it. However, according to others, my spontaneously-appointed intellectual ability makes me somehow obligated to contribute those genetic gifts to the greater good. "You should be curing cancer." "You should be working in genetic research." "You should be doing something more substantial than painting fingernails and managing salons."

For six years, I believed these statements. My career goal when I was in high school was to work in viral genetic research, using viruses to "infect" people with cures to genetic diseases. I only obtained my cosmetology license so that I could pay my way through college, which is exactly what I did. What I didn't anticipate is that I would develop an intense love of my profession that would supersede my love of science. That was information I gained over time—information that I was choosing to ignore because my guilt fueled my college career.

Although science excited me and kept me stimulated intellectually, I never felt sufficiently motivated to make it my sole purpose in life the way I did with my career in the beauty industry. I'm a motivated person. I live by the motto, "I want. I take. I have." If I really wanted to be a viral geneticist, achieving that goal would be simple. Instead, I pursued it lazily. Two classes one semester, one class the next, skip two semesters, another two classes...

I wasn't committing. And the more time passed, the less I wanted to continue with college. Finally, I had finished all of the courses required for my major (all of the courses that actually interested me). All I had left to complete were some ridiculous required courses, like humanities and other frivolous electives that colleges require students to complete so they can collect more of their money.

That's when I quit. I decided that I just didn't want it bad enough to skate through another three semesters of boring filler classes. I couldn't justify burning more money on a degree I knew I was unlikely to ever use. I let the new data change my path and finally refused to keep throwing good money after bad.

Do I consider the time and money I spent on college to be wasted? Absolutely not. I took the classes I enjoyed and learned a lot. It didn't result in a career but that doesn't mean the experience was without merit or value. I don't regret quitting either because college was becoming my personal Concorde.

During this time, my career in the beauty industry also evolved. In addition to feeling this guilt inflicted on me by my peers, I often reconsidered my career based on some unquantifiable factor causing dissatisfaction. I could not put my finger on it. About twice a year, I would have what my husband and friends started referring to as "career crises." Burnout.

During these periods, I would agonize over whether or not I made a big mistake sticking with my career instead of finishing college. I mistakenly assumed that I had grown to hate working in salon management. It took me up until three years ago to realize that I just don't like managing successful salons.

I was known in my area for taking a stagnating or failing salon and turning it into a money-making machine full of happy staff. However, after that turnaround was completed, I grew bored and that boredom made me incredibly unhappy. I started looking for reasons to leave and find a fresh, new job at a broken salon.

The problem wasn't the beauty industry. It was me. I need to be challenged regularly. I need to figure out why things are broken and determine how to fix them. I need to instigate and see growth, change, and improvement.

I never considered a career in consulting. I was aware that consultants existed, I just didn't think there would be a market for it since the majority of salon owners I knew were cheap, bullheaded, and preferred to fumble their way through business ownership rather than ask for assistance. I was wrong.

I no longer have career crises because I love what I do. You know what I do now? Exactly what I want. All the time. I left my salon to take care of my youngest daughter and make more babies. I read, I write, I consult, I teach, and I play video games. When my kids are in school, I'll probably return to full-time salon ownership, consulting, and educating. Maybe I'll decide that I actually do want to finish college and pursue a career in something awesome that caters to my strengths and my interests, like game development. Who knows? I'll figure it out when I get there, but I can tell you that I'll go into it without fearing the stigma of failure and without concern of public perception.

Persistence isn't always a virtue. Know when it's time to call it quits and don't be afraid to do so. There are a lot of blogs out there that promise that success is guaranteed if you apply yourself, never give up, and shoot for the stars. To perpetuate this, "If you're not successful, you're not dedicating yourself enough" advice is cruel. Sometimes, no amount of dedication, patience, sacrifice, or struggle will ever equate to success—and no amount of professional success is worth a damn if you're unhappy in the end.

At some point, you have to quit asking yourself, "What am I doing wrong?" and ask yourself, "Is this really what I want to do anymore?" Don't be upset if you come to the realization that it isn't. Failure doesn't define you. Refusal to accept failure when it is clearly in your best interest to do so is the biggest failure there is.

Raise the Bar

The first step to changing our industry starts with you. If we want to be treated with respect, we need to start showing our salon owners and our clients that we're worthy of it, not just by taking oaths and making promises, but by projecting a more professional image.

When professionals attempt to take action against owners who have wronged them, they often hit a brick wall. I believe that because of the "frivolous" nature of our industry, attorneys, judges, and state officials don't take us seriously. I suspect many of them perceive us as a bunch of silly women in an inconsequential industry that serves no purpose but to cater to the vanity and insecurities of others.

For too long, our industry has been over-casualized. We've Steel Magnolia'd ourselves. When people think of us as a group, instead of picturing professionals who are sleek, smart, and on top of their game, people picture the big-haired, big-mouthed, high school dropout—ditzy gossip queens in tank tops and skinny jeans. They see us as perpetual twenty-year-olds. Our image has suffered because of it. These are our careers and our professional reputations! We should be taking them seriously!

Moving forward in your career, I urge you to make a commitment to becoming an exceptional representative for our industry.

Get Involved. What did you say? You've been licensed for thirty-five years and you've never in your life gone to a single board meeting? Don't be lazy. Get involved and informed. If you can't go to board meetings, at least read the agendas, minutes, and executive summaries online.

Stick Together. Join Facebook groups composed of people in your profession in your state or county. If your area doesn't have one, take initiative and make one yourself. In that group, you can share knowledge, support one another, and keep each other updated on legislative changes that affect your businesses.

Be a Professional. Stop over-casualizing our industry. I'm not saying you have to dress and act like a six-figure attorney, but have some respect for your career and the others that work in it. Don't be the stereotypical airhead hairdresser, talking loudly about something inappropriate to a bunch of people who genuinely don't want to hear it.

Act Your Age. For the love of God, please, please start acting your age. If you are seventy years old with spiky, pitch black hair and fire engine red tips, it is incredibly unlikely that you're pulling that look off. What you are doing is making yourself and the rest of us that work in this industry look ridiculous. Unless you're one of those rare badasses who can rock a multicolored mohawk in their golden years, have some dignity. Please.

Consider Uniforms. I'm sick of seeing salon professionals dressed like slutty teens. Miniskirts and thigh high boots are not professional attire (unless you're working corners). They call that section "Juniors" for a reason. If you are not a "junior," your ass does not belong there unless you're buying school clothes for your kids. Some professionals say, "Well, you have to keep up with the trends." No. You don't. The only thing about you that should be "trendy" are your hair or your nails and even those need to be appropriate. It is not your professional duty to wear your bra on the outside of your shirt because you saw random model in Vogue wearing it that way. You're salon professionals, not clothing designers. It is possible to be trendy, professional, and age-appropriate.

Name Your Business Appropriately. Quit giving your businesses stupid names. I'm not talking about cutesy names like, "Curl Up & Dye" or "Too Much Lacquer." Those are clever, corny, awesome names. I'm talking about hard core stupid names. "Salon Ef-Fekts," "Hair 2 DYE 4," and "A Nu Do" are STUPID names. So stupid that I have to resort to using all caps to express how strongly I feel about it. Slang, purposeful misspellings, and numbers in lieu of letters don't belong in business titles. Please, I beg you. Stop this insanity.

Don't Let Others Humiliate Us. Oppose media that belittles our profession. Showcasing and disrespecting clueless owners and representing salon professionals as a bunch of idiots on national television harms us all.

I have an optimistic vision of our industry's future. I see mature, educated, well-dressed, responsible salon employees, keeping their conversations focused on polite discussion and educating their clients during their services. I see clean, organized salons. I see owners and staff members that know their rights and aren't scared to stand up for themselves if those rights are being infringed upon. I see judges, lawyers, and state representatives taking us seriously for once instead of rolling their eyes and pointing us to small claims. This is what I see, and hopefully you see it too.

A Note from the Author

I sincerely hope you enjoyed this book and that it helped you. I worked harder on this volume than I have ever worked on anything in my entire life and I hope it met or exceeded your expectations.

I am so incredibly thankful to have the opportunity to share the information I've gained over the course of my career with others and I love hearing from all of you. Your feedback keeps me going and contributes to my continual improvement. If you have any questions or commentary, you can write to me at tina.alberino@gmail.com and visit me on the web at www.tinaalberino.com.

If you have the time, I'd love it if you would leave an honest review of The Beauty Industry Survival Guide. (Seriously, be honest. I'm writing another book on salon management and ownership. If I made mistakes here, it's sort of important that you communicate them to me before I finish the next book.) I want to deliver the best I possibly can to this industry, so your feedback and suggestions are welcome.

If you really hated this book, you could bitch me out in person at one of the many trade shows I lecture at across the country. The schedule for those events can be found on both of my websites. (Be warned: I carry mace—but I'm not entirely skilled with it, so it could end up being a bad day for both of us.)

Thank you so much for reading!
-Tina Alberino
www.tinaalberino.com
www.thisuglybeautybusiness.com

Acknowledgements

This book would not have been possible without the support of my amazing husband, Jason, who tolerated my furious typing for fifteen hours a day, the raging tantrums I threw when things broke or my brain forgot how to form legible sentences, and my excessive bitching about the injustices that plague this industry. He's the best husband in the world. I'm still not entirely sure how I managed to convince him to marry me.

This book also would not have happened without my friend Jaime Schrabeck, who provided valuable insight, perspective, and humor. Without her guidance and encouragement (read: entirely necessary forceful insistence), I very likely wouldn't be educating at trade shows and this book probably wouldn't have been released until sometime in 2030, if ever. Without Jaime, this book also wouldn't be nearly as good. She did a thorough edit during her extremely limited spare time, which improved it greatly. Her similar passion for professionalism and ethical, organized salon management makes me feel a little less like a freak of nature in this industry. She has been my greatest inspiration and I'm incredibly grateful for her support, friendship, and enthusiastic endorsements (which I'm not quite certain I deserve).

I also want to thank my readers, who urged me to write this book to begin with. Their praise, encouragement, suggestions, and gratitude have kept me motivated. They are the reason I write, educate, and work to change this industry for the better. You guys are fantastic. Thank you!

Appendix

"You've Been Served"

A strange person approaches and greets you by name, asked in the form of a question. "Um...yeah?" you reply. They hand over a packet and say, "You've been served."

Holy crap! That packet of papers looks like it was written in another language! Your head spins, your heart pounds, and you feel like you're about to throw up all over your cute new boots. What are you supposed to do now?

Chill out. This chapter will help you form a plan and handle this difficult (and thankfully rare) situation.

Step 1: Deep Breaths. Recite the Jedi Code. "There is no emotion, there is peace. There is no ignorance, there is knowledge. There is no passion, there is serenity. There is no chaos, there is harmony. There is no death, there is the Force."

Relax, Padawan. You're going to get through this.

Don't panic. Keep calm and maintain your composure. Allowing your emotions to control you will affect your ability to think clearly. Don't get caught up feeling sorry for yourself or feeling angry at your boss. Don't waste your energy feeling anything. You don't know how this will end. Agonizing over it is counterproductive and will only hurt you.

Step 2: Read Until You Comprehend. If you don't understand the document, find an attorney.

Step 3: Evaluate the Claims. The burden of proof always rests with the petitioner. The owner or landlord will have to prove their claims against you. You're innocent until the petitioner proves you guilty. For each claim made in the petition, you need to be able to rebut it with proof or reasonable justification for violating. If the charges are bogus and you have no proof to rebut it, odds are that the petitioner can't prove it to begin with, so don't worry about it.

For example, let's consider a typical lawsuit filed by salon owners: the non-compete violation. The owner will have to prove you violated the NCA. She can do this by showing a printout of a salon website that lists you as a staff member or providing a business card of yours addressed to a salon within the NCA's radius. You will then be called upon to prove that you didn't violate the NCA (or that the NCA was not properly written and/or did not apply to you due to your employment classification and is therefore completely unenforceable).

Step 4: Prepare. Gather your evidence and prepare your counterarguments. Before you prepared your answer, you evaluated whether or not you could support yourself with proof. This is when you compile that proof. Gather evidence to support your claim. Hearsay is not evidence. You can bring in witnesses to testify on your behalf, but you want solid, legitimate, tangible proof—leases, contracts, receipts, pay stubs, phone records, text message transcripts, and emails. Those things are legitimate and tangible. They are admissible in court if properly submitted as evidence.

If you don't have an attorney, consider these five things:
- Does the law support the plaintiff's case? Let's go back to our NCA example from above. Perhaps our defendant in that example was classified as an independent contractor. Non-compete agreements directly conflict with that independent classification. In that case, the law likely wouldn't support the plaintiff's case.
- Does the law support your case? In contrast, if our NCA violator was a legitimate employee of Salon Beautilicious, then the NCA would be binding. The law would not support her case.

- Can the plaintiff prove their claims? Always assume the plaintiff has you dead to rights, even if you aren't certain. If you definitely didn't commit a transgression they've accused you of in their complaint (like eloping with a nonhuman primate), don't worry about proving otherwise. If they bring up a claim, they have to provide proof (like an inter-species marriage license or pictures of the two of you boarding a plane to Vegas). However, if you do have proof to the contrary (like medical records detailing your ongoing therapy to conquer crippling simian fear), gather it anyways.
- Can you prove your defense? You don't necessarily have to prove your defense, particularly if the claims are unfounded. However, if you can support your defense with documentation or proof, do so. It will help you immensely.

In our NCA example, to prove her defense, the defendant provides a listing of all salons in SmallTown, USA. On a separate form, the distance of each salon from Salon Beautilicious is specified and Google Maps are provided to illustrate this distance. She also includes the business license registration information from the state's website for each salon, which shows their establishment dates were all prior to that of Salon Beautilicious. The defendant can then argue that the plaintiff likely crafted her NCA to exclude all but one salon in town, making it impossible for anyone that left her salon to find work in SmallTown.

To support her argument that no competing salons were hiring, the defendant provides written rejection letters from all but one salon (the one she's currently employed at).

To support her argument that she hasn't solicited any clients from Salon Beautilicious, our defendant provides her appointment records dating back to her first day at Fancy

Pantaloons and her cell phone records to show she hasn't contacted any clients by phone.

To support her argument that she desperately needed employment, the defendant can provide bank statements and copies of her bills, illustrating her dire need for income.

- Do you have a claim against the plaintiff? My personal favorite. Sometimes, owners go to court and file—representing themselves—and have no idea that they're incriminating themselves by doing so.

In our NCA example, let's assume the owner hasn't been adhering to the FLSA. If the defendant can prove that she was required to work overtime without pay and that the owner didn't meet her minimum wage responsibilities, the defendant could win damages from the plaintiff. Moreover, the owner may face criminal penalties and joint investigations by the IRS, DOL, and State Attorney offices.

Step 5: Respond. In general, you have twenty-one days total (including weekends) to reply to a complaint in writing. The clock starts ticking the day that process server hands you those papers, so get your ass moving. If you don't file an answer, the court will enter a default judgment in the petitioner's favor, granting them everything they ask for plus attorney and court fees. FILE YOUR ANSWER IMMEDIATELY. Your answer must be in the courthouse and on file within a very specific time period after the day you were served.

Bad things will happen if you don't file an answer. The next paper you get served will be a Notice of Hearing, but that hearing will be for the default judgment. You can attend, but you won't be able to tell your side of the story.

Your response to each claim will be "Admit," or "Deny," but sometimes "answers" can be tricky. Let's refer back to the NCA example. Suppose the petitioner's NCA states that you can't work in another salon or similar beauty establishment within a three mile radius of their salon in the capacity of a stylist for six months. That is a reasonable, narrowly-defined NCA that will likely to be upheld in court. Let's assume she can prove that you violated the NCA by taking a job at a salon 2.9 miles away as a stylist. You're clearly guilty and nothing you can say will change that. However, you can plead your case to a judge.

To file an answer, first type up the heading found on your complaint. The court name, the case number, the petitioner name and the defendant name. All of that stuff up there: copy it. Next, type ANSWER below that heading. The complaint will have numbered paragraphs. You need to go through each one and number your answers to correlate with those complaints.

For example, if our sample complaint reads:

1.) Defendant willfully violated a signed non-compete agreement by taking employment as a cosmetologist at Salon Beautilicious as a cosmetologist shortly after resigning from Petitioner's salon,

2.) Defendant has solicited clients of Petitioner's salon since resigning, causing substantial loss of income for Petitioner's business,

3.) Defendant stole and eloped with Petitioner's pet monkey.

The response would read:

1.) **Admit.** *Only four beauty salons are in operation in SmallTown, USA. One is Salon Beautilicious. Another, Precious Hair Factory, Inc., is located within .5 miles of Salon Beautilicious. Cookie Cutterz Salon, located 4.1 miles away, was not (and still is not) hiring staff members (see attached rejection letter, labeled A). The third, Fancy Pantaloons Upscale Styling House, was the only salon seeking staff (see attached Craisglist posting schedules for March 1-14, labeled B). Fancy Pantaloons is located 2.9 miles away from Salon Beautilicious. Defendant desperately needed employment to continue paying her bills. Defendant realizes that she is violating the NCA by*

1/10th of a mile, but feels the filing of this motion is a frivolous, malicious attempt by the owner of Salon Beautilicious to restrict her employment. Defendant believes that Plaintiff intentionally constructed the NCA to make it impossible for ex-employees to find employment in SmallTown, USA.

    2.) **Deny.** Defendant willingly provides her cell phone and appointment records (see attached, labeled B and C) to prove that she has not contacted nor solicited any clients of Salon Beautilicious.

    3.) **Deny.** Defendant is terrified of monkeys, was not aware Petitioner even owned a monkey, and certainly would not elope with one since she is already happily married to a big dumb ape.

    ...you get the idea.

    Make three copies of your answer. File one in court, send the other to your ex-owner (or their attorney), and keep the third safe. Once you file your written answer (whether you admit everything or deny everything), the court will treat the case as contested and you will receive a Notice to Appear in court.

    Consider mediation. As I mentioned in Contracts 101, mediation is a great alternative to litigation. A good mediator will sit both parties down and show each of them what their best and worst day in court will look like. The plaintiff's best day in court would involve beating you entirely and getting a judgment against you. The defendant's best day would involve walking away without penalty. It's extremely unlikely that either of you will get exactly what you want at the end of a hearing.

    Hearings are expensive. Attorneys are expensive. Judges can be unpredictable. If the plaintiff is willing to attempt mediation, do it. You don't have to agree on anything in mediation if your opponent decides to be unreasonable. Just talk it out and see if you can come to an understanding.

Negotiate. Give and take. Compromise. If all else fails, go to court and put the decision in a judge's hands.

Courthouse Etiquette

How do you dress? What do you do? What can you say? How can you make sure that you won't make some horrifying mistake and be held in contempt? Read these tips. Many lawyers also have blogs that contain helpful advice, so do some additional research if you're still feeling insecure.

Dress conservatively and professionally. No sandals. No jeans. No tank tops. No t-shirts. Dress like you're going for an interview at a law firm or to a congressman's funeral. This isn't the time to make a fashion statement. Dressing sexy will win you no points here. If you chose to wear a skirt, make sure it's no shorter than two inches above your knee (and put on some nylons, you tramp).

Keep makeup minimal and natural. Don't get crazy with that eye shadow. You want to be taken seriously, so don't walk up in the courtroom looking like Bozo the Clown or Mimi from The Drew Carey Show.

Take the metal out of your face. If you normally wear facial piercings, take them out. They aren't appropriate to wear to court. Crazy makeup, provocative clothing, and piercings will distract from your argument.

Don't wear a belt or complicated shoes. You'll have to walk through a metal detector and remove these items before you can enter the courthouse. Make it easy on yourself by leaving your belts and metal accessories at home and wearing flats you can slip in and out of easily.

When it's your turn in front of the judge, follow these rules.

Don't speak unless spoken to. Even if the plaintiff spouts lies through their teeth, keep your mouth shut until you're addressed.

Never show emotion. You can be nervous, sad, and scared. You cannot be angry, loud, combative, or disrespectful. Don't roll your eyes, sigh, or draw attention to yourself during your opponent's testimony. If she lies, write it down on a piece of paper and bring it up when it's your turn to speak. Put on your best poker face and keep your mouth shut. Judges hate outbursts and disruptions. You do not want to look like a petulant child. You're an adult. Remember it.

Always address the judge with "Your Honor," or "Sir," or "Ma'am."

Never use slang or profanity. When you're asked a question that requires a yes or no answer, always respond with, "Yes, ma'am/sir/Your Honor" or "No, ma'am/sir/Your Honor." Never say, "yeah," "nope," or "I dunno." Judges hate that.

Drop your attitude. You don't bark orders at a judge or demand anything from them. You're interested in getting a peaceful, rational, reasonable resolution. You're not there to make the plaintiff/defendant look bad and you're not there to fight. Both you and the plaintiff are there to ask the judge to come up with a fair solution based on the information and evidence that each of you has collected.

Keep your testimony brief. State the facts and only state what you can prove.

Bring evidence in triplicate. Bring three copies of everything you're presenting: one for you, one for the judge, and one for your opponent. It is an amateur move to forget to bring evidence in triplicate.

Moral Considerations

I'm going to preface this with "your attorney often knows best." If you have legal counsel, follow their advice—but remember, you're the one that has to live with yourself at the end of the day.

When you're called to court, whatever the reason, I strongly advise that you be honest. Be honest with yourself, your lawyer, and the judge. If you did something wrong, take responsibility. The consequences may not be pretty, but I can guarantee you they'll be far less dire than if you get caught in a lie (or a series of them). Tell the truth not because you might get caught. Tell the truth because it's the right thing to do.

Everything we do, we should do with honesty, dignity, and integrity. People make mistakes every day. Nobody expects perfection. Whether the crime you committed was intentional or not, admitting fault and genuinely apologizing for that mistake is admirable.

Don't attempt to manipulate the justice system to justify your misdeeds. Don't walk into court with the mistaken assumption that you are smarter than the judge sitting on the bench. An ethical lawyer will advise you against compromising your integrity and potentially putting yourself in a position where you could be proven guilty or have your credibility called into question, but some attorneys may advise you not to admit guilt, to "plead the fifth" on inquiries that may be incriminating, or to utilize tactics during your deposition or trial that are intended to mislead or misdirect the judge and/or opposing counsel.

These pathetic, underhanded practices are disgusting. It's probably the best way to gain massive loads of negative karma, if you believe in that kind of thing. Sure, you may save yourself some money and walk away clean as a whistle, but are you willing to lower yourself like that? What kind of person do you want to be known as?

You may have lost the moral high ground when you committed the crime, but you can gain solid footing again by being apologetic and honest. Admit fault, apologize, and show that you truly want to rectify the wrong you committed.

Take responsibility and accept the consequences for your actions. We all (hopefully) have an innate sense of right and wrong. If something doesn't feel right, it isn't. There's nothing more liberating than the sense of freedom and serenity that comes with being honest and genuine. Being honest can be difficult sometimes, but making a habit of it will make you a better, stronger, and more respected person.

Online Resources

These are websites that I frequently reference. Sometimes links change, so if you find that these links are broken their updated versions can always be found at my website, http://www.thisuglybeautybusiness.com under the Resources menu.

IRS Resources

Internal Revenue Service:
http://www.irs.gov/

Tax Tips for the Cosmetology & Barber Industry:
http://www.irs.gov/pub/irs-pdf/p4902.pdf

Independent Contractor (Self-Employed) or Employee?:
http://www.irs.gov/Businesses/Small-Businesses-&-Self-Employed/Independent-Contractor-Self-Employed-or-Employee

Independent Contractor Defined:
http://www.irs.gov/Businesses/Small-Businesses-&-Self-Employed/Independent-Contractor-Defined

Behavioral Control Defined:
http://www.irs.gov/Businesses/Small-Businesses-&-Self-Employed/Behavioral-Control

Financial Control Defined:
http://www.irs.gov/Businesses/Small-Businesses-&-Self-Employed/Financial-Control

Type of Relationship Defined:
http://www.irs.gov/Businesses/Small-Businesses-&-Self-Employed/Type-of-Relationship

Present Law and Background Relating to Worker Classification for Federal Tax Purposes:
http://www.irs.gov/pub/irs-utl/x-26-07.pdf

Department of Labor Resources

Department of Labor:
http://www.dol.gov/
Summary of the Major Laws of the Department of Labor:
http://www.dol.gov/opa/aboutdol/lawsprog.htm
The Fair Labor Standards Act (FLSA):
http://www.dol.gov/compliance/laws/comp-flsa.htm
Employment Law Guide:
http://www.dol.gov/compliance/guide/
Wage & Hour Division:
http://www.dol.gov/WHD
File a Complaint with the WHD:
http://www.dol.gov/wecanhelp/howtofilecomplaint.htm

Cosmetology Resources

Beauty Schools Directory:
http://www.beautyschoolsdirectory.com/
Cosmetology License Requirements by State:
http://www.beautyschoolsdirectory.com/faq/state_req.php

Clients Behaving Badly Webinar:
https://www.youtube.com/watch?v=yIRZJTBH7as

Blogs

This Ugly Beauty Business
www.thisuglybeautybusiness.com
Precision Nails:
http://precisionnails.blogspot.com/

Nail Tech Reality Check:
http://www.nailtechrealitycheck.com/
Ask a Manager:
http://www.askamanager.org/
Employment & Labor Insider:
http://www.employmentandlaborinsider.com/
Screw You Guys, I'm Going Home:
http://employeeatty.blogspot.com/
The Middle Finger Project:
http://www.themiddlefingerproject.org/

Made in the USA
Monee, IL
20 December 2022